The Figure of FAUST
in Valéry and Goethe

For a listing of all titles, see page 257

The Figure of FAUST in Valéry and Goethe

AN EXEGESIS OF *MON FAUST*

Kurt Weinberg

PRINCETON UNIVERSITY PRESS

PRINCETON, NEW JERSEY

To Florence M. Weinberg and Arthur Henkel

Contents

Preface

IN DEFENSE OF A *PARTI PRIS*

MY INTERPRETATION of Valéry's *Mon Faust* does not trace this work back to its sources. It adds little to the existing influence studies—in particular those by von Richthofen, Kurt Wais, Fähnrich, Blüher, and Maurice Bémol.[1] Nor does it detract from them. I grant that "influences" are as old as the classical concept of *imitatio*, the imitation of established myths and great authors, and its rhetorical correlative, *inventio*, the invention of *ornatus*, of formal beauty. But I agree with Gide: influence "creates nothing"; rather, "it awakens" ("De l'Influence en littérature," in *Prétextes*, 6th ed., Paris, 1919, p. 32). Somewhat more forthright, Valéry's position comes close to Gide's: the writer feeds on everyone else's work but transforms and digests it into a substance of his own. Whatever one may think, Gide is no doubt right when he holds that the most important influences are those against which one reacts ("l'influence par réaction," *ibid.*, p. 34). For Valéry, influences may have their importance, but not so much

[1] Erich von Richthofen, *Commentaire sur* Mon Faust *de Paul Valéry*, Paris, PUF, 1961. Kurt Wais, "Goethe und Valéry's 'Faust,'" in *Mélanges de litterature comparée et de philologie offerts à Mieczyslaw Brahmer*, Warsaw, PWN (n.d.), 555 ff. Hermann Fähnrich, "Paul Valéry und Goethe," *Neue Folge des Jahrbuchs der Goethe-Gesellschaft*, 31. Bd., Weimar, 1969, 192 ff. Karl Alfred Blüher, *Strategie des Geistes, Paul Valéry's Faust*, Frankfurt a.M., Vittorio Klostermann (*Analecta Romanica*, Heft 10), 1960. Maurice Bémol, "Le jeune Valéry et Goethe. Étude de genèse réciproque," *Revue de littérature comparée*, vol. 34 (1960), 5 ff.

for what they *are* than for the *changes they undergo*, the
stimulus they provide, and the reaction they produce.
Their final result is a total metamorphosis of their substance into Valérian essence. It is perhaps in this sense
that an entry in the *Cahiers: "IIIeme Faust.* Tout ce que
Goethe a ignoré" (Cah. xii, 894), ought to suggest a
truth consistent with Valéry's intellectual egotism: *"Mon
Faust*; Everything Goethe *could* not know, because he
did not see through my eyes."

Literary criticism, if it is to elucidate a text, must start
with a *parti pris*, to use a term dear to Valéry. It is always
a wager with the odds on the side of probability, not unlike the hypotheses on which scientists build their investi-
gations and experiments. These experiments, more often
than not, are based on a lucky hunch. Intuition as surely
leads to induction and deduction, as "la trouvaille" precedes research—very much to the dismay of the positivists,
who would rather have it happen the other way around.
The scientist's conjectures and the critic's work partake in
varying degrees of the *als ob* ("as if") qualities that Kant
attributes to fiction, and that his commentator Vaihinger
generalizes into the very foundation of philosophising,
founding a school of "Philosophie des Als-Ob" ("Philosophy of the As-If").

Moreover, there is no such thing as an exhaustive analysis. Any exegesis is partial in both meanings of this word.
Its limitations are determined by those of the critic, whose
viewpoint is never impartial, however objectively he may
deport himself. Even with the best intentions, one can
only glimpse partial (i.e., incomplete) aspects of an ambiguous and complex text. Yet, any partial exegesis that
explores one or several levels, notwithstanding its incom-
pleteness and partiality, enhances understanding. It does

so, regardless of the extent to which it is bound to be partisan, specialized, or tentative—in other terms, despite its inevitable "as if" perspective.

In this sense, I have tried to add to the existing views on *Mon Faust*, by looking at it from a point of view that falls fully within the range of Valéry's own lifelong *parti pris* against Pascal and for Descartes. I have done so without denying the validity of other *partis pris* from which have come interpretations, glosses, and commentaries and that have greatly contributed to the elucidation of those texts whose fragmentary state and enigmatic richness allow a variety of readings. It would seem that my own "as if" conjectures might throw some light on areas that have hitherto been neglected. My assumptions, and the analysis I base upon them, are systematically predicated upon Valéry's linguistic experimentation, which, through charades, paranomasia, onomastics, and etymological puns, brings into full play the mystifying and mythologising aspects of language. Thematically, as already suggested, I examine the Cartesian potential inherent in Valéry's Faust. *Lust, la demoiselle de cristal,* curiously reflects the apparent misfortunes of the *cogito*, destined as they are to result from the mind's dependence on its body. This conflict somewhat lessens, in the light of Valéry's theories on *la sensibilité de l'intellect. Le Solitaire, ou les malédictions d'univers,* is partly envisaged as staging, on the scenery of Faust's brain, the *danse macabre* of Pascalian *pensées* (Act One), and the poetic temptation held out to Faust's mind by the bewitching forces of Imagination and Memory, as Cartesian *passions de l'âme (Les Fées).* The nightmarish as well as the lyrical aspects of *Le Solitaire* are brought into focus, *sub specie* of Descartes' three dreams, during the night of November 10, 1619.

Valéry's Cartesian Faust exhibits aspects of a "method" that coincides with Descartes' detached way of exploring his own potential, rigorously pursued to the very end—regardless of where it might lead. "Méthode, c'est lui" (Cah. xix, 803), is one of Valéry's most striking definitions of Descartes. It could be applied to Valéry's fictionalized Léonard da Vinci, as well as to fictional characters like Teste and Faust.

Thus, my first three chapters explore the Cartesian character of a Faust, bent upon carefully distinguishing between the myth that has grown about his figure and the reality of his own indefinable existence, which is capable of absorbing all fables that currently circulate concerning him, and those likely to arise in the future. The fourth chapter tries to establish essential differences between Valéry's and Goethe's protagonists, as well as between Goethe and his Faust. It aims to determine those paradoxical fallacies which Goethe's irony has embodied in Faust and Mephistopheles, but also in the minor characters: fallacies that serve his overall plan, Faust's salvation *malgré lui*—a grace less deserved through his actions than by the Lord's predestination and His unwillingness to lose a wager with the Devil. Chapter four must, therefore, concentrate on certain scenes in Goethe's vast play and on aspects of his thought which permit insights into patterns of Faust's behavior, strangely at odds with Valéry's rationalist hero (who mirrors his author's mind) and with Goethe's *Weltanschauung*.

An analysis of this order requires an exposition of the mature Goethe's ambiguous views on the "Northern Barbarian" world of "nebulous ideas and symbols" which, from circa 1797 onward, to his mind is incarnate in Faust. Furthermore, we must look at Goethe's epistemology, where the principle of systematic *Anschauen*—a term that

will be defined in chapter four—provides an intuitive way
of knowledge (even in the natural sciences), in a manner
similar to attempts by Renaissance humanists to intuit
"truth" through the contemplation of emblems and "hieroglyphs." Goethe's Faust, unlike his author, seems forever
incapable of differentiating between theory and its objects,
while Goethe's *Anschauen* is a method that coincides with
the etymological sense of speculation and theory. Faust
is the illusionist who, again and again, falls victim to the
illusions he creates, confusing aesthetics and libido, the
shadowy phantoms of ideals with the tangible substance
of reality. The complexities of these problems call for an
almost equally complex exegesis, where Goethe's thought
will provide antinomies to the strange failings of his protagonist, before the focus can be brought back to illuminate the differences between Goethe's and Valéry's Faust
figures, and to show the striking similarities between the
open and yet complete structures of Goethe's universal
mystery play and Valéry's fragments of liturgical dramas.

There are problems of style that the critic faces when
dealing with a fragmentary work like *Mon Faust*, consisting (as its subtitle explains) of sketches ("Ébauches"),
each one in a different tonality, ranging from the unre-
strained mirth of *Lust*, over the bitter, grotesque, and
sardonic (but nonetheless *grave*) exposure of the nightmarish side of Pascalian thought (*Le Solitaire*, Act One),
to the lyrical enchantment that accompanies Faust's dis-
enchantment in the interlude, *Les Fées*. I have tried to
cope with these abrupt changes in the tonality of *Mon
Faust*, by adapting the tone of my exegesis to the diverse
style levels of the text.

Altogether, this monograph owes much to after-wit,
l'esprit de l'escalier. It grew largely out of afterthoughts

on four lectures I was privileged to give in Professor Arthur Henkel's colloquium on Goethe's Faust during the summer semester of 1971, when I was a visiting professor at the University of Heidelberg (Germanistisches Seminar). I am deeply indebted to the stimulus derived from the probing discussions that ensued with Arthur Henkel and his brilliant group of *Doktoranden*.

My grateful acknowledgments go to Mrs. Joanna Hitchcock, Managing Editor of Princeton University Press, for her generous help, and to Miss R. Miriam Brokaw, Associate Director and Editor of Princeton University Press, for putting the final touches on the styling of this project. I wish to thank my friend and colleague, Professor Ralph Freedman of Princeton University, for his constant encouragement, the careful reading he gave to my first draft, and his valuable suggestions, which I was able to incorporate in the definitive version of my manuscript. My special thanks go to my wife, Professor Florence M. Weinberg, whose acute insights and astute reading of my typescript helped eliminate those perverse barbarisms to which foreign-born scholars, with a style of their own, seem to be prone when they face the more arcane pitfalls of the English language.

This monograph was completed with the aid of a Senior Fellowship of the National Endowment for the Humanities during a year's leave of absence from the University of Rochester.

Rochester, N.Y.   KURT WEINBERG
Fall 1974

Abbreviations

With the exception of *Faust I* and *Faust II* (see below, under GOETHE), Roman numerals refer to volume number, Arabic numerals to page numbers.

I. DESCARTES

AT   *Oeuvres de Descartes*, publiées par Charles Adam et Paul Tannery, Paris, 1897 ff.; 13 volumes.

Alquié   *Oeuvres philosophiques de Descartes*, Textes établis, présentés et annotés par Ferdinand Alquié, Paris, 1963 ff.; 3 volumes.

Baillet   A. Baillet, *La Vie de Monsieur Descartes*, Paris, 1691; 2 vols.

Gilson   Descartes, *Discours de la Méthode*, Texte et commentaire par Étienne Gilson, 3ᵉ éd., Paris, 1962.

II. GOETHE (If not otherwise indicated, all quotations are from *Gedenkausgabe*, see Bibliography, under *Goethe, Editions* used.)

Ausg. letzt. Hd.   *Goethe's Werke*. Vollständige Ausgabe letzter Hand, Stuttgart und Tübingen, 1827 ff.; 56 volumes.

Eckermann   Johann Peter Eckermann, *Gespräche mit Goethe*, Leipzig (n.d.), 3 volumes.

Faust I	J.-W. v. Goethe, *Faust, Der Tragödie Erster Teil*, ed. Erich Trunz, Hamburg, 1963.
Faust II	Same edition as above, *Faust I*.
MacNeice	*Goethe's Faust, Parts I and II*, an abridged version, translated by Louis MacNeice, New York, 1960.

III. PASCAL

Pensée	Pascal's *Pensées* are quoted in the numbering of the Brunschvicg edition: Blaise Pascal, *Pensées et Opuscules* publiés avec une introduction, des notices, des notes par Léon Brunschvicg, Paris (n.d.).

IV. VALÉRY

P.	Paul Valéry, *Oeuvres*, édition établie et annotée par Jean Hytier (Bibliothèque de la Pléiade), Paris, 1957-1960; 2 vols.
Cah.	*Les Cahiers de Paul Valéry*, Centre National de la Recherche Scientifique, Paris, 1957-1961; 29 vols. in facsimile.
Corr. AG-PV	*André Gide–Paul Valéry. Correspondance, 1890-1942*, Paris, [1955].

The Figure of FAUST
in Valéry and Goethe

Animi cibus est ita demum utilis, non si in memoria ceu stomacho subsidat, sed si in ipsos affectus et in ipsa mentis viscera traiciatur.

(The mind's food becomes useful only once it no longer lies in Memory as in a stomach, but is transferred to all the moods and entrails of the intellect.)

RATIO SEU COMPENDIUM VERAE THEOLOGIAE PER DE-SIDERIUM ERASMUM ROTERDAMUM

One.

LUST, LA DEMOISELLE DE CRISTAL

1. *The Liturgical Comedy of the Intellect*

Valéry's ideas on the drama parallel his thoughts on the novel. They matured in his early twenties, between 1891 and 1894, half a century before *Mon Faust*, under the impact of works as diverse as Huysmans' *A Rebours*, Mallarmé's *Hérodiade* and *Igitur* fragments, and Poe's *The Fall of the House of Usher*. They reject the complementary concepts of the stage as a world and the world as a stage, and they condemn narrative fiction on the order of *"La marquise sortit à cinq heures."* For Valéry, the only stage for drama and novel is the abstract theatre of the human mind, where reason and will enact their unceasingly comic feud with the *Puissances trompeuses*, the deceptions of desires, passions, memory, and imagination. The mind, both stage and audience, observes itself in the exercise of its functions. "J'ai relu le *Discours de la Méthode* tantôt, c'est bien le roman moderne comme il pourrait être fait," Valéry wrote to Gide on August 25, 1894. "A remarquer que la philosophie postérieure a rejeté la part autobiographique. Cependant, c'est le point à reprendre et il faudra donc écrire la vie d'une théorie comme on a trop écrit celle d'une passion (couchage)" (Corr. AG-PV, 213).

These sentences mark the prelude to *Monsieur Teste*, Valéry's cerebral non-novel about a true monster of intellect, shown in the process of watching, speeding up, and reversing his own thought processes. Monsieur Teste,

Valéry's transparent and lucid embodiment of Descartes' *cogito, ergo sum*, was invented in 1894. The last episodes were published in 1946, one year after Valéry's death. The elaboration of *Monsieur Teste*, like that of Goethe's *Faust*, spanned a lifetime. So did Valéry's ideas on Descartes' *Discours de la méthode* as an epic work on the life of the intellect, worthy of a place on a par with Dante's *Divina Commedia* and Balzac's *La Comédie humaine*. These remarks were made on July 31, 1937, before a Sorbonne audience, in Valéry's address to the Ninth International Congress of Philosophy. "Dans cette vaste Comédie de l'Esprit à laquelle je souhaitais un Balzac, si ce n'est un Dante, Descartes tiendrait une place du premier rang" (P.1, 799). And again, in 1941, the *Discours* is compared to *Hamlet*: ". . . le Discours de la méthode, est un monologue dans lequel les passions, les notions, les expériences de la vie, les ambitions, les réserves pratiques du héros sont de la même voix indistinctement exprimées . . ." (P.1, 818).

Maurice Bémol, in his excellent study on "Le jeune Valéry et Goethe,"[1] traces back to 1887 Valéry's first reading of Goethe's *Faust* in Nerval's rather awkward translation. His painstaking analysis leads to the conclusion that Goethe's *Faust* "semble donc avoir été pour Valéry, au cours de son Odyssée spirituelle, un repère assez constant, en dépit de ses intermittences" (*ibid.*, 12). It is hard to determine the exact date when Valéry decided to write his own version of Faust. *Mon Faust*, written down in 1940, but planned since 1932 at least, completes *Monsieur Teste* in more than one sense: it adds a body to the monstrous intellect bent upon the narcissistic pursuit of its own elusive image; *and* it releases Monsieur Teste from his

[1] *Revue de littérature comparée* 34 (1960), p. 9.

self-imposed isolation, from his habitual posture that shows him with his head turned towards the wall, *in contemptu mundi.*

Valéry's Faust is an aged but ageless, somewhat mellowed, wiser but also more foolish Monsieur Teste. He can be all that because a body has been added to the mere head that was Monsieur Teste: a body with all its frailties that, in the comedy *Lust, la demoiselle de cristal,* draws the mind in and out of love, causing it to succumb—however little—to the seductions of the senses, and to engage—temporarily at least—in the silliness of gamesmanship and one-upmanship. But, although endowed with human weaknesses, Valéry's Faust still remains predominantly a formidable mind, a *cogito* at work and watching itself at work, fending off the irrational forces of deception that are deeply rooted in his nature rather than in external reality. Unlike Monsieur Teste, Valéry's Faust has not divested himself of his humanity, although his methodical doubt à la Descartes, in its power of negation, even exceeds the very spirit of negation, Mephistopheles himself. In the end, what distinguishes Faust from Monsieur Teste is the social context where he is placed, a *milieu* that gives him a center of gravity and a stage where he acts out the comedy of consciousness in the company of fellow humans and surrounded by incarnations of essentially non-carnal temptations of the flesh that is willing while the mind, at times, is very weak. If it is Faust's task to embody the comedy of the *cogito,* distracted again and again by the passions, his antagonist, "the Other," Mephistopheles, represents the very opposite. Faust is the incarnation of thought, diverted by sleep and dream; Mephistopheles defines himself as the disincarnation of non-thought and non-sleep: "Je suis l'être sans chair, qui ne dort, ni ne pense" (P.II, 354). It is one among numerous classical alexandrines that are hidden in Valéry's prose, a practice that, in *Lust* (if not in *Les Fées*), seems to be related to a principle to which Valéry gave expression in 1939: "L'écriture des vers en lignes a nui à la qualité. Il faudrait que la lecture seule obligeât à dire en vers" (Cah. xxii, 238). Most Mephistophelian temptations are expressed in alexandrines, concealed in the text. They are perhaps meant to evoke the essence of Racinian tragedy, where passion, more often than not, tends to overcome reason. By defining himself as fleshless being without sleep or thought, Mephistopheles hints at himself as an allegory of human passions and fantasies which never sleep and which interfere with the human substance of being, with thought.[2]

There exists a link, although a most tenuous one, between the conception of *Monsieur Teste*, in 1894, and Goethe's *Faust*. In June of that same year, while in London, Valéry had seen Sir Henry Irving's production of Irving and Wills' more spectacular than faithful arrangements of scenes from Goethe's *Faust I*. This Victorian monstrosity had left Valéry with mixed feelings that he confided to his brother Jules: "The Machinery, the details, the deviltries are extraordinary—but: no drama, no art" (P.i, 22). We shall presently examine exactly what the twenty-three-year-old disciple of Mallarmé understood by

[2] This interpretation of Mephistopheles and his demonic servants as instinctive forces, opposing the thinking essence, is borne out by a parenthetical note in the *Cahiers* in which Valéry belatedly reflects upon the *Mon Faust* fragments one year after their publication: "(Les instincts seront figurés par le *Méphistophélès*—et toute leur diabolique ingéniosité, leurs séductions, tentations, leur faux 'infinis' "—clearly a hint at Pascal's "deux infinis"—"et tout l'art de se tromper soi-même. . . .)" (Cah. xxvi, 440-42; 1942; Valéry's italics).

"drama" and "art." For the moment, we note that the dubious spectacular at the Lyceum marks Valéry's first, and probably only, encounter with Goethe's *Faust* on stage. Almost half a century elapsed before the publication of his own two *Faust* fragments in 1940. They are titled: *Lust, La Demoiselle de Cristal, comédie* and *Le Solitaire, ou les malédictions d'univers, féerie dramatique.* An indefinite number of melodramas, comedies, tragedies, and pantomimes were planned to form Valéry's *Third Faust,* the preface informs us. This generous plan demonstrates that, despite his merely nodding acquaintance with Goethe's *Faust,* which he could read only in translation, Valéry must have had a keen intuition of Goethe's intention to use dramatic forms in *Faust II,* ranging from tragedy, comedy, opera, operetta, farce, and liturgical processions to mummery. There is no trace of Marlowe in *Mon Faust,* and although Gounod and Berlioz are indirectly mentioned in *Lust,* the preface makes it clear that Goethe alone gave the impetus to Valéry's *Faust.* What in particular attracts Valéry to the Goethean model is Goethe's typifying art. Rather than being cast as developing characters, Goethe's Faust and Mephistopheles express "extremes of humanity and the inhuman" (P.II, 276). They are, in Valéry's words, "liberated from any particular plot" (*ibid.*). Faust and Mephistopheles, as Valéry sees it, perform *tasks* rather than roles (*ibid.*), and it is precisely in the transcendence of their roles and in the subordination of plot to archetypal universality that Goethe's *Faust* reaches beyond the modern stage back to the liturgical genre of Allegory, of the Mystery and the Fool's play.

This brings us to Valéry's definition of "drama" and "art." Surprisingly, we find it fully fledged in another letter to Gide, dating back as far as December 5, 1891. As the then only twenty-year-old Valéry put it, affecting the esthetic mysticism and the esoteric dogmatism of the Symbolist vocabulary: ". . . tout Drame est impossible, après la Messe. Qui dit Drame, pense exotérisme, spectacle. Seule apparition de l'Art devant *tous—tous*. Et le drame liturgique est la Perfection—dans la Perfection" (Corr. AG-PV, 142 f.). These are words of an agnostic who has gone through the esoteric school of Des Esseintes. The essence of Mass is defined in the same letter of December 5, 1891, as "la Chair tenaillée puis abolie par la seule Puissance de la Pensée." This formula poetically summarizes the intense drama of Descartes' autobiographical account concerning his preparation for the *cogito*: that is, to strip away, through the sole power of thought, the flesh, the world and its seductions. What is amazing above all is the permanence of Valéry's thought. Decades later, comparing conventional theatre and liturgy, he comes out again in favor of the latter: "La *Cérémonie* plus noble que le théâtre, pas la grossièreté du simulacre . . ." (Cah. VI, 508). In the liturgy, "tout n'est pas—ou plutôt *rien* au fond *n'est pour le public*. Il faut savoir et *suivre*. (. . .) La messe peut être sans ou avec public" (*ibid.*). One might say that the *Mon Faust* fragments are, and are not, for an audience. Their exoteric spectacle presents minimal action, while their esoteric ironies are concerned with the misfortunes of the *cogito*—thought caught in the web of the body's passions and the mind's superstitions. The Cartesian *cogito* and its frustrating dialogue with the will of the body, so different from its own, are the elements that weave together into a unified fabric the strands of Valéry's theory on liturgical drama with those of his speculations on the direction in which the modern novel should move.

2. Art as an Exorcism of Nature

Valéry's thoughts on the drama of the intellect are tested in his lyrical poetry as well as in much of his prose, in the "melodramas" *Amphion* and *Sémiramis*, the libretto *Cantate du Narcisse*, and, last but not least, in *Mon Faust*. The liturgical comedy *Lust* presents, in a new *décor* and under new masks, the same allegory of the *cogito* that underlies most of his work. It is the secular drama of consciousness observing itself in the exercise of its very function. It dramatizes man's estrangement from himself, the circumstances and consequences of his fall from innocence into the irreversible state of reflectiveness. This drama turns into tragedy, if the hero stands with his back against a wall and has no choice left—in other words, when recognition comes too late for escape. It turns into comedy, when tragedy is averted by way of accommodation, when the *liber arbiter* has the resource of retreating into anticlimactic possibilities. Since it is the *cogito* that determines the *sum*, and since its domain is the exploration of countless possibilities, thought can always accommodate being, and—potentially, at least—avert tragedy. It can do so by shocking the mind with a touch of the unexpected, such as adding to the sublime an element of the ridiculous. The human mind is never totally consistent. Fantasies are always intruding upon thought. "Mélange c'est l'esprit" (P.I, 286) is Valéry's formula for the natural incongruity of consciousness, which mixes the sublime with the trivial, the pertinent with the impertinent. With the aid of some bad taste, one might well imagine Oedipus, at the moment of gouging out his eyes, wondering whether he has ordered the proper selection of wines for tonight's supper. If not in tragedy, in common life, such admixtures of

trivia and the awesome are certainly more frequent than
the total concentration of the tragic hero who is bent on
his own destruction.

It is on such discrepancies that Valéry draws for his
comic effects. In that, his comic vision is not so remote
from Lawrence Sterne's, whose *Tristram Shandy* owes
his pathetic non-nose to a distraction suffered by his
parents during the up-to-then quite enjoyable act of engendering their son. A flaw in concentration can indeed
give a comic twist to the potentially ponderous gravity of
the *cogito, ergo sum*. It can lend an element of farce or
operatic levity to the essentially tragic scene of Adam and
Eve consuming the fatal apple. This holds true, in particular, if the author is, like Valéry, an agnostic, and if,
like Valéry, he practices cogitation as an Art for Art's
sake, in the full knowledge that the only Being that the
cogito produces is the verbalization of Myth.

Valéry's thought, then, can play on the *cogito*, binding
it up inextricably with the idea of original sin, and with
the events that immediately precede the Fall of Man. They
are not events in a literal sense. Stories that never occurred
in history, their scene is the human imagination. They
never happened in time—even if one were to take them
literally: they would have taken place *outside* time, in the
extra-temporal setting of eternity. As myth, they recur in
the ever-repeated cycles of symbolic re-enactments of the
Fall of Man—in his inability to resist the temptations of
intellectual pride and of its allegorical struggle with the
distractions of demonic but very real appetites. Man fallen
from grace shares Lucifer's revolt against creatureliness
by erecting his own verbal creation, his *Art*, against the
creation of the divine Word. Through reflectiveness, man
may have lost his natural innocence. What he has gained is
the exploration of *le possible*, of the unlimited possibilities

that lie outside the fixed confines imposed upon everything in nature, including his own physical existence. Consciousness can invent its own universe, transcend nature and transcend even itself, by focusing upon the mechanics of its own contrivances. Thought and imagination can reverse and alter reality; they can project themselves instantaneously into the past and into the future, give lasting essence to a floating vision. Art is the exorcism by which man imposes the order of his mind upon the randomness of events in nature, in society, in history, in his own life.

At this point, it will prove useful to go back once more to the young Valéry's letter to Gide, dated December 5, 1891: ". . . En somme, je puis dire que tout Art est la mise en forme de cette fameuse parole: *Et eritis sicut dei* (*sic*). C'est l'opium difficile et rien de plus! C'est peut-être du Démon mais Tout ce qui s'égare hors de cette voie n'est qu'informe et chaotique" (Corr. AG-PV, 143). "And you will be like God," the serpent's words from Gen. 3:5 find their complement in the irreverent twist that, in 1916, Valéry gives to John 1:1 "Rien ne serait sans la parole" (Cah. VI, 456)—*la parole* being simply language: man's poetic word which, like the Divine Logos, can draw its creation *ex nihilo*, and bring order into chaos. "Au commencement était la Fable" (P.I, 394). The past exists only in the mind. It is nothing else but a conglomerate of fables, for *"ce qui fut* est esprit, et n'a de propriétés qui ne soient de l'esprit. (. . .) a la limite, il n'y a plus que du *toi*. C'est tout *du toi*: fable pure" (P.I, 394). Since all history turns into myth, it is little more than a hoax. Hence, "In the beginning was the Word" might as well read: "Au commencement était la Blague" (P.II, 694; Cah. VI, 456). Things invariably start out as fairy tales: Genesis, descriptions of the universe, babies born in cabbages (P.II, 694).

In short, myth is all that which cannot exist outside of language (Cah. xxiii, 159). These are the words of Valéry in 1940; they express in different terms what Valéry had said since the beginning: e.g., "Dieu est quelques mots" (Letter to Gide, dated August 10, 1891; Corr. AG-PV, 120). Human imagination (one may conclude, although Valéry does not clearly say so) invents those fictions of life which harden into facts of life. *Homo fictor* and *homo factor* are interchangeable with the idea of *homo faber*: man the maker fabricates his fictional universe of facts, that is, of reality transmuted through verbal interpretation.

In short, Valéry's meaning is clear and distinct: without verbalization, the flux of existence would leave no trace of its passage. Human language and art alone can transfigure existence into being, flux into permanence (or a semblance thereof). Art and language alone can mythologize the crude raw material of life into those mythical patterns which are universally accepted on faith, as theology, philosophy, history, and the passing show of highly volatile scientific hypotheses. For Valéry, they illustrate the human mind's ability to explore the vast realm of theoretical possibilities, and the skill of consciousness that imposes its arbitrary order upon the chaotic mixture of partly pertinent, but more often unrelated, events in nature, society, and history.

3. *The Misfortunes of Thought, or "La panse qui pense"*

I found it necessary to take this long detour to lead into Valéry's *Lust, la demoiselle de cristal*, a comedy almost devoid of plot, which is neither a comedy of character, à la Molière, nor a comedy of situation, à la Beaumarchais. It is predominantly a cerebral comedy, and its comical aspects must remain largely invisible to the English-speaking audience, for they are mostly enshrined in untranslatable puns. At best, *Lust* can be called a comedy of errors, and this in a threefold sense. To the first one we have already pointed: the comedy of the trials and errors of consciousness in its incessant struggles with phantoms of its own creation. Secondly, man's error in the Garden of Eden, his "original sin," forever repeated, and no longer "original" in the modern sense of the word. It has been rendered harmless by the obsolescence of faith in God or in the Devil. Twice Faust and Lust bite into the forbidden fruit, only to gain insights into the workings of the human heart, which remains opaque and a mystery to the forces it defeats: to Mephistopheles and his creatures, Astaroth, Bélial, and the incubus-succubus Goungoune. A third bite into the once fatal but now harmless fruit from the tree of knowledge—to be performed by the disciple—turns out to be abortive: the disciple can do without it. Finally, the third aspect of *Lust* as a comedy of errors is provided by Mephistopheles, who has lost his grip on humankind, and lets himself be tempted to commit, in his turn, a kind of "original sin" on the order of Eve's and Adam's.

By now, the reader may feel mystified. A comedy? he may wonder. The answer is a comedy, indeed: a comedy, frivolous, sparkling, but also anguishing. It is a promise held out by the very name "Lust," the crystalline Damsel.[3] It evokes delight, luster, refracting prisms, light refracted as spectrum, even the purifying rites of lustration. On the dark side, the name "Lust" suggests lust, sensuous appetites and temptations that may lead to the consumption of the forbidden fruit. *Act One, Scene 1*: The curtain

---

[3] For a thorough study of the name "Lust," and an equally impressive survey of research along these lines, see Erika Lorenz, "Der Name *Lust in* Paul Valérys erstem Faustfragment," *Romanistisches Jahrbuch*, XXII (1971), 178 ff.

rises on Lust's crystalline bursts of laughter, which temporarily interrupt Faust in the dictation of a hybrid
magnum opus, part *Memoirs*, part philosophical *Treatise*.
Faust reprimands Lust: "*Ici, on ne rit pas.*" His study is
no place for laughter. Nor is laughter itself a laughing
matter. Its essence is bestial, demonic, a spasmodic reminder of man's unhealthy condition, halfway between
angel and beast: variations on the theme of Baudelaire's
De l'Essence du rire. Lust apologizes, tries to explain:

> *Lust*: Pardon, Maître . . . C'est un peu votre faute. Je sais
> trop ce que c'est que le rire. Vous avez dicté, l'autre
> jour, que le rire est un refus de penser, et que l'âme se
> débarrasse d'une image qui lui semble impossible ou
> inférieure à la dignité de sa fonction . . . comme . . .
> l'estomac se débarrasse de ce dont il ne veut pas garder
> la responsabilité, et par le même procédé d'une con-
> vulsion grossière.
>
> *Faust*: Eh bien, n'est-il pas vrai? Et n'est-il pas très re-
> marquable que l'âme et l'estomac aient mêmement
> recours à la force brutale pour . . . repousser . . . (P.ii,
> 279).

Catharsis, in a figurative sense: a rhetorical device is
brutally likened to its literal meaning, purgation. The
psychological purge through laughter is compared to a
bowel movement. From the outset, Valéry strikes hard at
the root of human absurdity, the split between mind and
body, begun by the ancient Greeks and made irreconcilable by Descartes. Metaphysical comedy results from the
disproportion between the soaring aspiration of the mind
—its flight toward the infinite—and the plight of the
finite body to which it is wedded. The body's inescapable
gravity always brings the mind's genius crashing down to

the agonizing confines of its earthly, all too earthy, prison. Don Quixote begins the noble work. When he gives up the spirit, his work is carried on by Sancho Panza, on an even less sublime level of the absurd. The point is made in *Act III, Scene 1*, by Bélial, a minor servant of Mephistopheles: human beings are mongrels, half flesh, half ideas; bellies that ruminate. *La panse qui pense*—the paronomasia gets lost in the translation. It unmistakably evokes Sancho Panza, the pathetically idealistic stomach that continues the mind's work where the mind retreats into failure.

Lust reads back the dictation she has taken. When she comes to the words, *"Eros energoumenos,"* Faust realizes that they are not of his invention. But they *ought* to be. He promptly usurps them as his own, just as he incorporates into his *Memoirs* all the legends that circulate about his mythical figure, and claims as his own the discoveries of Cardano. *"Eros energoumenos,"* we find out later, was slipped among his notes by Mephistopheles. Faust's shameless way of appropriating it, together with all other mental fare he encounters, symbolizes the mind's capacity to imitate the animal stomach, its ability to assimilate and digest all nourishment in the service of its own growth. Terence's "I am human; nothing human is alien to me," is here adapted to intellectual life: "I am mind, I consider nothing mental is alien to me," or "everything mental *could* be, and consequently *ought* to be, my own product."

Faust's attitude recalls Goethe's defense for having imitated Job 1:6-12 in his "Prologue in Heaven," where the Lord allows Mephistopheles to tempt Faust: "Warum soll er [der Dichter] sich scheuen, Blumen zu nehmen, wo er sie findet? Nur durch Aneignung fremder Schätze

entsteht ein Grosses" (Letter to F. von Müller, dated
December 17, 1824) ("Why should he [the poet] shy
away from picking flowers where he finds them? Only
through the assimilation of alien treasures do great things
come into being"). Or, in Valéry's more direct words:
"Soit qu'il mange l'agneau, soit qu'il couvre la louve, le
loup ne peut que faire ou refaire du loup" (P.II, 187). The
Biblical "Le vent souffle où il veut; tu entends sa voix,
mais tu ne sais ni d'où il vient ni où il va" (John 3:8), is
quoted only in part by Lust: "L'esprit souffle où il veut."
Faust modifies her quotation, "L'esprit souffle où il peut,
ce qu'il peut (P.II, 288), "The wind blows wherever it can,
whatever it can," or, translated with equal literalness:
"The mind steals wherever it can, whatever it can," for
esprit, in French, does double duty for "spirit" and "mind,"
—and souffler, "to blow," "to breathe," is slang for "to
steal." A third variation on this theme, equally ambiguous,
makes clear that this meaning is implied: "L'esprit vole
où il peut" (P.II, 328) which suggests both: "The spirit
flies wherever it wants to," and "The mind steals wherever
it wishes to," since voler means "to fly" and "to steal."
Mental activity is brutally reduced to the assimilation of
mental theft, a reduction that may scandalize the reader,
but that ultimately conforms to Valéry's concept of the
mind's action as reflectiveness, as consciousness reflecting
itself and reflecting whatever is consciousness in the self
and in the other. Its reduction to a digestive mechanism,
to a sort of mental stomach, consistently continues and
extends the parallelism of physical and intellectual functions that, as a grimly comical theme, runs through all of
Mon Faust.

"Eros energoumenos," Faust approvingly muses. By
interpreting Eros energoumenos as "Eros source of extreme energy" (P.II, 282) he conveniently brings together

eroticism and the modern physical theory of energetics.[4] Wittingly or by default, he overlooks the *theological* meaning of *Eros energoumenos*, which is: "Love possessed by the Devil"—love, the means by which the desires abolish will, and love, the avenue through which sexual fantasies intrude upon consciousness. *Eros energoumenos*, the perturbance that he tries to ignore, overpowers Faust, who suddenly feels compelled to fondle Lust's ear, while he wishes her to be transparent, so that he may read her thoughts. Lust is wondering whether Faust has actually had commerce with the Devil. He answers, yes, *the devil is whatever one desires*.

4. *"Le Style, c'est le diable"*

Scene II: The Devil enters in clerical garb, very elegant. He offers his services if Faust wants to *"effeuiller une nouvelle Marguerite"* in the person of Lust. Faust denies such intentions. Mephistopheles replies that Faust has invoked him by thinking of him 3,200 times in the last eight days, since Lust has come into the house. All Faust wants from Lust is tenderness, which, one might say, is a reasonable restriction if one considers his very old age. He wants to use Mephistopheles and render him a service in return. What follows is the *temptation of Mephistopheles by Faust*. For, Faust tells Mephistopheles that his physics and his whole superstitious approach are outdated and absurd. No one believes in the Devil any more. Faust will rejuvenate Mephistopheles by teaching him modern methods, the modern recognition of chaos, the death of the indi-

---

[4] His interpretation is reminiscent of Baudelaire's observation in "La Fin de Don Juan": ". . . car ce n'est pas la qualité des objets qui fait la jouissance, mais l'énergie de l'appétit" (Baudelaire, *Oeuvres complètes*, éd. Pléiade, 1244).

vidual in numbers. In exchange, Faust wants to borrow
the Devil's pen for his planned book of false and true
memoirs—his own version of Goethe's *Dichtung und
Wahrheit* (*Fiction and Truth*). In order to record "toutes
[ses] voix diverses," all his contradictions (P.II, 297), he
needs the Mephistophelean STYLE "that weds itself to all
modulations of the soul and to all sudden shifts of the
mind and spirit to become the living body of the writer"
(P.II, 298). Giving a slight twist to an often misquoted
word by Buffon, both agree that "Le style . . . c'est le
diable" (P.II, 298). The word reaches beyond its literal
meaning to the very essence of Valéry's poetics: a pun on
the colloquial *C'est le diable à réussir*, it implies that it is
style that it is devilishly hard to bring off, while ideas,
topics, delicate states of mind and soul are a dime a dozen.
For all art is *l'art de persuader*, the seductive trickery of
rhetoric, the serpentine road of insinuation, leading the
reader through an enchanted forest of poetic symbols that
hold out the temptation of *Et eritis sicut Dii*, "Le style . . .
c'est le diable."

To come back to Mephisto's temptation by Faust: The
Devil is horrified by Faust's account of modern man who
has no style in life and letters, who believes in neither
vice nor virtue, whose religion is trivial, and who makes a
mockery of all sacraments. (Shades of Baudelaire!) Mephistopheles bares his arm to provide the drop of blood
with which to sign a new pact with Faust. Faust scorns
such infantilities. Pacts are more volatile in the Europe of
1940 than the Devil's word. In evil and in negation, man
has surpassed the Devil to the extent that, by comparison,
the Devil, naïve and innocent, can be tempted by man to
partake of the fruit from the tree of Man's own elusive,
deceptive, and highly destructive knowledge.

Scene III: Lust rushes in, calling for help to put out a

fire in the laboratory. Mephistopheles does so, demonstrating that that particular fire was an illusion of his
making. Since Lust still doubts his power, he forces her
to look deeply into his eyes. She cries out in horror: he has
shown her the abysmal depth of her most secret longings,
the hidden phantoms of her lust. *"Eros energoumenos,"* a
gross convulsion—no laughing matter.

5. Beware of Love

Act II: Faust walks in his garden. He is accosted by the
disciple, who is at first awed by the master, then shocked
by Faust's simplicity, which he mistakes for banality. He
pleads for an exciting experience, on the order of "the
bite of the serpent of wisdom in my flesh" (P.II, 313). The
serpent's insinuation, *"Et eritis sicut Dii,"* precedes its bite.
It haunts the disciple's mind like an inner voice, pleading
for the loss of innocence through the rather disappointing
sting of knowledge, as experienced by the first couple in
Paradise, and, more excitingly, by *La Jeune Parque*, as an
awakening of sense and senses. But far from tempting
(leave alone, awakening) the disciple, Faust plays the
innocuous role of *senex magister amoris: "Prenez garde à
l'Amour"* (P.II, 313) is his Cartesian advice against the
deceptive powers of passion. Faust, a physician who does
not heal himself, fails to heed his own warning, enam-
ored as he is with the Mephistophelean formula *"Eros
energoumenos,"* although it darkly mirrors his words to
the disciple: "Beware of Love!" The disciple asks for an
interpretation, and that Faust inscribe the words in his
copy of a book by the master. Faust refuses. He now only
dictates. His past experience with the Devil has made him
wary of writing down things and signing them.
    Scene II: Alone, the disciple vituperates against Faust,

who fails to live up to his image of what a master should be, which he specifies, by sketching a portrait resembling to a hair the platitudinous *persona* that is commonly ascribed to Goethe, posturing for posterity. In doing so, he commits the beginner's mistake of confusing the author's official pose with the fictitious character of his protagonist, and his intangible *creator spiritus* with the mask his critics have forced on him: "C'est pas naturel, d'être si naturel, tout en étant surnaturel . . . Non. Ma foi, j'aime les grands hommes qui ont l'air grand homme et Olympien, avec un énorme front et le doigt dessus . . . et l'œil . . . l'œil, tout est là! Enfin tout ce qu'il faut pour ressembler à ce qu'on veut paraître . . ." (P.II, 314 f.). Musing over the triviality of Faust's words, the disciple attempts to translate them into Latin, in the hope that a learned disguise will make them sound less asinine. But he runs into the kind of embarrassment that confronts every translator, the inherent ambiguity of language, and the obvious absence of style, that diabolical and devilish attribute of the accomplished master: "Je traduis: Cave Amorem. C'est moins nul en latin . . . Ou plutôt: Cave Amores? Non. Cave venerem, c'est mieux. Mais Cave amorem fait penser à Cave d'amour."

Scene III: Mephistopheles enters. The disciple mistakes him for Faust's secretary. The scene turns into a variation of Mephisto's impersonation of Faust in *Faust I* ("Studierzimmer") (1868 ff.), where the Devil inscribes the naïve freshman's album with well-known advice (slightly misquoted by Goethe): "*Eritis sicut Deus, scientes bonum et malum.*" In the present situation, Mephistopheles offers to write Faust's dedicatory note into the disciple's copy of a book by Faust. He even offers to add a touch of profundity: "Si vous voulez, je puis y mettre un rien de profondeur . . . C'est ma spécialité . . . Je suis assez connu comme Déprofondiste" (P.II, 317). The dramatic irony goes beyond a mere hint at the *De profundis clamavi* and at the Devil's true nature and habitat, of which the disciple is clearly unaware, although he now feels that Mephisto is carrying him off ("Hé! Pas si fort! Vous m'emportez, sapristi!"). The allusion to "profundity" rounds out the portrait of Goethe, which the disciple's wishful thinking would have liked to have seen in Faust. Valéry indeed had suspicions as to the genuine depth of Goethe's style. They were published in 1946 by René Berthelot: "Il y a quelque chose qui me gêne chez Goethe. J'ai l'impression qu'il a un *truc pour faire profond.*"[5] If the *cogito* is man's lucid side, style is his dark and Satanic aspect: "Le style—c'est le diable."

6. *Eros Energoumenos*

Scene IV: Lust looks for Faust. She is aware of her role as a mirror to Faust and the Other. She feels "as though there were no one inside [her]." She cannot think any more. "Is it because there is so much thought hereabouts?" (P.II, 317). A feeling of emptiness is overtaking her: "Après tout, c'est peut-être un vide, que l'âme? C'est peut-être seulement ce qui demande sans cesse ce qui n'est pas?" (*ibid.*). *Ame, anima,* the breath of life manifests itself by a negative power; emptiness, hunger, thirst, want, desire— the incessant search for nourishment and fulfillment—are the animal conditions that govern the existence of the soul as much as that of the body.

Scene V: Faust arrives. He presents Lust with a rose. He

[5] "Lettres échangées avec Paul Valéry," *Revue de Métaphysique et de Morale*, January 1946, p. 2. A similar observation, more laconic and more biting, can be found in the *Cahiers* (1931): "Goethe—comédien—de la profondeur" (Cah. xv, 142).

wants to dictate, but he finds that life, mere existence, is
fulfilling enough: "Je vis. Et je ne fais que vivre. Voilà
une œuvre . . . Enfin ce que je fus a fini par construire ce
que je suis. Je n'ai plus aucune autre importance. Me
voici le présent même" (P.ii, 321). Could this be Faust's
"moment of eternity," that instant of total fulfillment that,
in Faust's wager with Mephistopheles (*Faust I*, 1701 ff.),
would herald the Devil's victory? Is the art of totally living
in the present the answer to Lust's soliloquy on the perpetual state of want of body and soul? Faust is indeed
ready to merge with the infinite, but his senses are stronger.
In the first scene, a pervasive scent of strawberries, or was
it the memory of their aroma? had driven him to fondle
Lust's ear. Now the perfume of the rose aggravates his
reaction to Lust, who is touching his shoulder. Baudelairian anticipations of Satanic threats and arcana had been
in the air ever since Lust's and Faust's analysis of laughter,
which so closely follows Baudelaire's definition of *le rire*
as "une convulsion nerveuse, un spasme involontaire,"
without daring to jump to his conclusion: "Le rire est
satanique, il est donc profondément humain" (*Oeuvres
complètes*, éd. Pléiade, 715 f.).

There had been other Baudelairian hints of an unmistakable nature. The disciple had flattered Faust by calling
him "*le flambeau* même de ce temps" (P.ii, 310; my italics). Somewhat later, Faust had pontificated: "*L'homme
est donc une sorte d'éphémère* qui ne revit jamais ce jour
unique, qui est toute sa vie" (P.ii, 312; my italics). In Act
III, Mephistopheles will suggest to Lust, on whom he tries
to focus the disciple's concupiscence, that the latter is but
"un aimable jeune homme, ici venu, *comme vient un in-
secte à la flamme,* venu puiser la lumière Faustienne à la
source" (P.ii, 345; my italics). Altogether, these scattered
fragments of literary souvenirs, rebus-like, spell out a clear

and distinct allusion to the mysteriously amoral (and most likely, Satanic) nature of the artist's pursuits:

> L'éphémère ébloui vole vers toi, chandelle,
> Crépite, flambe et dit: Bénissons ce flambeau!
> ("Hymne à la Beauté," vv. 17 f.)

Wherever the senses overpower *le bon sens*, Mephistophelian forces are at work, and become manifest in Baudelairian symbols and synaesthesia. Now, in Scene v, the Baudelairian perturbance of the mind by way of olfactory experiences leads to a moment of temptation. But Faust returns to his dictation. He fabricates, or thinks that he is fabricating, the memory of a love adventure with a comely young widow. Lust nearly faints with jealousy. Faust tries to reassure her that the comely young widow is a poetic license of the kind needed to make *Memoirs* readable. The implied moral conforms to Valéry's concept of the past: purely a matter of the mind, its purported facts have turned into the stuff of which fiction is made. Faust stops dictating. He takes Lust on a tour of the garden. The temptation of present beauty eclipses the uncertainties of resurrecting intact memories of past beauty. Lust picks a ripe peach, bites into it, and gives it to Faust, who takes a bite and hands the fruit back to her. She takes his arm, and they go out left—*manu sinistra*, through the Devil's sinister exit.

Scene VI: Mephistopheles slides down from the peach tree in the form of a green serpent. He laments that while everyone eats the fruit from the tree of knowledge (*connaissance*), there is no tree of acknowledgment (*reconnaissance*). The Devil is always invoked, never thanked. And yet, it is he who organizes fantasies that lead to encounters with passionate young widows and their successors. "For," Mephistopheles informs us, "that passionate

young widow was a very passionate fact. . . ." For the force
that awakens lascivious desires, it is indifferent whether
they are satisfied or whether, as mere fictions, they haunt
the fantasies of the mind, disturbed by the body's passions.
As though to summarize the perturbing fantasies that he
controls, and that interfere with all rational controls, he
ties together Faust's exorcism of the spasms of *love* with
the rictus of *laughter*, the two phenomena he dominates:
"Ha ha! Érôs énergumène . . . Prenez garde à l'Amour
. . . Amour, amour . . . Hi hi hi! Convulsion grossière . . .
ha ha ha!"

7. *Nocturnal Forces and Phantoms at Work*

Act III, Scene I illustrates what exactly Mephistopheles
understands by love: Eros possessed by the Devil. The
setting, significantly, is Faust's library, the mausoleum of
the collected works and errors of the *cogito*. Significantly
too, the disciple is seen fast asleep, his head resting on an
open volume, as though he were to exemplify Faust's
contempt for all book learning, ten years after he earned
his doctorate ("Habe nun, ach! Philosophie, / Juristerei
und Medizin, / Und leider auch Theologie / Durchaus
studiert" etc., Faust I, 354 ff.). It is a sentiment that runs
parallel to Descartes' feelings on these matters, as we shall
see below, in chapter two. While the mind is asleep, the
never-sleeping passions torment it. They are represented in
deceptive embodiments of spirits from below who appear
in the form of three devils, lounging in conversation or,
rather, who are at work, as we shall instantly see. Each
one characterizes himself through his words. *Bélial*'s mission is to soil everything he touches: thoughts, glances,
words. He represents the negative side of truth, for who-
soever seeks truth finds the hideous, the obscene, the

degraded. *Astaroth*, patron of monotony and boredom, could have stood as model for Baudelaire's *Ennui* in the Preface *Au lecteur* of *Les Fleurs du Mal*. He gnaws at human hearts, bodies, glory, races of men, rocks, and at time itself, reducing all to the ultimate dust. *Goungoune*, incubus-succubus, supplies the sexual fantasies of which daydreams and night dreams are made. All three despair of ever knowing mankind in its impure mixture of flesh and spirit—in Bélial's words, which echo through all of *Mon Faust*: "la panse qui pense" (P.II, 337). Faust perplexes them as the soul that outwitted their master; is he indeed *plus malin* (shrewder) than *le malin* (the Devil) himself (P.II, 339)? If not more than a human being, Faust must be in some little way something else than a human being: "Mais l'Homme d'ici est comme un peu autre chose qu'un homme, sais-tu?" inquires Goungoune (*ibid.*). Meanwhile, in her ambivalent role as incubus-succubus, Goungoune inspires the disciple with the vivid imagery of sexual fantasies: "Je vois ton amoureux destin qui vient chargé de vie, au fil du riche fleuve de ton sang" (*ibid.*). In conformity with Descartes' mechanistic psychology, these amorous passions are carried by animal spirits in the blood stream to the dreaming mind.

Scene II: With a whip in his hand, Mephistopheles enters, cursing his assistants. It is his way of praising them: "Tristes brutes incorporelles, vermine de la fange du feu éternel, vous, mes sombres suppôts, valets ignobles du bourreau que je suis" (P.II, 340). The demons psalmodize together: "Satan, ayez pitié de nous," echoing Baudelaire's refrain, "O Satan, prends pitié de ma longue misère!" in "Les Litanies de Satan." Mephistopheles alludes to their role in the divine plan of the universe: ". . . blasphèmes figurés, instruments d'épouvante par qui s'exerce toute la bassesse de la Très Haute Justice" (P.II, 341). Goungoune, still engaged in insinuating obscene dreams into the disciple's mind, is ordered to suborn Lust and the disciple through sexual fantasies.

Scene III: Lust enters with a lamp. She looks for a book to keep herself from thinking: "Un livre . . . Un livre pour ne pas penser . . . Un livre entre mon âme et moi . . ." (P.II, 342). Not to think is not to be herself. She wants to block out her *cogito* (and being herself) with the fiction of "quelque autre vie que la mienne" (*ibid.*). Mephistopheles and his three helpers now appeal in unison to her prurient instincts. She feels their voices as hers, and not as hers; their *ensemble*, she vaguely intuits, combines into the voice of the Other: "O quelle voix me parle qui est la mienne et qui me tourmente comme une autre . . . (P.II, 343). The diabolical quartet insinuates: "AIME-TOI . . . AIME-TOI . . . AIME TOUS TES DÉSIRS!" They try to have her identify with her passive nature, her passions. Mephistopheles makes himself visible. He offers his services: "Je débrouille . . . Je simplifie . . . Les gens ont peur de leurs idées . . . Ils ont peur d'aimer ce qu'ils aiment . . ." (P.II, 344). With a rhetorical sleight of hand, he passes off lascivious fantasies for ideas, for acts of the intellect: "Lisez et relisez ce roman favori qui ne cesse, dans votre tête, de s'écrire, et de s'illustrer, de se refaire et parfaire, aussi vivant que vous-même . . . sinon davantage" (*ibid.*). His appeal to her imagination has the opposite effect. Horrified, Lust exclaims: "Le Monstre! . . . Toujours là . . ." (*ibid.*); perceiving him "there" and not "here"—as an insinuation of concupiscence coiled in her mind—but outside, she has resisted his persuasion. She discovers the disciple and fears that he is dead. Mephistopheles reassures her. He now tries to arouse her desires for the young man. Stichomythia marks the high drama of her struggle with the tempter:

Lust: Je vous hais, je vous hais!
Mephistopheles: Me haïr . . . c'est m'aimer!
                                        (P.II, 345)

It could stand as a worthy reversal of Chimène's indirect
confession of her love for Rodrigue:

Chimène: Va, je ne te hais point.
Don Rodrigue: Tu le dois.
Chimène: Je ne puis.
                              (Corneille, *Le Cid*, III, vi)

Although the three assistant devils, as pure spirits of the
impure, are invisible and inaudible to her, she senses the
presence of Evil, and pities the disciple for his vulnera-
bility. Lust's heart remains opaque to Mephistopheles.
Lust, the complex allegory of the human heart and its
crystalline labyrinth of contradictions, remains a mystery
to the simple and simplistic powers of Evil. Mephistopheles asks Lust whether she loves Faust. She does not know.
Lust and Faust, heart and mind in their physical bondage,
are uncertain of their inclinations. They need one another
as interpreters, and as refracting mirrors that reflect one
upon another with a certain degree of distortion. But she
can understand the Devil, "un déchu, un vaincu." It is in
negative terms that she apprehends the Spirit of Negation:
"Il n'y a point de musique en vous . . ." (P.II, 349). What
she perceives in him is the Satanic side of humanity, for
her definition echoes Baudelaire's "L'Héautontimorou-
ménos":

        Ne suis-je pas un faux accord
        Dans la divine symphonie?

Her next sentence—an apostrophe to her very essence, her
heart—opposes the indifference of beauty to matters of
good and evil: "O mon coeur, tu te moques du mal . . . et

même du bien. . . ." Again, her words sound like a para-phrase of Baudelaire's first question in "Hymne à la Beauté":

> Viens-tu du ciel profond ou sors-tu de l'abîme,
> O Beauté!

But they also reflect Baudelaire's answer to this question, in the poem's last quatrain:

> De Satan ou de Dieu, qu'importe? Ange ou Sirène,
> Qu'importe, si tu tends,—fée aux yeux de velours,
> Rythme, parfum, lueur, ô mon unique reine!—
> L'univers moins hideux et les instants moins lourds?

In the context, Lust's apostrophe to herself is a fervent reassertion of the heart's final triumph over good and evil, the triumph of the irrational side of life's creative forces, as Valéry so movingly affirms it in one of the last pages of the *Cahiers*, not quite two months before his death:

> *Il triomphe. Plus fort—en tout* que l'esprit, que l'or-ganisme—voilà le fait. Le plus obscur des faits. Plus fort que le vouloir vivre et que le pouvoir comprendre est donc ce sacré—C[oeur]—"Coeur"—c'est mal nommé. Je voudrais, au moins, trouver le vrai nom de ce terrible résonateur—Il y a quelque chose en l'être qui est *créateur* de *valeurs*, et cela est tout-puissant—irrationnel—inexplicable, ne s'expliquant pas. Source d'énergie *séparée* mais qui peut se décharger *aussi bien pour* que *contre* la vie de l'individu—Le *coeur consiste à dépendre*! En somme, je me sens dans un au-delà "Rien ne m'est plus"
>   c'est-à-dire = je ne vois pas ce qui me ferait plaisir dans ce qui est possible—(Cah. XXIX, 909; May 5, 1945)

Lust represents this irrational source of energy, this inexplicable force of vital resonance and creation that opposes the values of life and truth to the living lies staged by Mephistopheles, the master of sleep and death, in the pruriently dreaming mind. "J'endors comme un vrai maître," he boasts (P.II, 345); and, again, in a feminine alexandrine,

> Et puis, j'ai le sommeil. Là, je travaille à l'aise (P.II, 348),

true to the alchemist image of Satan Trismégiste in Baudelaire's preface "Au Lecteur":

> Sur l'oreiller du mal c'est Satan Trismégiste
> Qui berce longuement notre esprit enchanté,
> Et le riche métal de notre volonté
> Est tout vaporisé par ce savant chimiste.

8. *Temptation Gone Sour*

Scene IV: A servant enters, for comic relief; the going was heavy at the end of Scene III, where Mephistopheles reveals that the peach shared by Lust and Faust had come from his own orchard, and Lust admits: "Elle était presque trop bonne" (P.II, 350). The servant complains to Mephistopheles about spooky events in the kitchen. He calls Lust to the table. As they leave the library, Bélial blows out the lamp. Darkness and the powers of darkness take over; all hell breaks loose.

Scene V: Alone with the sleeping disciple, Mephistopheles ponders Lust's unfathomable mystery. Since she herself does not know what she wants, the crystalline Damsel is not truly transparent. But Faust, too, remains enigmatic and opaque to him. Both are as obscure and complex to the Devil as are the human heart and human thought, which he defines as a turgid mixture of what is known and what is unknown. The *cogito*, the intellectual act of experiencing existence through thought, is incomprehensible to him: "Penser, c'est ce qu'ils font quand ils ne font rien" (P.II, 354). The mysterious fire that animates Lust seems to have nothing in common with the flames known to Mephistopheles, this learned expert in the fires of Hell, alchemy, and prurient passions: "Serait-ce quelque feu que je ne connais point?" (*ibid.*). He gets hopelessly lost in Faust's mind and Lust's soul: "Perdition du Diable ... Je ne sais pas penser et je n'ai pas d'âme" (*ibid.*). He sees an easier victim in the disciple. He awakens him, who was under the Demon's spell. The disciple is aware that he fell asleep reading dull prose. His lascivious dream, inspired by the incubus-succubus Goungoune, leaves him with the impression of having lived through a poem: "Je sors d'un poème, mon cher, et non d'une pâteuse prose" (P.II, 355). The Devil, the master and connoisseur of style, pontificates:

> La prose n'est jamais qu'un pis aller, mon cher ...
> (P.II, 355).

His classical alexandrine is, no doubt, meant to underscore this bit of poetic wisdom. The disciple tries in vain to reconstruct his incomparable experience. It defies description: "Je dis des choses absurdes," he admits.

Mephistopheles pontificates again, this time with a parody of Pascal's "Le coeur a ses raisons que la raison ne connaît point ..." (*pensée* 277): "L'absurde a ses raisons, Monsieur, que la raison soupçonne" (P.II, 355). The disciple succeeds in resurrecting fragments of his voluptuous dream that was interrupted by a skeletal giant, black as glittering coal. He knows that this giant was much

thinner than Mephistopheles, "Et pourtant, je savais que
c'était vous" (P.II, 356). Mephistopheles politely points
out that dream is a masquerade, and, "Il se peut que ce fût
là un costume de rigueur pour circuler dans le carnaval
de vos nocturnes libertés" (*ibid.*). He is punning on the
disincarnate nature of libertine dreams, under the aegis of
eternal death and Lucifer, its minister: carnival, "carne
vale," "O flesh, farewell!" is a discrete paraphrase for
memento mori. But such subtleties are lost on the disciple,
who, instead, in his prosaic literalism wants to know what
role Mesphistopheles plays in Faust's household. Mephistopheles obligingly defines his mission in life: "Je fais ce
que l'on veut." He adds, "Et je fais même que l'on veuille."
He is a "professor of existence," and he pimps: "JE PRO-
CURE . . ." (P.II, 358). In one word, "JE SERS" (*ibid.*).
The disciple recalls that a certain Lucifer (whom he does
not name) had cried out against heaven: "I will not
serve!" That was in the old days, says Mephistopheles,
modestly. "Moi, je sers" (*ibid.*). He modifies for his own
purposes of persuasion the definition that Goethe's Mephistopheles gives of himself as "a part of that force, / that
always wills evil and always produces the good" (*Faust I*,
1335 f.): "Bref, je fais du bien, et je fais le bien que je fais
avec le plaisir même que l'on trouve généralement à faire
le mal" (P.II, 359).

His introduction of the pleasure principle blurs the
moral distinctions between good and evil, conveniently
shifting the meaning to concepts of permissiveness, i.e., to
gratifying experiences as contrasted with unpleasant ones.
It eliminates the ironies in the position of Goethe's Mephistopheles, who unwittingly enounces the prediction of his
preordained failure. But it moves Valéry's Mephistopheles
closer to the more cynical deceptions of Baudelaire's Satan

and his "oreiller"—a pillow that lulls suspicions and self-criticism into acquiescence and sleep. There follows a quid pro quo, with a bit of dramatic irony. The disciple exclaims: "Diable!" It is an expletive, meant to express his surprise. Mephistopheles chooses to take it in a literal sense, as an invocation to the Devil: "C'est un appel?" The disciple protests; it was nothing more than "une manière de parler" (*ibid.*). Mephistopheles throws out a bait; if the disciple could evoke the Devil, what would he ask for? The disciple counts on four fingers of his hand: to be handsome, loved, rich, powerful. But, on second thought, he finds himself well off and handsome already. As to love, he would settle for nothing less than "du grand amour"; he wants to be loved for his own sake, and not owing to the Devil's intervention. Money he scorns. Mephistopheles thinks he has understood the disciple's sin. In the banal setting of the twentieth century, the disciple holds up the mirror to the sin that, in a primeval and grandiose décor, had brought about the Devil's own downfall, the sin of Pride. The disciple's pride, in an age without faith, aims not at being like God (in whom he does not believe) but like the godlike Faust he imagines: "Dominer l'esprit par l'esprit . . . Par mon esprit" (P.II, 363), is his Luciferian ambition. It brings the supernatural aura of Satanic revolt down to the human *naturel*, to the reader's unconscious and hypocritical Satanism, his duplicity, in Baudelaire's preface "Au Lecteur."

Mephistopheles now reviews all branches of knowledge, as did his Goethean model, posing as Faust, in his first interview with the student (*Faust I*, 1868 ff.). He reduces all accumulated human knowledge to myth and dust, in a parody of Descartes' rejection of learned authorities (*Discours* I), but also in imitation of Faust's very first lines in

Faust I (354 ff.). With a glance at Faust's vast library, the disciple ironically echoes Pascal's "Le silence éternel de ces espaces infinis m'effraie" (*pensée* 206), bringing down its august anguish from the sublime to the ridiculous: "Le silence éternel de ces volumes innombrables m'effraie" (P.ɪɪ, 365). He rejects this compost heap of "the mind's excrements," a metaphor that takes us back to the beginning of the play, to Faust's cogitations on the parallelism of physiological and psychological processes of assimilation and elimination. Suddenly, the disciple recognizes Mephistopheles. First tentatively: "Et si je vous appelais SATAN, puisque nous jouons Faust" (P.ɪɪ, 371). The ambiguity of his "since we are playing Faust"—referring both to the Devil's cat-and-mouse game with the disciple and to the play in which they perform on stage—seems to shock the young man into facing a reality beyond his rather shaky reserves of belief. Incredulously, he exclaims: "Tu es le Diable! . . . ." Mephistopheles replies: "Vous êtes bien lent à comprendre, mon jeune ami!" ("It took you a long time, my young friend!"). He vanishes, while his shadow remains for some time, projected against the wall, symbolizing the ineffectiveness of his rule in a world that has discovered the far greater powers of evil that man sets in motion when he is left to his own devices.

Scene VI: The disciple is furious. He invites the Devil, who has already disappeared, to go to Hell, there to rejoin his devilish self. He now realizes that *chez* Faust he has found folly, not wisdom. Unwittingly, he falls into the trap Mephistopheles has sprung for him, for he finds that here "sleep is delightful," while the waking state is a nightmare. Altogether, the soarings of the mind, allegorized by Faust, in their vain flight toward the absolute, prove as foolish and unsatisfactory as the sexual illusion

the Devil's companions had dreamt up for him, but whose
deceptions are the only pleasurable benefit the young man
has derived from his visit to Faust's mad domain.

9. *"Hypocrite lecteur, mon semblable, mon frère"*

Scene VII: Lust enters with her lamp to put a few
books back on the shelves. With an obscure hint at his
experience with Mephistopheles, the disciple modifies
Faust's warning, "Beware of Love," into a caveat against
l'esprit: "Prenez garde à l'esprit" (P.II, 372). He means
the spirit of evil that insinuates itself into the mind while
one fancies he is alone. But Lust's reply: "Ce n'est pas
l'esprit que je crains" (*ibid.*) implies that she interprets
l'esprit as the intellect—whose incarnation is Faust. The
disciple indicates that he is still possessed by *l'esprit*, the
spirit of evil, Goungoune's inspiration. He does so, by
repeating Mephisto's insufflation: "Il est l'heure qu'il faut
qu'il soit (...) pour que les êtres qui doivent être ensemble
soient ensemble" (P.II, 372). They come to discuss Mephistopheles. The disciple admits that, in the end, the Devil's
presence frightened him. But that is all he can do, Lust
suggests. The Devil is reduced to the unruly chaos of our
own fears, desires, and anguish. The only temptation he
holds out to the young man is his desire for Lust herself,
who appears to him the very opposite of the Monster. That
he is still bewitched, still possessed with Goungoune's
voluptuous dream, unmindful of Faust's caveat "Beware
of Love," is discreetly suggested by further hidden refer-
ences to Baudelaire's warning preface "Au Lecteur." For
he now proceeds: "*Mais, parmi tous ces biens qu'il (Mephistopheles) prétendait me procurer si je l'écoutais, il en
est un qui me semble à présent le seul ...*" (P.II, 375; my
italics). If one takes into account Mephisto's sleight-of-
hand, which presents "evil" as "good," and if one con-

siders that the image of Lust planted in the disciple's mind
is but a diabolical deception—the combined creation of the
incubus-succubus Goungoune, the defiling devil Bélial,
and Astaroth, the spirit of *l'Ennui*—the disciple's word
fairly accurately paraphrases these verses in Baudelaire's
"Au Lecteur":

> Mais parmi les chacals, les panthères, les lices,
> Les singes, les scorpions, les vautours, les serpents,
> Les monstres glapissants, hurlants, grognant, ram-
>   pants,
> Dans la ménagerie infâme de nos vices,
>
> Il en est un plus laid, plus méchant, plus immonde!
> Quoiqu'il ne pousse ni grands gestes ni grands cris,
> Il ferait volontiers de la terre un débris
> Et dans un bâillement avalerait le monde;
>
> C'est l'Ennui!—

The demons' deception, still active, succeeds in deluding
the disciple into the belief that Lust is transparent to his
mind. He burns with concupiscence: "Je vous assure et je
m'assure que je ne pourrais plus jamais penser qu'à vous"
(P.II, 377). "Thought," the active part of the mind, is
perverted into prurient passion. Lust recognizes this:
"Voilà bien les conseils du Monstre . . ." (*ibid.*). The
disciple rejects "Ce Faust qui m'a déçu, blessé, remis à
rien" (*ibid.*). It is the ultimate refusal of the intellect by
burning, demented passion, which hypocritically blinds
itself to the understanding of its own nature. He does not
see Lust for what she is, the heart as the moderator between mind and blind passion. What he sees is the delusive
object of his lust, "Vous la seule raison, vous, la vie; vous,
l'humaine"; and, in Baudelairian terms, "*vous, ma semblable, ma soeur*" (*ibid.*), echoing the last line of "Au
Lecteur," but significantly omitting the first term of

Baudelaire's surprise attack on the reader, "Hypocrite
lecteur." The meaning of Baudelaire's original "—Hypocrite lecteur,—mon semblable,—mon frère," is distinctly
paraphrased in the title of Valéry's preface to the *Mon
Faust* fragments, addressed "Au Lecteur de bonne foi et
de mauvaise volonté" (P.II, 276). The disciple's own hypocritical lapsus is driven home to him by Lust, who
gently rejects his attempt to take her hands into his own,
thrice repeating Faust's caveat: Beware of Love. She
knows that love is "un bien qui fait mal . . . Très mal . . ."
(P.II, 378)—a sickness, a passion, beclouding the heart as
much as the mind. Her words are ambiguous, meaning
"Love, a good thing that does evil, great evil," but also
"love, this good thing which hurts; hurts very badly." She
leaves him. "Vous me rendez au diable! . . ." he cries,
unaware that, ironically, she has just tried her best, by her
voluntary departure, to deliver him from evil. But, ironically, by refusing his love, she has also precipitated him
back into the hell of his fantasies about her, the inferno
of his ennui.

Halfway between Faust, the allegory of thought, and
the disciple's diabolically inspired passions, only Lust is
fully human. Neither excessive as mind aspiring to the
infinite, nor excessive as the body, ridden by uncontrollable
prurience, she holds up the mirror to the golden mean.
The center of man and his life—as the exemplar of the
human ideal with all its flaws, neither entirely good nor
totally evil, Lust, woman, the heart—tries to keep body
and mind in harmonious balance.

10. *Conclusion*

There exist two fragmentary outlines for Act IV. Faust
tells Lust that tenderness remains as the ultimate value,

after glory, power, and wealth are reduced to ashes. In tenderness, one gropes through beauty, through intellect, to find the Self in the Other. All of Faust's efforts to feel existence through the thinking act of the *cogito* are abolished, in the end, by the heart mirroring its tenderness in its own reflection, in Lust. Faust's efforts to reach her are "effort pour se faire. Oui, l'idée à l'état naissant, et la tendresse qui est l'amour toujours à l'état naissant et renaissant" (P.II, 1413). One must always return "*au coeur et a l'ésprit qu'on a*, ces deux répondants de la vie même" (*ibid.*).

It is Lust, the human heart in its innocent cupidity, who has eaten the forbidden fruit with Faust, thus teaching him the meaning of tenderness. But rather than fulfilling wishes, the promise of *Et eritis sicut Dii* remains only wishful thinking. For Faust's vision of a moment of eternity resembles the illusory copulation of Goethe's Faust with a Helen of Troy he has himself drawn out of his own inner depths—a moment of poetry: "Nous serions comme des Dieux, des harmoniques, intelligents, dans une correspondance immédiate de nos vies sensitives, sans parole— et nos ésprits feraient l'amour l'un avec l'autre comme des corps peuvent le faire" (P.II, 1414). These harmonies will reach beyond the copulation of thought: "n'est-ce pas là du reste l'accomplissement de la promesse, en quoi consiste la poésie qui n'est après tout que tentative de communion? Nous ferions des moments comme l'on procrée des moments qui seraient dérobés au désordre de la vie ordinaire qui est accidentelle et faite de lambeaux" (*ibid.*). The conditional tense indicates that Faust still moves within the confines of wishful thinking. But his anticipation of order created and procreated by poetry is the point where the 69-year-old Valéry of 1940 rejoins the theory of the liturgical drama, which the 20-year-old Valéry had so

strikingly formulated in his letter to Gide, of December
5, 1891, and to which can be added the stylistic lesson of
Mon Faust that "Le style . . . c'est le diable."

The ever-repeated bite into the forbidden fruit, the tantalizing foretaste of a never-coming fulfillment, is trans-
figured by the bewitching and devilish magic of *Art*, into
moments of eternity, i.e., into POETRY, into moments
that have the momentum of a temporary escape into para-
disiac timelessness. *Moment d'éternité*, dictate the stage
directions. But, like all human aspirations, Faust blending
with Lust, the beatific vision of two minds copulating in
the embrace of *poetry*, this unorthodox vision of *La grande
oeuvre*, Faust's alchemical purification through lustral
reflection and rarification, a kind of Ciceronian introspective *lustrare animo*, falls short of its goal. In the end, it
turns into the myth of Narcissus drowning in his own
deceptive image, for "une oeuvre est l'action naïve qui veut
trouver cet autre hors de nous" (P.II, 1414) concludes
Faust. Faust's final lesson on *"das Ewig Weibliche,"* on the
eternally feminine that attracts us, leads to the very center
of the self, to *egocentrism* and solipsism: whatever we
look for is within ourselves—elusive and intangible. What
we find *outside* ourselves are illusions, projected outside
by the Spirit within us, which is never entirely godlike, or
by the Devil within us who is never as simplistically bestial
as the Demon himself, tempered as his deceptions are by
the more tender and more insinuating deceptions of the
human heart. It is a lesson that nonetheless does not end
the folly of man's reflective narcissism, his search for the
Other within *and* without: outside himself in the ever-
repeated comedy of the fall from innocence, and within
himself, as he reaches for the forbidden fruit of the
Cartesian *cogito* that gives him the Faustian foretaste of a
knowledge that is *not* to come.

Two.

LE SOLITAIRE, OU LES MALÉDICTIONS D'UNIVERS. ACT ONE

> Ce n'est qu'un Loup garou, du Soleil ennemi,
> Qu'un animal sauvage, ombrageux, solitaire,
> Bizarre, frenetique, à qui rien ne peut plaire
> Que le seul desplaisir: né pour soy seulement,
> Privé de coeur, d'esprit, d'amour, de sentiment.
>
> Guillaume de Salluste, Seigneur du Bartas,
> *La Sepmaine ov Création dv Monde*, 6ᵉ Jour, 955 ff.

> El sueño de la razón produce monstruos
>
> (The sleep/dream of reason produces monsters)
>
> Don Francisco Goya, *Los Caprichos*

1. *A Cartesian Faust*

After the monstrously cerebral Monsieur Teste, after Valéry's methodical Leonardo, and his Narcissus, who is curious only about his own essence (cf. P.i, 128), Faust represents a last attempt by the author to portray "ce que serait un Descartes qui naîtrait de notre époque" (P.i, 826). His Cartesian version of Faust would be possessed by the same Nietzschean "will to power" that Valéry attributes to Descartes (P.i, 807). Like Valéry's Descartes, he would be intent upon showing and demonstrating "ce que peut un Moi" (P.i, 808). He would, to put it in Descartes' own

terms, "chercher la vraie méthode pour parvenir à la connaissance de toutes les choses dont [son] esprit serait capable" (*Discours* ii; AT, vi, 17). A Cartesian contemporary
of ours, he would have overcome his outdated whirlwind
theory and minor shortcomings in his speculation on the
mechanisms of the Universe and the human body.

The reader who is familiar with Goethe's *Faust* may
easily detect the first link in a chain of associations that
connects Valéry's hero with the image of Descartes. Are
not the very first words of Goethe's Faust like an echo of
passages in the *Discourse on Method*, where Descartes
enumerates the disciplines he had studied at La Ferté and
in Poitiers, without learning anything useful about Nature,
or the conduct of his own reasoning?

Goethe's Faust I:

Habe nun, ach! Philosophie,
Juristerei und Medizin,
Und leider auch Theologie
Durchaus studiert, mit
   heissem Bemühn.
Da steh ich nun, ich armer
   Tor,
Und bin so klug als wie
   zuvor!
   Faust I, 354 ff.

In Nerval's translation:

Philosophie, hélas! jurisprudence, médecine, et toi aussi,
triste theologie! . . . je vous ai
donc étudiées à fond avec ar-
deur et patience: et mainte-
nant me voici là, pauvre fou,
tout aussi sage que devant.

Descartes' Discours:

   J'avais parcouru tous les
livres, traitant de celles [sci-
ences] qu'on estime les plus
curieuses et les plus rares, qui
avaient pu tomber entre mes
mains. (. . .) [Je savais] que
la théologie enseigne à gagner
le ciel; que la philosophie
donne moyen de parler vrai-
semblablement de toutes choses, et se faire admirer des
moins savants; que la jurisprudence, la medecine et les
autres sciences apportent des
honneurs et des richesses à
ceux qui les cultivent. . . .[1]
   Discours de la Methode, i;
AT, vi, 5-9

[1] Marlowe's Dr. Faustus (1604), questioning the value of his
own studies, had enumerated these disciplines almost in the same

The wager of Goethe's Faust with the diabolical inventor of human self-consciousness (*Et eritis sicut Dii*), and Descartes' discovery of self-consciousness as the very foundation of the individual's existence (*cogito, ergo sum*) are guiding forces for Faust in his explorations of the small and the great world, and, for Descartes, in travels abroad that ultimately lead to an ever-deepening exploration of the self and of the physical universe, in a never-ending effort of learning "to distinguish Truth from Falsehood, to understand my actions clearly, and to progress with certainty in this life" (*Discours* 1; AT, vi, 10). If Goethe's Faust, like Marlowe's, resorts to black magic to overcome his scholastic training, the young Descartes, in a similar effort to penetrate the occult sciences, had secretly sought, in 1619-1620, to contact the Rosecrucian Fraternity in Germany. His enterprise turned out to be as fruitless (Baillet, 1, 87-91) as was Faust's alliance with the Devil. In his resolve to seek no other science than "that

---

order, but naming jurisprudence before medicine (Verses 29-64). Goethe's Faust uses the same sequence as Descartes, with this difference: theology takes the last place in Faust's enumeration, while it occupies the first place in Descartes'. The great humanist Vives, as quoted by Gilson in his commentary (p. 102), enumerates the three disciplines of post-graduate learning in this order: ". . . Medicinae, Theologiae, et perititiae Juris, quas supremas artes disciplinasque nominamus." They were taught in the universities, while *philosophia* was studied in Jesuit colleges during the last three undergraduate years (one year of Logic, one year of Physics, and one year of Metaphysics, the latter two disciplines based on Aristotle, see *Gilson*, 118 f.). On the preference given by Descartes to *wisdom* as contrasted with a wealth of useless knowledge accumulated through memorization, and on the origins of this preference in Seneca and Montaigne, see Etienne Gilson's Commentary to Descartes' Discourse, René Descartes, *Discours de la méthode*, Texte et Commentaire par E. Gilson, Paris, Vrin, 1962, p. 93 (to p. 3, l. 9), hereafter mentioned as *Gilson*.

which could be found in [himself], or in the great book
of the World," the young Descartes travels, guided by his
consciousness, as Faust travels, guided by Mephistopheles,
"à voir des cours et des armées, à fréquenter des gens de
diverses humeurs et conditions, à recueillir diverses expériences, à m'éprouver moi-même dans les rencontres que
la fortune me proposait, et partout à faire telle réflexion
sur les choses qui se présentaient, que j'en pusse tirer quelque profit" (*Discours* 1; AT, VI, 9). One feels that, following the irresistible temptation of striving for ever-greater
self-consciousness and knowledge of the universe, Descartes' salvation, like Goethe's Faust's, may ultimately
come to pass by virtue of the very constancy of his intellectual endeavors, or rather by the very quality of his
searching mind, bent on discovering the occult mechanism
of Nature and the thinking essence that distinguishes him
and all sane human beings from the rest of the physical
world.[2]

No wonder then, that Valéry's vision of a Descartes
born in our time comes on stage, in *Le Solitaire*, under
the mask of Faust, acting out in a literal sense the metaphor suggested by his historical model in Descartes' early
Cogitationes privatae (January 1619): "Vt comoedi, mo-
niti ne in fronte appareat pudor, personam induunt: sic
ego, hoc mundi theatrum conscensurus, in quo hactenus

---

[2] Cf. the saving angels in *Faust II*:

Gerettet ist das edle Glied
Der Geisterwelt vom Bösen,
Wer immer strebend sich bemüht,
Den können wir erlösen.   (*Faust II*, 11934 ff.)

(Saved, saved now is that precious part
Of our spirit world from evil:
"Should a man strive with all his heart,
Heaven can foil the devil.")   (MacNeice, 298)

spectator exstiti, larvatus prodeo" ("As the actors, admonished not to show their shyness on stage, put on masks: so I, as I enter this theatre of the world where hitherto I was but a spectator, move forward behind a mask" [AT, x, 213]). The *Discourse on Method* reveals that, in the intervening nine years, Descartes, the new "actor" on the world's stage, chose whenever possible to wear the mask of a traveling "spectator," reflecting on the passing show rather than actively taking part in it:

> Et en toutes les neuf années suivantes, je ne fis autre chose que rouler ça et là dans le monde, tâchant d'y être spectateur plutôt qu'acteur en toutes les comédies qui s'y jouent; et faisant particulièrement réflexion, en chaque matière, sur ce qui la pouvait rendre suspecte, et nous donner occasion de nous méprendre, je déracinais cependant de mon esprit toutes les erreurs qui s'y étaient pu glisser auparavant. (*Discours* III; AT, VI, 28 f.)

It is as a spectator, rather than an actor, that Valéry's Faust, in his travels through the world, reaches that icy, nocturnal, and mountainous scene above the timber line, where, having left Mephistopheles behind, he views with suspicion and some amusement the confused metaphysical anguish of the benighted Solitaire.

2. *The Play as a Charade*

The technique of giving literal readings to figurative expressions, and its inverse, the metaphorical use of literal imagery, are interpretative devices that may appear far-fetched. Yet they seem justified in the light of Valéry's concept of plays as "charades": "Toute pièce de théâtre est une *charade*" (Cah. VI, 230). The definition is excessive, for it obviously does not apply to "all plays." It is, however, justified with regard to the Symbolist idea of theatre, to which both Valéry's lyrics and his dramatic poetry are deeply indebted. The concept of "plays as charades" merely secularizes Valéry's lifelong obsession with "theatre as liturgy." For indeed, in the strictest sense of the word, the Liturgy (in the Eastern rite, the term for the Mass in the Western Church), i.e., the Eucharist, is a ritual charade that symbolically enacts the Sacrifice of the Blood and the Body of Christ.

Valéry's formula of the play as a charade goes to the heart of *Mon Faust*. In *Le Solitaire* even more than in *Lust*, action and dialogue are indeed charades that provide clues to the models for Faust and for his antagonist in Act One; and, in the Interlude, to the poetic temptations of memory and imagination, allegorized by the two Fays. In the performance of these charades, mimicry and the unspoken word contribute to the mythical portrayal of an antagonist whose *persona* conceals the features of a historical character, encountered by Valéry's Faust in Act One. The same holds true for the allegories, who try to enchant him in the interlude, *Les Fées*. Transparent under their masks from the outset, their identities assert themselves by degrees. Rather than any developing plot, it is this slow revelation that engages the audience's attention. The spectator is guided toward the unfolding of characterization through thought, imagery, and gestures, implied as much as expressed, which are pregnant with literary reminiscences, pointing to a meaning *concealed within* their meaning. Since elements of dramatic suspense are conspicuously absent, interest shifts to the play behind the play, or, rather, to the rebus hidden in its cycles. Rather than advancing in a straight line, the play moves around the circles of Faust's rise and fall in a pattern where there is "ni haut ni bas," and in the ever-repeated cycles of charades, whose variations reinforce increasingly clearer hints as to the identity of the characters and the implicit significance of the action.

Like one of Valéry's favorite hieroglyphs, the Ouroboros, "whose tail passes an infinity of times through its mouth, each time by way of one more envelope" (Cah. VII, 750), the hidden charades of Le Solitaire are swallowed by action and dialogue and wait coiled inside this envelope, ready to strike the mind's eye, invited to follow their convolutions. When all is said and done, attention is less focused on the conflicts or on their dénouements than on deciphering those coded messages which lead beyond (i.e., inside the verbal "envelope" of) the play, to a drama of consciousness. On the stage of his mind, Faust is assaulted by forces hostile to Cartesian *bon sens*. On the lifeless heights of metaphysics, he sustains the theological onslaught of the Solitaire's irrationalism, which ultimately plunges him into those lively and abysmal regions of his mind where passions try to draw him into their enchanting orbit. Whatever happens on this abstract stage of thought represents a symbolic play that enacts itself, and beyond itself signifies a mystical presence: the quite tangible presence of a mystery. In this sense, as liturgy and charade, the theatrical fiction transcends mimesis, the imitation of reality. Instead, it symbolizes the reality of a fiction, whose stage is language itself, its rhetorical devices coming to life and entwining their metaphorical charades with those performed by the actors, and those which become manifest in scenery, backdrop, and stage accessories.

In short, language as poetry, a creative force in its own right, is the invisible actor that, rather than obeying action, commands its motion. Language thus ceases to be the mere vehicle of thought, action, and of a plot that is

practically nonexistent. The processes of rhetoric occupy
the center of the stage: literal, figurative, and etymological
meanings combine with puns and literary memories,
clashing to produce those verbal fireworks of periphrastic
imagery which explode into bursts of rebus and charade.
The audience is challenged to perceive, at the same time,
what is represented and what is concealed by the glittering
skin of the Ouroboros-like drama. All gestures and metaphors are incorporated into the play, as *instantanés*, snap-
shots frozen into miniature charades, and swallowed to
add to the inner wealth of nuances, whose total enhances,
underscores, and punctuates the larger charade of the
play as a whole. They are hidden in word figures that
Valéry, a Góngorist in his own right, pushes to the very
limits of their associative potential. Hardened into *boutades*
and *calembours*, their presence can be detected even prior
to action and dialogue in the unspoken word of stage
directions, names, and *décors*.

3. *The Solitaire, Mimicked in Onomastics, Rebus, and Tableau Vivant*

Before even the first word is uttered on stage, panto-
mime and charade combine to intimate the identity
hidden under Le Solitaire's mask. His generic name, his
posture, the very stage set and backdrop instantaneously
convey a *tableau* teeming with ciphered hints.

There are onomastic puns, or what's in a name. The
nameless and unnamed Solitaire points beyond his ancho-
ritic anonymity to the abbey of Port-Royal, whose Jansenist
recluses were called *les Solitaires de Port-Royal*. This tacit
suggestion is borne out by an onomastic pun in reverse,
the Góngorist device of concealing a name in a periphrastic image: "Un lieu très haut" (P.II, 380), the first stage

direction, designating the place, figuratively paraphrases "Montalte," the pseudonym under which Pascal published his *Letters to a Provincial*. They appeared in 1656-1657 as *Lettres de Louis de Montalte à un Provincial de ses amis aux RR.PP. Jésuites sur la morale et la politique de ces Pères*. Stripped of their devastating irony, their inflexible views on the uncertainties of divine grace, and their imprecations are mimicked and echoed (in substance, if not in tone) by the exhortations that the Solitaire launches against his unwelcome visitor, Valéry's Cartesian and urbane Faust.[3] The still tacit onomastic puns are reinforced by the *tableau vivant* offered by the Solitaire as the curtain rises. At first barely visible, "couché à plat ventre sur une roche plate," his very posture implies the Pascalian self-sacrifice ("le moi est haïssable," *Pensée* 455, *et passim*), on the altar of the Church. Both altar and Church are symbolized by the rock of the Apostolic Succession (cf. Matt. 16:18) on which he is prostrated in an attitude of "humility" and "mortification"—the Pascalian antidotes to "pride" and "concupiscence" (*Pensée* 493). His precarious and dramatic position in the midst of precipices, "roches, neige, glaciers," strikingly conforms to Valéry's vision of Pascal—ostentatiously fragile, and surrounded by "perils and solitude" (P.I, 461). Soon he will reveal himself as "cet anachorète [radouci] en homme de lettres" (P.I, 466), spewing forth his anathema, in a pastiche of Pascal's style that Valéry once characterized as a "mélange de ses terreurs et de ses dégoûts avec un espoir intime d'éblouir et

---

[3] L. J. Austin recognized the Pascalian model in the Solitaire: "Or Valéry avait certainement Pascal en vue lorsqu'il fit parler son Solitaire des 'sottises' que le ciel étoilé, 'cette grenaille et ses poussières ont semé (. . .) dans les cervelles.'" L. J. Austin, "Paul Valéry, 'Teste' ou 'Faust'?" *Cahiers de l'Association Internationale des Études Françaises*, XVII, 1965, p. 250.

d'être admiré" (P.i, 466). In his frightened and frightening isolation, a thousand feet above the last vestiges of life, he seems a replica of Valéry's Pascal: a "French Jansenist and Hamlet," "qui frissonne et songe, sur une terrasse opposée à l'univers . . ." (P.i, 465).

The cosmic backdrop against which he is projected adds another nuance to this rebus: "Autant d'étoiles au ciel que sur un cliché de la Voie Lactée" (P.ii, 380). It sets the stage for the Solitaire's forthcoming lamentations on the Pascalian theme of the eternal silence of these infinite spaces, already parodied in *Lust*, and most cruelly analyzed in Valéry's "Variation sur une pensée": "A ce nombre d'étoiles qui est prodigieux pour nos yeux, le fond de l'être oppose un sentiment éperdu d'être soi, d'être unique,—et cependant d'être seul" (P.i, 469).[4] Against this excessively starry backdrop, the Solitaire will soliloquize in the posture of Valéry's Pascal, speaking to himself "sur la marge du néant où il paraît exactement comme sur le bord d'un théâtre" (P.i, 465). His confused and uncertain apologetics

---

[4] Faust will exhibit an indifference toward this stereotype of the Milky Way, which reflects Valéry's cautious attitude in the presence of this overwhelming experience à la Kant: "3ʰ. —Nuit étoilée— Aussitôt toutes les pensées vaines et absurdes—s'ébauchent à l'appel de l'auguste perception. Je m'essaye à ne pas donner un sens à cette exposition de feux froids." (Cah. xxii, 611 f.)

It may be worth noting that the combination of this farcically starry background and the Solitaire's isolation, which is anything but beatific, seem like a savage travesty on Faust's romantically lyrical outburst on the "plains of Hungary," in Scene One of Berlioz's *La Damnation de Faust* (libretto by Berlioz, Gandonnière, and Gérard de Nerval, "after Goethe" [sic]):

Des cieux la coupole infinie
Laisse pleuvoir mille feux éclatants
(. . . . .)
Oh! qu'il est doux de vivre au fond des solitudes,
Loin de la lutte humaine et loin des multitudes!

will invoke *le néant* ("*rien*"), night, darkness, and ignorance. Swelling to whirlwind proportions, his mad
litanies are meant to terrify himself, more than anyone
else, into an attitude of blind faith, while they hurl into an
abyss of verbal damnation Faust, the intruder, suspected of
trying to usurp this privileged site *in excelsis*, seemingly
so near, and yet so far from the seat of divine grace.

4. *On the Stage of Faust's Mind*

We may now surmise what is the nature of the play
behind the play, and on whose theatre of the mind its
metaphysical action takes place. As the curtain rises, the
ambiance is Pascalian, but only in the hostile anticipation
of Faust's arrival on the scene. And Pascalian, as we shall
see, by reaction to a Cartesian Faust, whose mind is the
very scene where the abstract drama of the intellect paral-
lels the nightmarish action performed on stage. Clues are
provided by Valéry's essays on Descartes. After demonstrating how Descartes gives himself "un Diable, pour les
besoins de son raisonnement" (P.I, 829), Valéry mentions
the three fateful dreams of the night of November 10,
1619, which the young philosopher himself considered as
the intellectual turning points in his life. It is my contention (1) that the Pascalian Solitaire plays the role of the
malin génie that a Cartesian Faust elects as the opponent
who ideally fills the needs of his very demanding reasoning; and (2) that the oneiric ambiance of the play boldly
transposes the essentials of Descartes' method and of the
first two of his three dreams. They are distorted only by
the telescoping of chronology and events. By substituting
vivid imagery for the vivacity of sensations, Valéry seems
to adhere to Descartes' own observations on the psychological effects of dreams and their difference from those

of consciously experienced reality (cf. *Traité de l'Homme*, AT, XI, 197 ff.).

Together with flashes from the *Discourse on Method*, the *Dioptrique*, and the Treatises on the World and on Man, Descartes' two first dreams are fused into one unique nightmare, where the Pascalian Solitaire logically plays the only *mauvais génie* worthy of a Cartesian Faust. In much the same way, Pascal plays his negative role opposite Descartes in Valéry's essays on Pascal and Descartes. In short, the Solitaire is quite literally Faust's *Diable* (from Greek διάβολος, "slanderer," but also "he who crosses," "throws over," "sets at variance," etc. [from διαβάλλω]). The Solitaire's whirlwind of slanders, howls, and curses, rising to a crescendo throughout Act One, obstructs Faust's progress in much the same way as Descartes is tempted and kept off balance in his first dream by what he knows to be his "evil genius."

5. *Exit Mephistopheles*

Act One, Scene One: Like the puppets of the original puppet play, and as though emerging from a Delacroix lithograph, Faust and Mephisto enter, one after another, "serrés dans leurs manteaux" (P.II, 380). Mephisto resents being dragged to these heights, where he suffers from vertigo. Faust's lesson in relativity "qu'il n'y a ni haut, ni bas," is lost on the poor devil.[5] Or, rather, does he feel exorcized by Faust's heretical values, which call into question the Devil's very validity as the embodiment of

[5] Valéry describes his Mephistopheles, who is outmoded, superstitious, and out of touch with modern science, in these terms: "[Méphistophélès] un pauvre diable, sans cervelle . . . que les transformations du monde moderne déroutent et déprécient." *Lettres à Victoria Ocampo*, 101. Quoted by Blüher, 49.

absolute evil? For does not his negation of "high" and
"low," "sublime" and "humble," conform to Descartes'
psychology, which rejects the Platonist concept of struggles between the "inferior" and "superior" parts of the
soul?[6] It anticipates and gives the lie to the Pascalian
argument, soon to be acted out by the Solitaire, that "qui
veut faire l'ange fait la bête," and vice versa. As the would-
be tempter, Mephistopheles had already outlived his usefulness in *Lust*, where the tables were turned on him to
the point that he had indignantly recognized in Faust his
own, Mephisto's, tempter. No wonder that, faced with the
rarefied atmosphere and the dizzying heights that Faust's
unconventional ideas have reached, the very conventional
and orthodox Prince of the infernal depths must now bow
out. No match for a consciousness in search of mathematical precision, he is cast out both from Faust's mind,
the theatre of thought, and from the stage of the theatre,
where thought is enacted. He surrenders the scene to an
"evil genius" more befitting a Cartesian Faust. Who,
indeed, could be better suited to replace the trivial Mephistopheles as a more sophisticated spirit of negation than
the Pascalian Solitaire—*abêti* by blind faith, inhuman and

[6] By reducing all inner conflicts to those occurring between the
soul (mind) and the body, and by locating all thought and sensations in the brain, Descartes can indeed do away with the distinction between the heart and the mind, which still plagues Pascal's
psychology; and he can eliminate the Platonist idea of a constant
struggle between the "inferior" and the "superior" parts of the
"soul" (mind)—the charioteer and the two horses in the *Phaedrus*:
"Et ce n'est qu'en la répugnance qui est entre les mouvements
que le corps par ses esprits [i.e., esprits animaux] et l'âme par sa
volonté tendent à exciter en même temps dans la glande [pinéale],
que consistent tous les combats qu'on a coutume d'imaginer entre
la partie inférieure de l'âme qu'on nomme sensitive et la supérieure,
qui est raisonnable, ou bien entre les appétits naturels et la volonté." (*Les Passions de l'âme*, I[e] Partie, art. 47; AT, xi, 365.)

dehumanized by the uncertainties of his apologetics? And whose rhetoric could rival Pascal's in opposing to Descartes' "ni haut ni bas" (the Cartesian exclusion of both mysticism and irrational passions from the realm of reasoning), the "haut" and "bas" of supernatural pleas addressed to the "highest" emotions and to the "basest" instincts at once?

6. Faust and the Essence of Solitude

Act One, Scene Two: "On this roof of the world" (P.II, 381), and surrounded by precipices—or in Pascalian terms of "haut" and "bas," "between these two abysses of the infinite and nothingness" (*Pensée* 72)—Faust's reactions are anything but Pascalian. Undisturbed by his precarious position between the two infinites, he feels neither fear, despair, nor vertigo. He reacts as a scientist, with detachment and dispassionate curiosity: "Je puis regarder le fond d'un abîme avec curiosité. Mais, en général, avec indifférence" (P.II, 381). If Faust feels vaguely ill at ease ("une ombre de malaise," *ibid.*), his malaise belongs to the rational soul, for "sentir" is a function of the mind, which communicates sensations to the body's machine *after* they have become conscious. Faust's malaise, rather than springing from existential anguish, arises from his constant conscious striving toward the rational definition of an essence. In his systematic search for certainty, Faust has chanced upon a wilderness so nightmarish that it can be taken for the very essence of a solitude beyond the confines of humanity. The yawning void of this nocturnal, icy, and starlit mountain peak, unreal in its extreme and lifeless exaggeration, threatens to annihilate the Self by swallowing it up: "La solitude essentielle, l'extrême de la raréfaction des êtres . . . ," observes Faust. "Personne, d'abord; et puis, moins que personne" (P.II, 381).[7] On this inhuman summit, where the nihilism of rarefied being extends its menace to body and mind, all clear and distinct notions are in danger of dissolving into a muddled and indistinct confusion of contradictory ideas and emotions, each one emerging in its turn, and all of them seeming equally valid or invalid.

The external stage, where Valéry's "féerie dramatique" takes place, blends with the intimate theatre of Faust's mind, appearing to reflect the experience of the young Descartes, on the verge of discovering his method. The process of Descartes' discovery was described by Baillet as "ce qui se passa dans son esprit, et dont il fut le seul acteur" (Baillet I, 77). In addition, these stark surroundings, where there is nothing but "pierre, neige, un peu d'air, l'âme et les astres," recall the oppressive atmosphere that pervaded Descartes' dream, and his uncertain state between sleep and waking, accompanied by the hallucinatory vision of innumerable "sparks of fire." Transported into a Pascalian nightmare of uncertainty, thought has carelessly risen to metaphysical heights, where it is in peril of transcending sanity and the boundaries of its own humanity.

Faced with these antibiotic extremes of a solitude, so alien to his urbane tastes, Faust shows no signs of losing either his wits or his countenance. Like Valéry's Descartes, who "opposes being to man" (P.I, 791), he confronts the life-destroying forces of rarefied "being" with the self-assertion of the inquiring intellect, keenly aware of the enormous amount of Nothingness in the All, where a minute trace of life barely animates a thin layer of dust.

[7] Cf. Paul Valéry on Pascal's *Pensées* as the product of a type of paralysis that results from the mind's realization that one is nothing while one feels that one is everything: "On voit alors le solitaire par essence, l'esprit, se défendre par ses pensées (. . .)" (P.I, 470).

But this minute crust of life contains a disproportionate quantity of mind that suffices to impose its order upon the chaotic whole. Why did Faust climb these nightmarish heights? Certainly not out of despair and existential anguish, nor in a spirit of penance and self-humiliation. The whole experience must be oneiric, for a Cartesian Faust would be aware "qu'on se rendroit ridicule de vouloir grimper sur les rochers, ou descendre dans les précipices, sous prétexte d'aller plus droit" (Baillet 1, 80). Faust conjectures that he may have come here in the hope "d'atteindre un lieu de notre monde où l'on peut mettre tout juste le bout du nez hors de ce qui existe" (P.ii, 382). This inference seems to confirm the suspicion that he is indeed dreaming, i.e., in a passive state of mind where thought is asleep and deceived by imagination's fantasies. For, what exists *for* Faust, exists *in* Faust when Faust truly exists himself, i.e., when he *thinks* himself, God, and the world in the Cartesian experience of the *cogito, ergo sum*.

7. The Eternal Silence Exorcised

At this point, where thought is asleep, language is ready to leap into metaphysics, the unreal realm of dreams of transcendence. Promptly, the monstrous Solitaire draws himself up ominously, uttering a long, modulated howl, as though to incarnate and voice the metaphysical threat of Pascalian *pensées*, which hangs in the thin and icy air. It sounds an inarticulate warning against Faust's progress in a climate hostile to his quest for clear and distinct ideas. His endeavors to adjust his opinions in a Cartesian way to reason (*Discours* ii; AT, vi, 15 f.) seem doomed at these very limits of life, where *le bon sens* can hardly breathe. Aware of Pascalian *idées reçues* in the air, Faust asks himself with some amusement whether, perchance, "the eter-

nal silence" is preparing to end itself: "Quoi? . . . La solitude hurle? . . . Le silence éternel voudrait-il en finir avec
lui-même?" The frustrated Solitaire emits another long
and modulated howl. He intones a confused hymn to the
Night, full of praise and imprecations. His psalmody
thrusts nihilist curses at the world and the firmament,
which indifferently sings whatever one wishes to hear, "A
l'un parle de Dieu / A l'autre oppose un froid silence"
(P.II, 383). He closes his Cyclops eye to the rotations of
time and planets, exalting the powers of darkness and
oblivion. His litany of negation, acclaiming the virtues of a
self-imposed ignorance, rises in this inhuman and in-
humane atmosphere as though to confirm the Cartesian
assertion that "confused and obscure ideas" pertain to the
realm of "Nothingness": "En sorte que, si nous en avons
assez souvent [i.e., des idées ou notions] qui contiennent de
la fausseté, ce ne peut être que de celles qui ont quelque
chose de confus et obscur, à cause qu'en cela elles participent du néant, c'est-à-dire, qu'elles ne sont en nous ainsi
confuses, qu'à cause que nous ne sommes pas tout parfaits"
(*Discours* IV; AT, VI, 38). If, on one hand, the psalmodiz-
ing Solitaire represents *le néant*, chaotically invading the
dreaming mind—his memorized fragments of commonplaces are, no doubt, meant to recall the reasons for Descartes' determination to reject the authority of this kind
of intellectual rubbish, and, for his decision, exclusively to
rely on the strength of his own reason. "Mais ayant appris,
dès le collège, qu'on ne saurait rien imaginer de si étrange
et si peu croyable, qu'il n'ait été dit par quelqu'un des
philosophes (. . .) je ne pouvais choisir personne dont les
opinions me semblassent devoir être préférées à celles des
autres, et je me trouvai comme contraint d'entreprendre
moi-même de me conduire" (*Discours* II; AT, VI, 16).
The Solitaire invokes the tenebrous forces of Night and,

using scrambled commonplaces, he seems to exorcise
Faust, in an attempt to stop him in his chosen course.

The scene is like a charade, where the Solitaire, with his
quick, ready-made solutions, acts out the metaphor of the
powers of darkness that Descartes invents to illustrate the
intellectual perils that stalk the lone seeker for truth:
"Mais comme un homme qui marche seul et dans les
ténèbres, je me résolus d'aller si lentement, et d'user de
tant de circonspection en toutes choses, que, si je n'avançais
que fort peu, je me garderais bien, au moins, de tomber"
(*Discours* II; AT, VI, 16 f.). The Solitaire's dithyrambic
incantations are incompatible with Faust's efforts to think
clearly and distinctly. They frighten away all potential
thought: "Mais ce hurleur est assez effrayant" (P.II, 382).[8]

[8] Descartes' *Méditation Sixième* provides a Cartesian objection,
avant la lettre, to Pascal's "eternal silence," by pointing out the
"perversion" and "confusion" of the senses, when confronted with
natural phenomena. Since sense perceptions tell us nothing about
the true order of nature, their function is limited to alerting us to
the usefulness or danger of phenomena to our own well-being. It
is a bold rhetorical device (but also a sleight of hand) to suggest
metaphysical conclusions to be drawn from a purely existential
anguish like the one purportedly produced in the psyche of Pascal's
libertine, reduced to fear and trembling by "the eternal silence."
The passage in Descartes' *Méditation Sixième* reads as follows:
"De même aussi, quoiqu'il y ait des espaces dans lesquels je ne
trouve rien qui excite et meuve mes sens, je ne dois pas conclure
pour cela que ces espaces ne contiennent en eux aucun corps; mais
je vois que, tant en ceci qu'en plusieurs autres choses semblables,
j'ai accoutumé de pervertir et confondre l'ordre de la nature,
parce que ces sentiments ou perceptions des sens n'ayant été mises
en moi que pour signifier à mon esprit quelles choses sont con-
venables ou nuisibles au composé dont il est partie, et jusque là
étant assez claires et assez distinctes, je m'en sers néanmoins
comme si elles étaient des règles très certaines, par lesquelles je
pusse connaître immédiatement l'essence et la nature des corps
qui sont hors de moi, de laquelle toutefois elles ne me peuvent

The meaning of this supercilious remark is unmistakable. The Solitaire evokes Pascal's claims that "the eternal silence of these infinite spaces frightens" him (*m'effraie*); Faust uses the same verb *effrayer* in its adverbial form (*effrayant*). He attenuates it to a courteous whisper, to litotes, by adding the limiting "assez," cutting down to mundane proportions the threat of metaphysical fright. What Faust finds "assez effrayant," i.e., "fairly ghastly," is the plebeian noise made by the Solitaire in his attempts to block out the "eternal silence," which has such a terrifying grip on him.

The Solitaire's misanthropic yells and their thundering echoes fill Faust with mixed feelings of distaste and amusement; rather than awing him, they strike him as being pretty *awful*. With his closed Cyclops eye, and in his selfish contempt for mankind, life, and knowledge, the Solitaire mimics Pascal's translation of I John 2:16: "Tout ce qui est au monde est concupiscence de la chair, ou concupiscence des yeux, ou orgueil de la vie: *libido sentiendi, libido sciendi, libido dominandi*." To these three "fleuves de feu," which are said to burn down a "malheureuse terre de malédiction," the Solitaire closes his only eye. Remote from all human flames of passion, lying prone on his flat rock, surrounded by ice and night, lamenting all "malédictions d'univers," and thirsting for a glimpse of the Holy Jerusalem, he remains "immobile," "affermi," "non pas debout, mais assis dans une assiette basse et sûre," like those who may be saved, and who do not rise from

---

rien enseigner que de fort obscur et confus." (AT, ix, 66)

Pascal prods his reader into deriving faith from the implied fear of *le néant*, the fear of Nothingness (yawning abysses of the "two infinites," etc.). In the *Discours*, Descartes had argued, on the contrary, that he could not deduce the idea of God from the contemplation of Nothingness ("car, de la tenir du néant, c'était chose manifestement impossible" [*Discours* iv; AT, vi, 34]).

this lowly position "avant la lumière" (*Pensée* 458). In this frightful and frightened posture, he fails to impress, let alone frighten, Faust. Blown up to nightmarish proportions, and in the midst of a rarefied atmosphere where the tensions of his antithetical style clash in a nonsensical dialectics without syntheses, the Solitaire indeed incarnates Valéry's Pascal: the mystical skeptic whose lamentations on "the eternal silence" are not *thought*, but *poetry*. On these glacial heights, where the contradictions of his fearful declamation, without being resolved, literally dissolve into "thin air," the Solitaire, like Pascal, pampering his fragility, seeks to be "everywhere surrounded by perils and solitude" (P.i, 461). The arid setting with its unsociable hermit reflects the hopeless ambiance of that horrifying "desert island" which Pascal uses as perhaps his most poignant metaphor for the misery and the blind, irreparable ignorance of postlapsarian man, face to face with a "mute universe" that answers none of his anguishing questions:

> En voyant l'aveuglement et la misère de l'homme, en regardant tout l'univers muet, et l'homme sans lumière, abandonné à lui même, et comme égaré dans ce recoin de l'univers, sans savoir qui l'y a mis, ce qu'il y est venu faire, ce qu'il deviendra en mourant, incapable de toute connaissance, j'entre en effroi comme un homme qu'on aurait porté endormi dans une île déserte et effroyable, et qui s'éveillerait sans connaître où il est, et sans moyen d'en sortir . . . (*Pensée* 693)

Conspicuous to the point of obscenity in this inhuman solitude, the deranged Solitaire spews forth an apologetics gone out of control. He exhibits his dramatic agony and the fury of his frustrations from the *templum* of his altar-shaped rock, a site of bad omen for Faust. His emotional *contemplations* stand in sharp contrast to Faust's methodical *considerations*, a polarity that is in accord with the etymological distinction Valéry makes between Pascal's *contemplation* of the heavens (with stress on the root *templum*), and Descartes' scientific *consideration* of constellations (*sidera*).[9]

8. *Two Types of Solitude*

Like all believers, Valéry's Pascal conforms perhaps to an instinct derived from "our vertical structure" when he reaches "towards the site's zenith, *vers le haut,* for the highest point" (P.I, 467). *Exhausser,* "to uplift," and *exaucer* "to hear a prayer"—Valéry postulates—are one and the same woıⅎ (*ibid.*). This commentary allows an almost literal interpretation of the Solitaire's isolation on high, as against the urbanely Cartesian concept of the thinker's solitude. Cues are provided by the meanings of Latin *solitudo.* It denotes (1) "a desert, or wilderness," like the site chosen by the Solitaire for his retreat from the world; (2) "a state of want or frustration," not unlike his spiritual and psychological condition. It is this arid type of "solitude," remote from all terrestrial roots, that serves as the breeding ground for an apologetics, drawn from accepted authorities. It is used in the Solitaire's flight from himself, as an exorcism against his own fears and doubts. It provides his last defense against the Cartesian forces of common sense that have come to beleaguer him in the person of Faust.

But there is a third meaning of *solitudo*: to live incognito in the midst of a multitude, whence an urbane Faust

[9] "En insistant un peu sur les étymologies, on pourrait dire, avec une sorte de précision, que le croyant *contemple* le ciel, tandis que le savant le *considère*" (P.I, 466).

has temporarily strayed to this nightmarish and truly
"supernatural" site, where he finds himself exposed to the
Solitaire's aggressive proselytizing. One feels that he will
strive to return to this mundane type of isolation that
benefits from the *busy-ness* that surrounds it. There, far
from attempting to convert others to his views, he can
freely pursue his search for ever greater knowledge—like
the young Descartes, who developed his thought in the
poële, the stove-heated room, during the winter of 1619-
1620 (cf. *Discours* II; AT, VI, 11), and like Monsieur Teste,
who thinks with his head turned to the wall. Or like the
mature Descartes of the *Méditation Première* who felt
carefree enough in the peace and quiet of "une paisible
solitude" to revise his own opinions, having already reminded us in the *Discours de la Méthode* that, withdrawn
in the busy heart of Amsterdam, "jamais mon dessein ne
s'est étendu plus avant que de tâcher de réformer mes
propres pensées, et de bâtir dans un fonds qui est tout à
moi" (*Discours* II; AT, VII, 15).

In short, the Solitaire's misanthropic isolation *on vertig-
inous heights*, which he jealously defends against any
intruder, is diametrically opposed to Descartes' treasured
anonymity *in the Netherlands*, literally *below sea level*, in
the midst of the hustle and bustle of a prosperous Amsterdam. The intellect functions with greater ease when
on the level of human reality and natural phenomena
than when erring on the glacial and treacherous mountain
peaks of transcendental uncertainties. This truth, which
helps to explain Faust's uneasiness in the Solitaire's antibiotic wilderness, is exposited by Descartes at great length
in a letter to Guez de Balzac, dated May 5, 1631, where he
tries to persuade his friend to settle (as he himself did)
in Amsterdam; his argument is summed up in the last
sentence of Part III of the *Discours* (quoted in part by

Valéry, P.ɪ, 823, and alluded to, P.ɪ, 847): "Parmi la foule
d'un grand peuple fort actif, et plus soigneux de ses propres affaires que curieux de celles d'autrui, (. . .) j'ai pu
vivre aussi solitaire et retiré que dans les déserts les plus
écartés."[10]

Descartes' greater wisdom is reflected in Faust's "il n'y a
ni haut ni bas"—an axiom that applies as well to the
"infinite spaces" as to the intellect, which has no distinctive
site and, in its indivisibility, escapes all tangible forms and
all crisp formulations. By contrast, the Solitaire, like
Valéry's Pascal, seems to ignore this fundamental truth
that "neither the First Cause, nor the Pure Act, nor the
Spirit have proper sites of their own, nor figures, nor any
parts" (P.ɪ, 467).[11]

---

[10] Descartes' definition of solitude "parmi la foule d'un grand
peuple" finds an echo in this exchange between Faust and Lust:

Faust: J'ai couru plus d'un monde . . . Mais j'ai pesé mes désirs
et mes expériences dans la solitude.
Lust: Dans le désert?
Faust: Pourquoi? La solitude est un produit qu'on fait partout.
(*Lust* ɪ, iv; P.ɪɪ, 320)

[11] Or in Descartes' words, in support of "the first principle for
the philosophy he sought," the "I think, therefore I am":

"Puis, examinant avec attention ce que j'étais, et voyant que je
pouvais feindre que je n'avais aucun corps, et qu'il n'y avait aucun
monde, ni aucun lieu où je fusse; mais que je ne pouvais pas feindre, pour cela, que je n'étais point; et qu'au contraire, de cela
même que je pensais à douter de la vérité des autres choses, il
suivait très évidemment et très certainement que j'étais; au lieu
que, si j'eusse seulement cessé de penser, encore que tout le reste
de ce que j'avais jamais imaginé eût été vrai, je n'avais aucune
raison de croire que j'eusse été: je connus de là que j'étais une
substance dont toute l'essence ou la nature n'est que de penser, et
qui, pour être, n'a besoin d'aucun lieu, ni ne dépend d'aucune chose
matérielle." (*Discours* ɪv; AT, vɪ, 32 f.)

9. Scatological Eschatology

Under such adverse conditions, there is little hope for any kind of mutual understanding between Faust and the Solitaire. Faust may well be aware of this dilemma; nonetheless, he makes a polite attempt to communicate with the howling hermit: "Pardon, Monsieur . . ." (P.ii, 383). He does not get very far. The boorish Solitaire interrupts him with (1) a rhetorical question actually meant to define the intruder; and (2) a brutal rejection, neither of which make Faust lose heart: "Une ordure? Va-t'en!"[12] The two parts of this exclamation taken together, spell out, by way of charade, Pascal's marginal remark to a

[12] A first, dark hint at the Solitaire's diabolical character, the idiomatic "Va-t-en" provides an insight into Valéry's technique of metamorphosing "sublime" metaphors by transposing them onto the low style level (*sermo humilis*). It is a way of modernizing, mocking, and deflating expressions that would strike us as representing an outlived type of pathos or bathos. One may playfully assume that the idiotism "Va-t-en" is a humorous transposition of the pathetic warning "*O homo fuge!*" in the *Historia von D. Johann Fausten* that Gérard de Nerval inserted in his fragmentary translation of Goethe's *Faust*, in Widmann's version (1599). The French adaptation by Palma Cayet had been published in 1608 under the title *Légende de Faust, par Widman* (*sic*). Here is the passage in the original German version: "Als diese beyde Partheyen (Mephistopheles and Faust) sich miteinander verbunden, name D. Faustus ein spitzig Messer, sticht jhme ein Ader in der lincken Hand auff, vnnd sagt man warhafftig, dass in solche Hand ein gegrabne vnnd blutige Schrifft gesehen worden, *O homo fuge, id est*, O Mensch fleuhe vor jhme vnnd thue recht, etc." *Volksbuch vom Dr. Faust*, Halle, 1911, p. 20. (When these two parties [Mephistopheles and Faust] had reached an agreement, Dr. Faustus took a pointed knife, pricked a vein in his left hand, and it is truly said that in that Hand could be seen engraved in blood an inscription, *O homo fuge*, O man, flee from him and choose righteousness.)

pensée dealing with "Divertissement"—a term that, in theological jargon, is related to the opposite of "conversion," "Que le coeur de l'homme est creux et plein d'ordure!" (*Pensée* 143). In the best tradition of hellfire and brimstone apologetics, scatology provides the arsis for eschatology.[13] Faust remains courteous, despite the rude injunction to leave (contemptuously uttered in the second person, singular), and notwithstanding the scatological insult hurled at him, which likens his courage—both his heart and the valor that fills it—to a garbage can full of refuse.

He tries again: "Pardon, Monsieur, je me suis égaré dans ces montagnes . . . ," indicating, once more, that the thin air of this anchoretic solitude is not precisely an element where he feels at home. Throwing Cartesian caution to the winds, he has obviously strayed from those "large roads which, twisting between mountains, by dint of being heavily traveled, become so smooth and comfortable that it is better to follow them than to climb over rocks, and to descend into the depth of precipices" (*Discours* II; AT, VI, 14). Having lost his way, by taking a steep shortcut that brought him to this rocky and snow-capped peak, he is carelessly exposing himself to the two dangers Descartes always thought to escape: to "prevention," the error of judging on the basis of prejudice, and "precipitation," the fallacy of judging before all the evidence is in (*Discours* II; AT, VI, 15). "Prevention" and "precipitation" threaten him—both in the literal sense and

---

[13] "À quoi sert le Pascal des *Pensées?* / Pascal apporte terreurs, dégoûts, désertion de toutes choses,—raisonnements insupportables —vomissement total et amer aux pieds de Dieu" (Cah. XIX, p. 359; 1936). And: "Sur Pascal: Pascal est peut-être un *excitant*, donc devait être apprécié au XIXme [siècle]—mais ce n'est pas un *aliment*" (Cah. X, 886; Valéry's italics).

in their Cartesian meaning—in the person of the rhapsodic
Solitaire, who, after trying to "prevent" Faust's progress,
will "precipitate" him into the abyss, while the "prevention" and "precipitation" of the Solitaire's apologetics—
leaping to judgments based both on prejudice and on
lack of evidence—attempt to captivate his mind. A dis-
gruntled reference to Pascal's "precipitated" and "pre-
ventive" dictum on the "natural hatred" of all humans for
all humans, issues from the Solitaire's lips, informing
Faust: "Que tu ne me plais pas!" His utterance adds a
strongly personal touch to Pascal's "Tous les hommes se
haïssent naturellement l'un l'autre" (*Pensée* 451), for it
reflects by implication the Pascalian dislike for Cartesian
thought (cf. *Pensées* 76, 77, 78, 79). Simultaneously, it
prolongs one of Pascal's major themes, paraphrased some
twenty odd times in his *Pensées*: *"Le moi est haïssable"*
(*Pensées* 284, 286, et passim).

Wondering exactly why he incurs the Solitaire's scorn,
an amused Faust learns that his very existence is believed
to sully, to stain: "Tu es. Tu souilles" (P.II, 384), is the
Solitaire's scatologically eschatological answer. It darkly
hints at the Cartesian *cogito, ergo sum*—interpreted, reversed, completed, and rejected, from a Pascalian perspective, to read: *es, ergo cogitas, i.e., inquinas,* "you are, therefore you think, i.e., you defile." A proud refusal of the
Pascalian "abêtissement" in blind faith, and of emotional
appeals to instinctive fears, the Cartesian *cogito* represents
the bold efforts of consciousness to break through the hard
shell of "being." It echoes forth in Faust's reasoning about
the incomprehensible impulse that prompted his ascent to
these unwholesome heights, an impulse that, we recall,
he had tentatively identified as the irrepressible oneiric
urge, to sample just once the unknown that lies "a tiny bit
outside the things which exist." To Faust's mocking

question: "Et vous . . . n'êtes donc pas?"—which implies
non-thinking on the basis of non-being—the Solitaire replies by an apparent gesture of self-effacement: "Non. Dès
qu'il n'y a que moi, il n'y a personne." In other terms,
non cogito, ergo non sum. Faust's "tip of his nose," his
flair, has indeed succeeded in breaking through to the
essence of non-being. Non-being by virtue of his non-
thinking, the Solitaire represents in a new disguise that
living *néant*, the very spirit of negation that Faust had
dealt with before in the primal and more primitive person
of Mephistopheles, who had defined himself by using a
similarly enigmatic paradox: "Je suis l'être sans chair, qui
ne dort, ni ne pense" (P.II, 354).

The Solitaire's Pascalian apologetics address themselves
with devout rhetoric and diabolical skill to *la panse qui
pense.* Confusing the mind (*l'esprit*) by an unfair appeal
to instinctive fears of the body (*l'automate*), they are
clearly meant to bewilder Faust, not unlike the temptation
held out to Descartes by the "evil genius" in his first dream,
when a heavy windblast kept him from attaining a college
chapel, toward which he was driven against his will, while,
simultaneously he failed to come within the reach of a
"melon" brought to him as a gift from a "strange land."
Descartes' interpretation of this dream, as reported by
Baillet, provides important clues to the meaning of Faust's
encounter with the Solitaire: "Le melon dont on vouloit
luy faire présent dans le premier songe, signifioit, disoit-il,
les charmes de la solitude, mais présentez par des sollicita-
tions purement humaines" (Baillet I, 85)—images that
could serve Valéry as a charade for the Solitaire's ungodly
isolation, with a dark hint at the forbidden fruit (μῆλον.
any tree-fruit, hence *malum*, "apple"), at a malignant
(μέλας) force, and at the "object of care and worry"
(μέλω) which the Solitaire's example and words repre-

sent to Faust. Descartes' explanation for the divine wind
that prevented him in his first dream from reaching the
college chapel bears out *le mot de l'énigme*, which points
to the violent Solitaire as a tempter figure:

> Le vent qui le poussoit vers l'Eglise du collège, lorsqu'il
> avoit mal au côté droit, n'étoit autre chose que le mau-
> vais Génie qui tâchoit de le jetter par force dans un lieu,
> où son dessein étoit d'aller volontairement. C'est pour-
> quoy Dieu ne permit pas qu'il avançât plus loin, et qu'il
> se laissât emporter même en un lieu saint par un Esprit
> qu'il n'avoit pas envoyé: quoy qu'il fût très-persuadé
> que c'eût été l'Esprit de Dieu qui luy avoit fait faire les
> premières démarches vers cette Eglise.   (*Ibid.*)

10. *Personal Imperialism*

Like Descartes, Faust refuses to be moved by eschatological arguments, based on the "authority" of men who
pretend "d'être plus qu'homme" (*Discours* I; AT, VI, 8).
No doubt skeptical of proselytizers who lay claims to their
pretended initiation into divine mysteries (*ibid.*), Faust is
reluctant to accept the Solitaire's renewed invitation to
"prevention" and threat of "precipitation": "Va, ou je te
jette en bas. Va, ou au précipice" (P.II, 384). The Solitaire's
base attempts to convert him—to "turn" or "whirl" him
"around" (the original meaning of Latin *converto*)—go
against his grain. Faust, by the nature of his myth forever
greedy for new experiences, and by virtue of Valéry's
own thought insatiably thirsting for greater consciousness,
will reject, like Descartes, any effort to force others to share
his own view. Contenting himself with setting an example, he would not invite others to follow in his foot-
steps. He remains true to Descartes' polite *captatio benevo-*

lentiae: "Que si, mon ouvrage m'ayant assez plu, je vous en fais voir ici le modèle, ce n'est pas, pour cela, que je veuille conseiller à personne de l'imiter" (*Discours* II; AT, VI, 15); and, earlier: "Ainsi mon dessein n'est pas d'enseigner ici la méthode que chacun doit suivre pour bien conduire sa raison, mais seulement de faire voir en quelle sorte j'ai tâché de conduire la mienne. Ceux qui se mêlent de donner des préceptes, se doivent estimer plus habiles que ceux auxquels ils les donnent; et s'ils manquent en la moindre chose, ils en sont blâmables" (*Discours* I; AT, VI, 4). To the Solitaire's impatient call for "prevention" and "precipitation," he answers with irony and self-assurance: "Monsieur, pardon . . . Il se pourrait, Monsieur, que votre précipice eût l'embarras du choix" (P.II, 384).

It is obvious that, in the Solitaire's view, Faust now comes to personify in a quite literal sense his own abysmal qualities, the Pascalian: "je vois mon abîme d'orgueil, de curiosité, de concupiscence" (*Pensée* 553). It is a vision that the anchorite would like to thrust back into the very abyss whence, incarnate in Faust, it had risen. His ill will toward Faust resembles Pascal's intention to destroy, in his apologetics, "those who go too deeply into the natural sciences," naming as an example, Descartes (*Pensée* 76). In his spiritual wilderness, where there is nothing valued by man, neither "grain, nor gold, nor wench" (*garces*): "Il n'y a rien. Le rien s'ajuste au seul, et seulement au seul" (P.II, 384). In his deathlike expectation of death bringing salvation, the Solitaire vaguely echoes Pascal's: "on mourra seul. Il faut donc faire comme si on était seul" (*Pensée* 211). But his words reach far beyond the Pascalian rejection of any of this worldly *joie de vivre*; they embrace a Satanic nihilism, a willingness to sacrifice the whole universe in order to guarantee the immortal survival of the "Only One," *le seul, le Solitaire*—for only Nothingness

would admit as its sole ruler the Devil, no matter what
guise he may choose. What at first seemed to be the
Solitaire's humble self-effacement, now reveals itself as
the acme of an individual imperialism. Its selfish aim is to
quench an immoderate thirst for immortality by swallowing up everything in one violent spree of annihilation that
would only be outlived by the sole "être sans chair, qui ne
dort, ni ne pense." The Solitaire's "Je suis seul de l'espèce,
seul, et le seul à être seul" (P.ii, 384) resounds with Satanic
pride, but also with the frustrations of Unamuno's "¡O
todo o nada!"—his totally exclusive "either All or
Nothing":

> De no serlo todo y por siempre, es como si no fuera, y
> por lo menos ser todo yo, y serlo para siempre jamás.
> Y ser todo yo, es ser todos los demás. ¡O todo o nada!
>
> (Not to be everything and forever, is like not being, and,
> at least [I must] be everything myself, and be everything
> forever and ever. And to be everything myself is to be
> all the others. Either everything or nothing!)
>
> *El sentimiento trágico de la vida*, ch. iii

In terms of Faust's "il n'y a ni haut ni bas," Faust and the
Solitaire come to illustrate two irreconcilable attitudes
toward Unamuno's "¡Quiero serlo todo!" (I want to be
all and everything): On the part of the Solitaire, it is an
insatiable instinct for total absorption of all, a reduction of
the World to Nothingness, in a titanic effort to usurp an
exclusive immortality *in excelsis*. On Faust's part, it is the
terre à terre precision of his reasoning, verified wherever
possible by experiments and cautious observation, which
boldly derives the Self, the Universe, and God from the
strength of human consciousness, safeguarded by methodical doubt.

11. *A Herd of Swine and Pascalian "Pensées"*

The Solitaire's previous remark, "Si l'on est deux, ce n'est plus une solitude," constitutes more than a simple rejection of the Cartesian separation of body and mind. It is meant as a warning that, on this wretched summit, there is room only for his own greedy *instinct* for eternity and a wholeness impeded by the duplicity of human nature, of which he is unpleasantly reminded by the *rational* presence of Faust ("Instinct et raison, marques de deux natures," Pascal, *Pensée* 344). The Pascalian theme of man's lost "wholeness," which faith and divine grace alone can restore after death, is darkly suggested by the etymological root of *solitude, solus* (*sollus*), as a noun denoting "the only" but also "the whole," and as an adjective, "alone," "only," "solitary," "forsaken." His reiterated warning—"Alors va-t'en puisque je suis seul, et je suis seul comme on est chien ou singe ou vache" sounds like "instinct's" injunction to "reason," to vacate a scene where Faust, the presence of reason, would incarnate the sin of intellectual pride. It mirrors Pascal's: "La nature de l'homme est tout nature, *omne animal*" (*Pensée* 94)—a fraudulent reduction of man to a mere animal existence, in an attempt to portray the only type of "wholeness in wretchedness," Pascal can conceive of for man on earth. It is a reference to the "bestiality" of postlapsarian man, whose animal instincts, paradoxically, may provide a better guide to the love of God than his reason, corrupted since Adam's fall.

Faust counters by opposing the Cartesian *duality* of mind and body to this Pascalian reminder of man's *duplicity*, and to the Solitaire's sleight of hand, which diminishes man to pure animality: We are all as lonely as our body, severed from thought, and yet we are married to thought, which is solitude and its echo (P.II, 384). This image intimates the echo chamber of the mind, reverberating with the Solitaire's deceptive "Thoughts," echoing in turn Pascal's *Pensées* which—I recall—in Valéry's definition are not rational "thoughts" at all, but rhetorically well structured *poems* (P.I, 458). Resounding with an "angoisse presque animale" (P.I, 464), they are poetic incantations in the form of those *malédictions d'univers* that linger in the play's subtitle. Although they differ in tone from those other, more intimate, enchantments that Imagination and Memory hold in store for Faust in the interlude, *Les Fées*, they are nonetheless a cruder version of *carmina*; and, like the Fays' neoclassical *charmes*, they evoke by indirection the title of one of Valéry's major collections of poems. The Solitaire's admonitions stress the animal isolation of post-lapsarian man, as the Solitaire had construed his own wretched loneliness, comparing it to that of "dog or monkey or cow" (P.II, 384). Like the ever-repeated calls of the nymph Echo, seeking Narcissus in search of himself (and unwilling to lie in her embrace), the echoing rings of the Solitaire's *pensées* haunt Faust's consciousness, which tries to evade their murky enchantment, while pursuing its own image in its quest for clear and distinct ideas. The Solitaire's *charmes* recall Circe's incantations. They had turned humans into swine, a fate that would obviously fail to tempt Faust, the intellectual *par excellence*.

The hermit leads Faust by stages to insights that establish a link between his Pascalian lamentations, Circe's bestialising charms, and a notorious Biblical herd of swine. He begins by metamorphosing Faust's narcissistic image of "thought" as "solitude and its echo" into a transparent metaphor for Pascal's *Pensées*, viewed as a legion of devils beleaguering Faust, and cast out from their habitat in the Solitaire's body and mind. The Solitaire's sudden boast,

"Je suis LÉGION" (P.II, 385), points to the encounter of Jesus with a madman in the country of the Gadarenes, who, when asked for his name, answered: "My name is Legion: for we are many" (Mark 5:9); "because many devils were entered into him" (Luke 8:30). The Solitaire's demonic incantations, which pose as religious "thoughts," are legion. A chaotic pandaemonium, they reflect in the antitheses of their rhetoric each other's terror and anguish. Their fugal reverberations tempt the listener to enter the Solitaire's personal labyrinth of wretchedness, where, like Pascal, he rages against corrupt mankind in general, and against himself in particular. The infernal character of his litany is demonstrated by way of metaphor. Meanwhile, the work designates itself through its author, defining both him and itself in periphrases where Pascalian "thoughts," unnamed, are invoked as anonymous and demonic "ILS" and "UN et UN et UN." By their disjointedness, they mark the fragmentary character of the *Pensées*, and by their masculine gender they indicate, no doubt, that they are to be regarded as *poèmes*: "On peut dire qu'ILS" (i.e., the LEGION I am) "sont plusieurs . . . ILS sont UN et UN et UN, et ainsi et ainsi, qui ne s'additionnent pas . . . (. . . .) Chacun est un présage, un souvenir, un signe . . . et non un être," etc. (P.II, 385).

While suggesting the chaotic migration of the legion of devils, whom Jesus drove out of a madman's mind and body, allowing them to take refuge in a herd of swine— pearls cast before the unworthy reader?—the Solitaire's words also mirror Pascal's design to demonstrate that his topic cannot be treated in an orderly fashion. Pascal had exemplified his design by refusing to impose any semblance of order on his *Pensées*: "J'écrirai ici mes pensées sans ordre, et non pas peut-être dans une confusion sans dessein (. . . .) Je ferais trop d'honneur à mon sujet, si je le traitais avec ordre, puisque je veux montrer qu'il en est incapable" (*Pensée* 373). Speaking again with the author's voice, the Solitaire imitates the rhetorical device of Pascal's antithetical isocola, which so often, rather than leading up to a synthesis, leave everything in a dramatic state of suspense: "And all this is like a creation of my mind, and is not a creation of my mind" (P.II, 385). His words seem to point once again to the evangelical legion of devils for whose actions the mind, possessed by them, cannot be held responsible, although he speaks with their tongues. Faust's commonsensical and dubitative: "Vous croyez? Et pourquoi non?" ambiguously seems to question both the validity of the Solitaire's extravagant claims and his "good faith." The latter replies: "Parce que je n'ai pas d'esprit (. . . .) Que pourrait être mon esprit quand ILS son là?" The implications of his retort are at least fourfold: (1) They suggest the mind's witless fear and trembling in the presence of Pascal's *Pensées*, and the existential anguish they are intended to produce. Appealing to instinct rather than reason, they aim to paralyze *le bon sens*, depriving the Solitaire (and those willing to listen to him), of that precious gift of common sense which, according to a generous Descartes, "est la chose du monde la mieux partagée" (*Discours* I; AT, VI, I). In his paradoxical role as the *advocatus diaboli* of Christianity, the Solitaire defends what Pascal calls in his own words, "la seule religion contre nature, contre le sens commun (. . .)" (*Pensée* 605).

(2) By tacit cross-references both to Mark 5:9 ff. and to *Lust*, the Solitaire's terms define him as exactly the one we had always suspected him to be, i.e., a very Cartesian Faust's unmistakably Pascalian "evil genius," who abolishes the cognitive power of thought in a sort of mental stagnation: Twice in *Lust*, Mephistopheles is said

to *have* no *esprit* because he *is esprit*; for, the reasoning goes, one cannot *have* what one *is* (P.II, 293, 295).

(3) The Solitaire's lamentations, like Pascal's apologetics, are pieced together with arguments drawn from many sources; hence, by referring to the LEGION he is, the Solitaire follows Pascal's advice to writers that they should always use the collective "we" rather than the exclusive "I," when apostrophizing their readers, "vu que d'ordinaire il y a plus en cela du bien d'autrui que du leur" (*Pensée* 43). His discourse shows the imperfections which Descartes discovers "dans les ouvrages composés de plusieurs pièces, et fait de la main de divers maîtres" (*Discours* II; AT, VI, 11). Curious only of clearly delimited knowledge that can be demonstrated and verified by his ever cautious and vigilant consciousness, Faust had forsaken long ago—to be exact, since his very first lines in Goethe's *Faust I*—his trust in books that are based on mere conjecture and "authority." Thus, he might say with Descartes:

> Et ainsi je pensai que les sciences des livres, au moins celles dont les raisons ne sont que probables, et qui n'ont aucunes démonstrations, s'étant composées et grossies peu à peu des opinions de plusieurs diverses personnes, ne sont point si approchantes de la vérité que les simples raisonnements que peut faire naturellement un homme de bon sens touchant les choses qui se présentent. (*Discours* II; AT, VI, 12 f.)

(4) In the light of these inferences, the LEGION of exorcized devils, driven into a herd of swine, and drowned in the equivalent of Pascalian *Pensées*—the Solitaire's cascade of divagations—"ILS" can be identified as Spirits of Negation, as nonsensical *poltergeister*, haunting the premises of *le bon sens*. The Solitaire's scorn for reason

may faintly echo Saint Paul's "We are fools for Christ's
sake" (I Cor. 4:10); but, more clearly, it recalls Pascal's:
"Les hommes sont si nécessairement fous, que ce serait
être fou par un autre tour de folie, de n'être pas fou"
(*Pensée* 414). Altogether, the Solitaire's surrender of his
mind to THEM, the LEGION, suggests an affinity with
the madman in Mark 5 and Luke 8, and with the "many
devils (that) were entered into him." In an aside, Faust
diagnoses also: "Il est rigoureusement fou . . ." (P.II,
385). What strikes him as the Solitaire's rigorously *consistent* madness is, no doubt, his refusal to share in what
Descartes had called the world's best distributed com-
modity, common sense. He sees in him something worse
than the Devil's rather simple-minded evil; for the Solitaire exhibits an ambivalence that Valéry finds in Pascal's
apologetics: it excites "le bestial et l'idéal tour à tour" (P.I,
468). Faust is vaguely aware of conflicting forces at work:
"Au fond, [il est] bien pire que le diable. Ce fou est beaucoup plus avancé." But he is puzzled, as yet, lacking the
key to the understanding of the Solitaire's complex in-
sanity, which is compounded of Biblical elements and
Pagan taboos. The Solitaire provides a clue: "A quoi te
sert ton esprit? A être bête"—meaning (1) in Cartesian
terms, that intelligence is of service only to those who
know how to use it: "Car ce n'est pas assez d'avoir l'esprit
bon, mais le principal est de l'appliquer bien" (*Discours*
1; AT, VI, 2); (2) on the level of Pascal's critique of reason, that the mind must be humiliated, for ". . . le malheur
veut que qui veut faire l'ange fait la bête" (*Pensée* 358);
and (3) in the light of Mark 5 and Luke 6: the "unclean
spirit" that possesses man debases him to animal proportions; if it is driven out, it is allowed to enter into swine,
and is even further reduced to base animality. The Soli-

taire's "Si le coeur avait de l'esprit, on serait mort" paraphrases the fideist argument that faith and grace, intuited
by the heart, can alone show the road to God, and, perhaps to immortality, while trust in the redeeming power
of reason would condemn man to eternal wretchedness.
Or, in Pascal's words: "C'est le coeur qui sent Dieu, et non
la raison" (*Pensée* 278).

12. *Halfway Between Beast and Angel*

In this context, one easily understands the Solitaire's
confession that, having once been very intelligent—a hint
at Pascal's scientific career—he has long since come to
realize that his mind is of little service to the true concerns
of life. What is meant by "life," has nothing to do with
the certainties of this-worldly existence: it refers to the
Pascalian "wager," by which one loses nothing while
potentially gaining eternal "life" through a simple act of
faith. In the Solitaire's own case, *l'idole Esprit* has "only
offered him the fatiguing fermentation of its malignant
activities" (P.II, 386)—one more clear allusion to the
LEGION of devils that made up the "unclean spirit" of
the madman in the country of the Gadarenes. Since the independent "creations" of these "activités malignes" are the
equivalent of Pascal's *Pensées*, their author, possessed by
THEM, is revealed once again as the embodiment of that
very "malin génie," who, to Descartes' mind, had caused
his first two dreams in the November night of 1619, and
whose nightmarish presence has come to haunt Valéry's
very Cartesian Faust. The Solitaire's confession paraphrases Pascal's: "On se fait une idole de la vérité même;
car la verité hors de la charité n'est pas Dieu" (*Pensée*
582). He seems to intimate that charity and the quest for

God are (1) diametrically opposed to the diabolical fermentation of his mind, and (2) irreconcilable with Faust's intellectual curiosity, with its reliance on *le bon sens*.

Pascal's contempt for philosophers "qui ne discutaient pas l'immortalité de l'âme" (*Pensée* 220) is brought up to date, and takes on a modern savor in the Solitaire's sarcastic variations on Kant's awesome feeling, whenever he considered the "moral law in his breast" and the starry heavens above him. Endeavors to derive ethics from the categorical imperative and the like only provoke "senseless desires, vain hypotheses, absurd problems . . ." (P.II, 386). Mocking the Kantian maxim, he invites Faust: "Regarde un peu là-haut . . . Hein? Le beau ciel, le célèbre ciel étoilé au-dessus des têtes!" (*ibid.*) Like Mephistopheles in *Lust*, the Solitaire in his role as "malin esprit" takes a clerical posture when he callously apostrophizes Faust: "Minime Ordure," parodying the patronizing view of the spiritual shepherd who regards his sinful flock as *infima pecora*. Conforming to Pascal's skepticism toward man's corrupted reason—"L'homme n'est qu'un sujet plein d'erreur, naturelle et ineffaçable sans la grâce" (*Pensée* 83, et passim)—but consistent, too, with the evangelical story of the demons that were allowed to seek refuge in a herd of swine in the country of the Gadarenes, the Solitaire can now expound:

> Songe, Minime Ordure, à tout ce que cette grenaille et ces poussières ont semé de sottises dans les cervelles; à tout ce qu'elles ont fait imaginer, déclamer, supposer, chanter et calculer par notre genre humain . . . Oui, Ordure, le ciel et la mort ont rendu les hommes pensants plus stupides que mes pourceaux. (P.II, 386 f.)

It is now that we learn of the Solitaire's way of life: "Je vis de mes pourceaux parmi mes anges" (P.II, 387).

Having exorcised his "unclean spirits," he is living on the very swine that now harbor them in a stable, a thousand feet below his seat on high, where he lies suspended halfway between bestiality and angelism. He is unaware that both are united in *his* fallen angels, the demons that now inhabit his herd of swine. In short, in his proud ascension *beyond* the human condition, he has made no progress whatsoever, although he has placed himself high above those whom his apologetics have turned into his swine. While they wallow in their *abêtissement* for the sake of faith (*Pensée* 233), or in their pagan Pyrrhonism, bewitched as they seem by Circe, the Solitaire himself closely resembles those who, in Descartes' view, "se mêlent de donner des préceptes," and "se doivent estimer plus habiles que ceux auxquels ils les donnent; et s'ils manquent en la moindre chose, ils en sont blâmables" (*Discours* 1; AT, VI, 4). In his situation, midway between beast and angel, the Solitaire may resemble Everyman. Yet, in terms of his own principles, he is to be blamed: for, by elevating himself above everyone else, he has debased himself by the sin of pride—unlike Faust, who has only chanced upon these heights by following the purely human dreams or reveries of his intellect, a natural and fairly innocuous bent that at best can benefit everyone else, and at worst can bring harm only to himself.

13. *The Intellect, That Prostitute*

The Solitaire's swine are a choice lot. When Faust suggests that, down there, a thousand feet below, someone might steal them, the Solitaire self-assuredly brags: "Mes pourceaux? . . . Ho ho . . . Il n'y a que le diable qui pourrait s'y prendre, et encore . . . Ho ho . . . Ils sont des pourceaux enchantés . . ." (P.II, 387). Descending "en droite ligne des meilleurs sujets de la porcherie de Circé, la magicienne," and from those "famous swine who were once so rudely driven out and pushed into the sea, *pleins d'esprits*" (*ibid.*), they represent the full range of inherited demons: i.e., of those deceptive powers, both Pagan and Christian, which survive as deeply ingrained prejudices in the scholastic teachings, rejected by Descartes as well as by Faust, and doing the devil's bidding in the *Pensées* of Pascal, the former scientist turned theologian. The Solitaire's own mind and spirit inhabit one of his swine, jealously guarding his "belle et grasse truie" from any potential usurper (*ibid.*). "Vous lui laissez l'amour?" asks Faust (P.II, 388). Why not, the Solitaire replies. Is not prostitution the very principle of spirit and intellect? (P.II, 388.) His rejoinder corresponds to Valéry's critique of Pascal's apologetics, which, like all works of this nature, prostitutes the mind in the service of *propaganda fide*: "Faire de bons chrétiens avec de mauvais raisonnements, utiliser la logique et la mort, etc. Le Serpent peut-il faire pire?" (P.I, 468). "More subtil than any beast in the field" (Gen. 3:1), prostrate, and only occasionally rearing up like a snake that is ready to strike, inimical to mankind and poisoning human life: the Solitaire is, indeed, the very image of the postlapsarian Serpent in Paradise (cf. Gen. 3:14 f.).

Valéry's criticism of Pascal echoes, in more violent terms, Descartes' critique of the school discipline of *disputationes*, in which he took part at La Flèche; they cannot lead to new truths, "car, pendant que chacun tâche de vaincre, on s'exerce bien plus à faire valoir la vraisemblance, qu'à peser les raisons de part et d'autre; et ceux qui ont été longtemps bons avocats ne sont pas pour cela, par après, meilleurs juges" (*Discours* VI; AT, VI, 69). As though he were confirming his total identification with

Pascal, the Solitaire now gives Pascal's own example for the fragility of the human mind: "La moindre mouche le débauche" (P.II, 388). Or, in Pascal's words: "une mouche bourdonne . . . ; c'en est assez pour le rendre incapable de bon conseil" (*Pensée* 366; cf. *Pensée* 367; also: Montaigne, *Essais* III, xiii, and "Lettre de Madame Émilie Teste" [P.II, 26]). The mind is a whore "[il] s'offre, se pare, se mire, s'expose" (P.II, 388), not different in this from Pascal's description of "reason offering itself," but being "ployable à tous sens" (*Pensée* 274), and "flexible à tout" (*Pensée* 561). Language is a pimp "qui introduit en nous n'importe qui, et qui nous introduit en qui que ce soit"—"insinuating anyone into us, and inserting us into anyone" (P.II, 388).

Pascal expresses the same idea a number of times in less crude metaphors, e.g., in *Pensée* 15: "[Eloquence] consists of a correspondence to be established between the minds and hearts of those to whom one speaks, on the one hand; and on the other, between the thoughts and expressions one uses; which presupposes a thorough study of the human heart in view of knowing its motives, so that, as a consequence, one finds the exact proportions of the discourse suitable to their needs." Faust objects to the Solitaire's cynicism with arguments worthy of both Descartes and Valéry: "Mais . . . Mais les créations par le verbe, les chefs-d'oeuvre, les chants très purs (. . .) les architectures de la déduction, les lumières de la parole?" (P.II, 388). The Solitaire's very Pascalian retort demonstrates that he has by no means cast out all his devils, for his words paraphrase Bélials' pun, in *Lust*, on "*la panse qui pense*" (P.II, 337), and also those of a former incarnation of Faust (in *Lust*): "Must we protest again that every work of the intellect is but an excretion by which it delivers itself, in its own way, of its excessive pride, despair, lust or boredom?"

14. *Language Equals Myth*

The Solitaire had come to these conclusions when he "was still an *ordure*," he admits. Here, on his site on high, he can say: "j'ai enfin trouvé . . . ce qu'on y trouve . . ."—an ambiguous statement, since *trouver* means many things, among others: "to find" as well as "to guess," "to imagine," and "to invent." That he is referring to the latter two meanings becomes clear in the Solitaire's didactic axiom: "Tout ce qui peut se dire est nul." It recalls Valéry's definition of "myth" as "toute existence qui ne peut se passer du langage et s'évanouit avec un mot ou nom" (Cah. XXIII, 159), but also his somewhat blasphemous pun on the interchangeability of μῦθος and λόγος, which allows the Biblical "In the beginning was the Word" (John 1:1) to be turned into "Au commencement était la Fable" (P.I, 394; P.II, 189, et passim). While pointing to the Pascalian belief that the only truth that counts escapes both formulation and comprehension, the Solitaire's "All that can be put into words is nil," also amounts to a diabolical—if perhaps unintentional—denial of the Creative Word that was at the beginning (John 1:1). True to the Pascalian "qui veut faire l'ange fait la bête," the Solitaire's LEGION of demons, far from being exorcised, now begin their deception by turning upside down their Pascalian repertoire. For the Solitaire now suggests that there is nothing more banal than miracles: they astound naïve minds who can be impressed with "l'extrême grandeur ou la petitesse extrême" (P.II, 390). More and more, the Solitaire reveals the rhetorical trickery of his apologetics, which uses to its advantage the mathematical truth of infinitesimal calculus, passing off as a "miracle" the Pascalian axiom that "deux infinités (. . .) se rencontrent

dans toutes [choses]: l'une de grandeur, l'autre de petitesse" (*De l'esprit géométrique*, Brunschvicg, p. 174).

The more Faust hears, the more he realizes that, on these
dizzying heights, his 'raison y trouve l'air trop rare, et se
sent défaillir en [lui]" (P.II, 390). An experimentalist
who is anything but prone to leaps of faith or speculation,
his cautious reasoning is like Descartes', who modestly
proposes to *explain* rather than to *prove* the potential relations between effects and causes (*Discours* VI; AT, VI, 76).
He does not wish to astonish his reader by extraordinary
novelties, but rather to show him fairly clearly "ce que je
puis, ou ne puis pas, dans les sciences" (*Discours* VI; AT,
VI, 75). Thus he exposits only his own opinions "si simples
et si conformes au sens commun" (*Discours* VI; AT, VI,
77), which he has cautiously weighed throughout the
years, and which he holds by virtue of deduction, "seulement parce que la raison me les a persuadées" (*ibid.*).
Addressing Faust again as an embodiment of "filth" and
"weakness" (*imbécillité*), who should return to "the
gutters" (*aux égouts*), the Solitaire now exhibits a self-
reliance that would seem incompatible with his earlier
pronouncements on the order of the Pascalian "le moi est
haïssable": "Va, je ne t'ai rien dit que tu n'eusses pu tirer
de toi-même, si tu n'étais ordure et imbécillité" (P.II, 390).
His words echo Valéry's condemnation of Pascal's self-
centered speculations, so remote from empiricism: "Il a
tiré de soi-même le *silence éternel*" (P.I, 473). The Solitaire's threat that Faust, if he did not instantly leave, would
be "saisi par le mal des montagnes" evokes that type of
vertigo which had kept Descartes off balance, during his
first dream of the November night in 1619. Beyond their
literal meaning, the Solitaire's words contain a veiled
hint at the *mal*, the "evil," he himself represents, and that

will be swelling to whirlwind proportions with the arrival
of his companions. For he announces: "Mes Amis vont
venir . . . Va! Retombe, suis ton poids, Monsieur-je-ne-sais-
qui . . ." (P.II, 390). Faust acquiesces regretfully: this
"rigorously mad" monster is best left "rigoureusement
seul" (*ibid.*), but his curiosity gets the better of him. He
hides behind a rock, with this aside: "Je voudrais vraiment
voir la suite de ce fou" (*ibid.*)—the literary *terminus tech-
nicus* "suite" = "continuation" indicating that he, Faust,
is aware of watching a fiction, as a sort of participating
spectator.

15. *"Walpurgisnacht"*

Fancying himself to be *seul* again, the Solitaire now
conjures up his "friends," who, one gathers, are the
"fiends" driven out into his swine. With grotesque gestures
of execration, he prostrates himself, rises again, and vo-
ciferates with outstretched arms, invoking the "Splendeurs
du pur"—an Absolute beyond the reach of man, which
can be perfect "good" or absolute "evil." The latter is
meant, as it becomes clear with the next qualifiers: "peuple
superbe" (with a reference to *superbia*, Satanic pride),
"Puissances de l'instant," purely temporal powers, etc.
(*ibid.*). The diabolical litany calls on "Voix sans parole et
Parole sans voix," on negative forces of non-creation, and
on Satanic laughter annihilating night and day ("Riez,
Rires du rien [. . . .] Riez, la nuit n'est rien, le jour n'est
rien"). It is a Faustian *Walpurgisnacht* without Faustian
participation, but surreptitiously attended by Faust, the
hidden observer and scientific *voyeur*, and staged by the
Pascalian Solitaire, who is frightened by the "eternal
silence of these infinite spaces," which are to him a yawn-

ing Nothingness, while, for other mystics, they resound with the voice of God (cf. P.ɪ, 459 ff.).

The absence of God is filled with the presence of unclear and indistinct notions, beseeched by the Solitaire in an absurd attempt to silence the eternal silence: "Forces sans formes, puissances sans prodiges, / Exterminez mystère, énigmes et miracles, / [. . . . .] / Mes grands amis sans corps ni âmes"; he evokes them "Contre tout ce qui fut et tout ce qui peut être, / Contre ce qui connaît et contre ce qui sent; / Contre moi-même, que je hais comme une épouse, / Et contre toute mort qui ne soit pas Quelqu'un de Vous" (P.ɪɪ, 390 f.). Negative powers of total negation, forces of destruction, to be unleashed against life as it is and against all its possible future forms, his demons are called back from their habitat in his swine to haunt, as Pascalian *pensées-poèmes*, a world stained with original sin, and hence denied, as unworthy to exist. The Solitaire's "malédictions d'univers" are invoked, in particular, against the Cartesian "âme raisonnable" ("Contre ce qui connaît et contre ce qui sent"), against the Pascalian "moi haïssable"—that Self who has become hateful like Adam's spouse—and against death brought about by any other power than that of the devil (afflicting mankind with the curse of mortality). Unclear and indistinct, the Solitaire's curses and demons fulminate against God's "silence" throughout the "infinite spaces" of his universe. From a Cartesian perspective, their confusion and obscurity would suffice to indicate their inherent falsehood, their diabolical origins, and their participation in Nothingness: "En sorte que, si nous en [i.e., des idées] avons souvent qui contiennent de la fausseté, ce ne peut être que de celles qui ont quelque chose de confus et obscur, à cause qu'en cela elles participent du néant. (. . .) Et il est évident qu'il n'y a pas moins de répugnance que la fausseté ou l'imperfection procède de Dieu, en tant que telle, qu'il y en a que la vérité ou la perfection procède du néant" (*Discours* IV; AT, VI, 38 f.).

The Solitaire's *litanie de Satan* had begun with an invocation ("A moi Splendeurs du pur," etc.); it had continued with a eulogy ("Troupe sans nombre et non pas innombrable," etc.); and, like its beginning, and middle, it ends, in the best tradition of prayer and ode, with a supplication: an invitation to his LEGION, dispersed as *pensées* in his apologetics, and thence, in his readers—the swine kept a thousand feet below his lofty heights—to return and to take again possession of him:

> Oh . . . Passez en moi, Vents superbes! (. . .)
> Rompez les ronces du savoir,
> Foulez les fleurs de ma pensée,
> Broyez les roses de mon coeur,
> Et tout ce qui n'est pas digne de ne pas être!
> Je veux que l'air glacé que vous soufflez me lave
> D'une faute commise avant que rien ne fût!
>
> (P.II, 391)

Desirous to be "washed clean of a sin committed before anything was," the Solitaire invites precisely the power that had committed this sin, to become embodied in him— in strict observance of the Pascalian "qui veut faire l'ange fait la bête." The "Vents superbes," a transparent metaphor for Lucifer's *superbia*, before the beginning of time, combine with the "espèce de tourbillon" in Descartes' first dream (Baillet, I, 81), in which he thought to recognize his "mauvais génie." The charade thickens, as the Solitaire speaks like Dante's Gate of Hell: for "Une faute commise avant que rien ne fût!" roughly corresponds to "Dinanzi a me non fur cose create" (*Inferno* III, 7). He opens him-

self indeed wide to the devils who want to enter Pandaemonium, as Mephistopheles describes it in *Faust II*, Act
IV (10075 ff.).

Now suddenly, the Solitaire's site on high, where he
tries to come as close as possible to transcendental mysteries, assumes a ferociously ironic meaning. In the light
of Faust's initial "il n'y a ni haut, ni bas," but this time
seen from the Devil's cosmogonic perspective, the Solitaire's high mountain reveals itself as analogous to the
"Hochgebirg" ("high mountains"), of *Faust II*, Act IV,
which—now turned upside down—had once been the
"bottom of hell" ("Denn eigentlich war das der Grund
der Hölle" *Faust II* 10072). "Hochgebirg" is the vantage
point from which Mephistopheles shows Goethe's Faust
the treasures of this world, in imitation of Christ's temptation by the Devil. Mephistopheles describes its topog-
raphy in terms of the reversibility of concepts of "haut"
and "bas," according to sound diabolical doctrine that
turns all value systems upside down:

> Was ehmals Grund war, ist nun Gipfel.
> Sie (die Teufel) gründen auch hierauf die rechten
>   Lehren,
> Das Unterste ins Oberste zu kehren.
>
> (What formerly was bottom, now is summit,
> They [the devils] upon this, too, found the proper
>   doctrine,
> To turn the bottommost into the Uppermost).
>   (*Faust II*, 10088 ff.)[14]

---

[14] This good doctrine is proclaimed elsewhere by Mephistopheles, in the *Mummenschanz* scene (*Faust II*, Act I), where he appears disguised as Zoilo-Thersites:

> Das Tiefe hoch, das Hohe tief,
> Das Schiefe grad, das Grade schief,

But the Solitaire's highly suspect summit also recalls
the *Harzgebirg*, locus of *Walpurgisnacht* in *Faust I*. Altogether, the Solitaire's litany paraphrases Mephisto's
"moral" self-portrait when he first introduces himself to
Faust:

> Ich bin der Geist, der stets verneint![15]
> Und das mit Recht; denn alles, was entsteht,
> Ist wert, dass es zugrunde geht,
> Drum besser wär's, dass nichts entstünde.
> So ist denn alles, was Ihr Sünde,
> Zerstörung, kurz das Böse nennt,
> Mein eigentliches Element.

> (I am the Spirit who forever negates!
> And rightfully so: for whatever
> springs up, deserves to perish.
> Hence, it were better if nothing
> arose. Thus, all that which you
> call Sin, Destruction, in short,
> Evil, is my true element.) (Goethe, *Faust I*, 1338 ff.)

"Hâtez-vous, hâtez moi!"—the Solitaire's wishful identification with his fallen angels (the "vous" becoming
"moi") leads to an anticipation of "qui veut faire l'ange

> Das ganz allein macht mich gesund,
> So will ich's auf dem Erdenrund

> (What's deep [I want] high, what's high, deep,
> What's crooked, straight, what's straight, crooked,
> This alone makes me feel well
> This is the way I want it on Earth.) *Faust II*, 5467 ff.

[15] This line is quoted once in the original German, in Cah. vii,
857, where it occurs as a marginal remark to an aphorism on the
insincerity of any "sacrifice." It is meant as an affirmation of
Valéry's own and very specific type of "methodical doubt" (not as
an anodine affirmation of what might be mistaken for "satanism").

fait la bête," in these terms: "Il est l'heure, il est temps que je me change en loup!" (P.II, 391). Watching the Solitaire fall on his belly as he utters a long howl, Faust concludes: "Quel monstre de bon sens que ce terrible individu! J'ignorais jusqu'à lui qu'il pût exister une espèce au-delà de la démence . . ." (*ibid.*). Worse than the devil, and different from him, the Solitaire *s'abêtissant*, turning willingly into a demented beast and recalling the demons of his nihilism, totally mystifies Faust.

16. *Angel or Beast? The Precipitation of Faust*

At this moment, Faust feels an icy wind: "Mais quelle bise!" (P.II, 391). Once again, his metaphor paraphrases the Thanatos touch of Pascal's *Pensées*, their disharmonious and negative effect on the mind, and their essential lack of love and charity, when measured by the standards of Descartes' *Olympica*, where "warmth means love," and all things are animated "by a single force: love, charity, harmony."[16] Simultaneously, Faust's imagery evokes the paralyzing wind in Descartes' first dream, and the presence of his "evil genius," who attempted to drive him by force towards a place of worship where his own devotion would have commanded him to go, but which a divine power kept him from reaching under such malignant auspices. Faust now decides to leave this uncanny place of worship, where the Solitaire celebrates his Black Mass. His gesture, once again, conforms to the Cartesian refusal to accept irrational works of apologetics.

The Solitaire suddenly realizes that his metamorphosis into a beast of prey and his prayer for total destruction of

---

[16] Vna est in rebus activa vis, amor, charitas, harmonia.
   Sensibilia apta concipiendis Olympicis: (. . .) calor
      amorem (. . .)
   Omnis forma corporea agit per harmoniam. (AT, x, 218)

life are taking place before an unwelcome audience. In a
rage, he jumps at Faust's throat, shouting: "Ordure! Il
était là!" Once more, Faust finds himself apostrophized
as the hollow and garbage-filled heart in the Pascalian
Pensée (143). As a "witness" ("Il était là!"), he will soon
be martyrized ($\mu\acute{\alpha}\rho\tau\upsilon\rho\sigma\varsigma$ = "witness") by the Solitaire,
whose vanity is so seriously affected by the presence of this
redoubtable rival that, in order to rid himself of Faust, he
is willing to humiliate and destroy the whole species, not
unlike Valéry's Pascal, boundlessly jealous of Descartes:
"Le commencement de son entreprise de destruction
générale des valeurs humaines se trouve peut-être dans
quelque souffrance particulière de son amour de soi. Il
est des rivaux si redoutables qu'on ne les peut ravaler
qu'en rabaissant toute l'espèce" (P.i, 462).[17] Although
Faust politely protests: "Mais je m'en vais . . . ," the
Solitaire, after a desperate struggle, precipitates him into
the abyss. Faust's presence was too much for him to bear;
he felt threatened by him in his solitary uniqueness, very

---

[17] There are strong affinities between Valéry's and Nietzsche's
views on Pascal. To quote only two passages from *Beyond Good
and Evil*: Nietzsche speaks of Pascal's "*sacrifizio dell'intelletto*"
(Aphorism 229)—in Dante's language, the equivalent of a surrender to diabolical impulses ("Ch'hanno perduto il ben dello
intelletto" *Inf.* iii, 18). Pascal's faith is characterized by Nietzsche
as "jener Glaube Pascals, der auf schreckliche Weise einem
dauernden Selbstmorde der Vernunft ähnlich sieht—einer zähen
langlebigen wurmhaften Vernunft, die nicht mit einem Male und
einem Streiche totzumachen ist" ("Pascal's faith which in a terrifying way resembles a continuous suicide of reason—of a tough,
longlived, worm- and serpent-like reason, which cannot be killed
once and for all, with one single stroke" [Aphorism 46]). On two
occasions, at least, Valéry calls Pascal an "enemy of the human
race." In 1924: "Pascal, ennemi du genre humain" (Cah. x, 194);
and again, in 1933: "En somme, ennemi du genre humain" (Cah.
xvi, 201).

much like Pascal, in Valéry's view, by Descartes: "Il ne lui suffit pas d'être Pascal . . . Qui sait s'il n'a pas trop profondément et amèrement ressenti la gloire de *Des Cartes*, dont il a constamment essayé d'abaisser les mérites et de railler les grands espoirs; et si une pointe de jalousie atroce, une épine secrète dans son coeur. . ." (P.I, 462). Valéry's use of aposiopesis, breaking off the sentence before its conclusion, prolongs and deepens its abysmal implications. Translated into Pascalian terms, they would read: "Que j'aime à voir cette superbe raison humiliée . . ." (*Pensée* 388), a wish that could stand as an oblique metaphor for Faust's "precipitation" into the abyss, an irrational conclusion to a rational career, suiting the Solitaire's "prevention," his deeply rooted prejudices.

"Bruit de chute," indicate the stage directions. Combined with the starry backdrop, which resembles "a stereotype of the Milky Way," the loud noise of Faust's fall into an abyss—a sort of Lucifer's fall in reverse!—evokes Descartes' second bad dream, "dans lequel il crût entendre un bruit aigu et éclatant qu'il prit pour un coup de tonnère. La frayeur qu'il en eut le réveilla sur l'heure même: et ayant ouvert les yeux, il apperçût beaucoup d'étincelles de feu repanduës par la chambre. . ." (Baillet, I, 82). The stage of the mind and its chamber correspond to the theatre's stage, where, with a cosmic thump, Faust, the incarnation of the Cartesian *bon sens* falls—a victim of the Solitaire's bestiality. For, in his overreaching *angélisme*, the Solitaire has dulled and "bestialized" himself, brutally ridding himself of his rational rival. He now rules in total isolation from reason on these antibiotic and loveless heights, possessed by his demons, as the living proof of the inhumanity of the Pascalian "tous les hommes se haïssent naturellement l'un l'autre" (*Pensée* 451), and of Mercator's *Lupus est homo homini* in the *Asinaria* of Plautus

(ɪɪ, iv, 88). In his final apotheosis, having tumbled Faust
into the abyss ("Va . . . Tombe comme une ordure . . ."
[P.ɪɪ, 392]), the Solitaire feels himself metamorphosed
into a wolf who cries "wolf" in the presence of his own
hateful human nature: "Ah! ah . . . Au loup! au loup!
Ah!" (P.ɪɪ, 392). Thus, as the curtain falls, he most strikingly dramatizes Valéry's Pascal, "une des plus fortes in-
telligences qui aient paru," but who "se ressent, (. . .) se
peint, et se lamente, comme une bête traquée; mais de
plus qui se traque elle-même. . ." (P.ɪ, 461).

17. *Conclusion*

We have seen that, in Valéry's Cartesian transposition,
the Solitaire's metamorphosis into a wolf who flings Faust
into the abyss serves to illustrate the "evil genius" whom
Descartes thought he recognized as the author of his first
two dreams in the fateful night of November 10th, 1619,
when in a burst of "enthusiasm" he experienced the
revelation of his future quest as a methodical searcher for
mathematically clear and distinct ideas. We have also seen
that the Solitaire's essential inhumanity culminates in a
negative apotheosis of Pascalian thought, as envisaged from
Valéry's pro-Cartesian vantage point. It exemplifies the
abêtissement in blind (rather than in good) faith, recom-
mended by the *Pensées*. It does so figuratively and etymologically, signifying a sort of self-inflicted "dullness"
and a voluntary "stupor," hostile to human passions and
to intellectual curiosity. But it does so, too, by showing
quite literally the unexpected byproduct of such an inhuman retreat from the proper pursuits of the inquiring
mind. The anchorite's Ovidian metamorphosis into a wild
beast serves as an exemplary demonstration of the validity
of Pascal's famous axiom that "qui veut faire l'ange fait

la bête." It points to the misanthropic ironies of a type of solitary meditation in the wilderness, selfish and selfless at once, in its uncharitable distance from the cares of life, and deriving self-hatred from a fanatical contempt for secular mankind, stained, as it appears to the Christian mind, by the indelible corruption of original sin. The "evil genius" that looks upon man as the natural enemy of all men, begetting the notion of "le moi haïssable," vitiates reasoning by rejecting the golden mean and the natural gift of common sense.

This Pascalian force, so inimical to Descartes' key notion of the intellect's progressive growth through its own methodical search, might well stand as an image for Mephisto's definition of "meditation" as "un vice solitaire" (*Lust* i, ii; P.ii, 291). Since vitiated virtue and vice alike do not suffer spectators lightly, it is not surprising that Faust, Valéry's detached and itinerant embodiment of the ever-observant Cartesian *bon sens*, is hurled into the abyss, as a human sacrifice offered by the Solitaire while the latter is turning into a wolf. In his lycanthropy and in his sacrificial offering of Faust to the "eternal silence" of *deus ignotus*, the unknown God, the Solitaire, like Valéry's Pascal, sacrifices human life on earth to a Moloch-like Deity. Simultaneously, on the level of classical myth, he resembles Lycaon, the Arcadian king, who was transformed into a wolf after serving a dish of human flesh to Zeus, his guest, whose divine presence he failed to perceive (Ovid. *Met.* i, 209-239). What Valéry, the agnostic, holds against Pascal is not his religious fervor but his insensitivity, which blinds him—in terms of religious values—to the world as God's image (*mundus imago Dei est*). It also causes his deafness to His voice in those "infinite spaces" where the prophets and mystics had thought to hear it in the harmony of the spheres. On the nocturnal stage of

Act One, where, in morose confusion, Pascalian *Pensées* hurl their *malédictions d'univers* against a divine order that they deprive of all signs and portents, Faust, the rational witness (or the presence of reason), must be felt as an infuriatingly embarrassing presence. On these liminal heights of transcendental silence, where Pascalian *Pensées* perform their *danse macabre*, in an icy climate of necrophilia, no Cartesian Faust can be tolerated. Nor is there room here for warmth, light, and harmony, those qualities dear to the youthful, slightly mystical, and Pythagorean Descartes of the *Olympica*. In this nocturnal twilight, so far from the "light that signifies knowledge," and in an air so rarefied that no "corporeal forms" could live here "in conformity with universal laws of harmony," there can prevail only negation, the absence of all "warmth which signifies charity" (cf. AT, x, 218).

In short, I have attempted to show that Act One can be seen as a dramatic charade, transposing the young Descartes' first two nightmarish dreams of the November night in 1619, with Descartes' identity hidden under the mask of Valéry's Faust. Erring on unfamiliar heights of metaphysical rarefaction that his dreams have erected in his sleeping mind, he stumbles onto the antics performed by the "evil genius" of Pascalian thought—not as the *Pensées* would affect a sympathetic reader, but in the guise of their unfavorable exposure by Valéry in "Variation sur une pensée" (P.I, 458 ff.).

In Cartesian terms, Faust's fate at the hands of the Solitaire was sealed by the mind's sleep, reason's temporal lapse into the fantasy world of dream, where a nightmarish "evil genius" led him astray from the broad path of *le bon sens*. Possessed by this *malin génie*, he had been misled like those misguided seekers for truth whose efforts Descartes had condemned, since they resembled travelers, "lesquels, ayant laissé le grand chemin pour prendre la traverse, demeurent égarés entre des épines et des précipices" (*La Recherche de la vérité*; AT, x, 497). His shortcut had brought him face to face with the lycanthropic madman, the very incarnation of suffering (the figurative meaning of "épines"), whose bestial assault hurls him from a precipice. The deranged Solitaire represented accepted opinions and superstitions, accelerated and heightened to climactic whirlwind proportions. He allegorized the dilemma of the insane passions invading the sleeping mind. A captive audience, Faust can judge the Solitaire's madness, but he cannot free himself from its antics in order to make *tabula rasa*, and to use methodical doubt in a fresh start from a point zero, searching for certainty in a systematic quest, based on the mind's inherent potential for discovery and invention. Thus, the Solitaire turned out to be a nightmare, the ultimate obstacle on the road to cognition, a point of no return and no advance—a mirage made of reason's sleep and dream. Faust's fall from these barren and misanthropic heights will prove, once again, the validity of his dictum that, in terms of the absolute, Nature, dream, and human consciousness know "ni haut ni bas." For he will fall into an abyss of enchantment, where his mind rises to new dimensions—more endearing but equally as treacherous as the Solitaire's metaphysical peaks of despair.

Three.

LES FÉES

1. *The Cartesian View of Passions*

Consistent with the Baroque origins and Stoic training of his historical model, Valéry's Faust had correctly diagnosed the Solitaire's behavior as symptomatic of a mental disease. In the language of the Stoics, the Solitaire would indeed be considered mad. He is possessed by uncontrolled passions that have overwhelmed a mind refusing (in Cartesian terms) its total union with the body's carnal functions, so necessary for its sanity. The Solitaire's uncontrolled passions, stripped of their Pascalian disguise as "thought," reach their climax when they triumph over Faust, the impassive and amused embodiment of the "rational soul," precipitating him into the abyss. It is a dubious victory at best, dramatizing once again a major theme of *Mon Faust*, the paradox of "la panse qui pense"; or, in the words of Valéry's Faust, the problems of *Le Corps de l'Esprit*—a title that might well serve to paraphrase Descartes' *Les Passions de l'âme*. If Act One shows the dangers of *mediocritas* refused, the Pascalian imbalance of an asceticism that unleashes the passions with a vengeance, *Les Fées* demonstrates the Cartesian wisdom of giving the passions their due but checking their excesses by the controlling "actions" of Reason through the will, its efficient agent.

On the level of human psychology, Faust's plunge from the Solitaire's icy heights into the fairyland palace of the Fays tends to prove once again the validity of Faust's dictum "qu'il n'y a ni haut ni bas." This time, the proof derives from Cartesian physio-psychology, which places the seat of the union between body and mind in the pineal gland toward which, he supposes, all nerves converge. Descartes conceives of them as tubular conduits containing networks of thin threads that connect the brain with all parts of the body. The latter convey pressures and information on injuries to the former, where they are instantaneously translated into sensations that then release corresponding "passions" (= sufferings) of the soul. They in turn are immediately communicated back to the affected part of the body, where only then they are felt as pleasure or pain. Only those images which are carried by the "animal spirits" to the surface of the pineal gland, where they leave their impression on the imagination and the common sense, can be called "ideas," i.e., "les formes ou images que l'âme raisonnable considérera immédiatement, lorsque étant unie à cette machine elle imaginera ou sentira quelque objet" (*L'Homme*, AT, XI, 177). "Ideas" are seen as the physical condition of sensations; their carriers, the "animal spirits," are "like a very subtle wind or rather like a very pure and lively flame"; they "constantly and in great abundance rise from the heart to the brain," and from there descend through the nervous system into the muscles, giving movement to the body's members (*Discours* V; AT, VI, 54).

Although they incorporate much of Hippocrates' and Galen's categories, these views are radically novel. The "heart" is no longer seen as the seat of emotions. The "ideas" of these latter, like all sensations, are mechanically conveyed on the bloodstream to the "concavities of the brain," heart and arteries functioning much like the "bellows of an organ" (*L'Homme*, AT, XI, 165), blowing and pressing the "animal spirits" into the direction of the pineal gland. Psychological reactions are reduced to mechanical processes, and sensations are seen as originating in the brain's pineal gland, the physical seat of "imagination," "memory," and the "common sense" (which coordinates all sense impressions), but also the physical locale where body and "rational soul" unite. "Passions" and "emotions" are seen by Descartes as "willed" by the body, passed on to consciousness; they are felt, although their causes may remain unknown. They denote the "passive" side of the soul, for they originate and end in the body, by contrast to the soul's "actions," which both begin and terminate in the mind (like man's aspirations toward God, and the *cogito*). Body and soul are at once united and separate. At their point of union, the pineal gland, both the "passions" endured by the rational soul and its actions turn into volition. In short, Descartes distinguishes between two types of the will: the volitions of the body (or "passions of the soul") and those which are caused by the soul, its "actions" which are purely rational. Since Descartes conceives of the pineal gland as the locale where all intellectual activity starts but where also all passions (lofty and base) enter consciousness, he can dismiss the traditional distinctions between "inferior" or sensitive and "superior" or rational parts of the soul.

For Descartes, the indivisible unity of the soul is the sign of its divine origin and superiority over the body, since the latter is divided into parts: "Car il n'y a en nous qu'une seule âme, et cette âme n'a en soi aucune diversité de parties: la même qui est sensitive est raisonnable, et tous ses appétits sont des volontés" (*Les Passions de l'âme* I, art. 47; AT, xi, 364). It is purely a matter of strength whether the rational soul resists carnal passions by warding them off with its own weapons; whether it opposes different passions to those which are beleaguering it; or whether it surrenders to their onslaught (*ibid.*, I, art. 48). *Le bon sens*, equally well distributed among all sane human minds (*Discours* I; AT, VI, I) is the arbiter, and a *liber arbiter* indeed, whose freedom of choice determines which "actions" to choose, to dispose of *les passions de l'âme*. For the young Descartes of *Olympica*, the rational soul contains *semina scientiae*, "seeds of knowledge," which, like "seeds of fire" in a flintstone, await their liberation (AT, X, 217). In their latent stage, *semina scientiae*, too, are "passions" of the soul. Enthusiasm, reason, and imagination are the mental conditions releasing them, and turning them into potential "actions" of the intellect.

These somewhat tedious disquisitions on Descartes' fanciful speculations about "passions" and "actions" of the soul will prove useful to an analysis of *Les Fées* and, in retrospect, to an understanding of the "passive" (i.e., "unhealthy") nature of the Solitaire's emotionally violent "thoughts." In Cartesian terms, his metaphysical anguish qualifies as a *passion de l'âme* that has hopelessly overpowered the intellect's freedom of coping with it. But since in Descartes' psychology there are no "inferior" and "superior" parts of the soul, the Solitaire's Pascalian *Pensées* have their seat on the same level of the brain, in the pineal gland, where, indistinctly, all rational thought, all carnal passions, all dreams and daydreams, become conscious.

With his pellmell invocation of contradictory school opinions, the Solitaire could well stand as a symbol for those doctrinaire books and ideas—rejected by both Goethe's Faust and the young Descartes as useless ballast— that had only contributed to the realization of their own ignorance.[1] In Faustian as well as in Cartesian terms,

---

[1] Cf. *Faust I*, 354 ff., *Discours* I; AT, VI, 4 ff. Descartes' lifelong search for truth by the use of his "natural light," relying on ob-

Faust's encounter with the Solitaire may thus be seen as a
temptation of the mind by the useless quibbles of theolo-
gians who—most likely without divine guidance—think
"d'être plus qu'homme" in their examinations of "revealed
truths" (cf. *Discours* i; AT, vi, 8). These blundering and
acrimonious ravings are met by the mind with Faustian
rejection and Cartesian doubt. Their universal curses, their
"malédictions d'univers"—far from hurling the rational
soul from metaphysical heights into the bottomless pit—
merely thrust its incarnation, Faust, back onto his own
inner resources, where a new temptation lies in wait for
him, in the form of the Fays' enchantment. If the Solitaire
represented the mind's seduction by fallacious school opinions and *idées reçues*, beleaguering the rational soul from
without, the Fays' enchantment constitutes the magic and
poetic spells which threaten it from within, tempting it
with "passions" and fairy tales in efforts to lure it away
from the path of reason and methodical doubt.

2. *Faust's Fall from Metaphysical Heights*

Faust's plunge into the innermost recesses of the mind
was "fatal" only in a figurative way; for he now finds
himself in the fantasy palace of Fays, who will eventually

---

servation and experimentation rather than on *auctores*, is perhaps
best expressed in *La Recherche de la Vérité*, AT, x, 497: "Mais je
ne veux point examiner ce que les autres ont su ou ignoré; il me
suffit de remarquer que, quand bien même toute la science qui se
peut désirer serait comprise dans les livres, si est-ce que ce qu'ils
ont de bon est mêlé parmi tant de choses inutiles, et semé confusé-
ment dans un tas de si gros volumes, qu'il faudrait plus de temps
pour les lire, que nous n'en avons pour demeurer en cette vie, et
plus d'esprit pour choisir les choses utiles, que pour les inventer de
soi-même."

reveal themselves as those forces of imagination and memory whose poetic *charmes* will play a decisive role in determining his destiny. As Fays, they literally allegorize his personal *Fates*—*fée* and Fay being derived from the vulgar Latin *Fata* "goddess of destiny," a noun stemming, like *fatum* "fate," from *farior* "to speak." They are foremost among the oracular powers of language, guiding its mythologizing qualities toward the expression of both the mind's "passions" and "actions." On the theatre of Faust's mind they can and will stage a repertory of *les passions de l'âme* from childhood memories of fairytale wonders to concupiscent dreams and daydreams of future glory. But it is also on this very scene that Faust will be tempted by glimpses of that rare conjunction of philosophy and wisdom—so disappointingly lacking in the Solitaire's and the philosopher's thoughts—that Descartes in his third dream ascribes to the works of the poets, conceived under the influence of "enthusiasm" (Baillet 1, 84).

In the end, Faust's terrifying "fall" from the lifeless heights of sterile metaphysics will reveal itself as the prelude to a temporal liberation similar to the one experienced by Descartes when he awakened from "l'épouvante" of his second dream, which affected him with "sa syndérèse, c'est-à-dire, les remords de sa conscience" (Baillet 1, 85). When applied to Valéry's Faust, this metaphor can be extended to embrace his consciousness "remordue," i.e., which has another go at life after having strayed from the path of reason into the mad and antibiotic world of the Solitaire's misanthropic and existential anguish. To sum up, Faust's "fall" had been little more than a breaking away—at once Faustian and Cartesian—from the nightmare of orthodox doctrine and preconceived notions. It had marked his exit from the icy and lifeless disputes of scholastic learning, where he had been less an actor than a contemptuous spectator. He has now moved on to a more intimate stage for another, by far more enjoyable but in the end equally tantalizing, act of the same *drame de l'intellect*, which takes place in the theatre of his brain.

In chapter two, I had intimated that the conjunction of Faust's precipitation by the loudly howling Solitaire and the very scenery of Act One, with its backdrop showing "as many stars as on a stereotype of the Milky Way," produces a charade, suggesting the "numerous fiery sparks" that Descartes saw when he awakened from his second dream, to the accompaniment of "la foudre dont il entendit l'éclat" (Baillet 1, 85). This "thunderbolt" was taken by Descartes to be "le signal de l'Esprit de vérité qui descendoit sur luy pour le posséder" (*ibid.*). Upon falling asleep again shortly thereafter, Descartes had a third dream, which, he felt, took place under the aegis of his "good genius," unlike the two preceding nightmares that, to his mind, had been the work of his "evil genius." Regarding this third dream as a good omen, he believed it augured well for a future to be spent in efforts to bring to fruition *semina scientiae*—his innate "seeds of knowledge"—through the relentless and methodical pursuit of clear and distinct ideas that might ultimately reveal the coherent unity of all sciences.

Thunderbolt—"Foudre se dit fig. Du Courroux des Dieux"—suggests the *Dictionnaire de l'Académie Françoise* (1694). On the metaphorical use of "foudre," it adds: "On dit fig. *Les Foudres de l'excommunication*, pour dire L'excommunication. *Les Foudres du Vatican. Les Foudres des censures Ecclésiastiques*" (*ibid.*). In this sense, it can be applied to the "malédictions d'univers" that accompanied Faust's fall. They may well be construed to be anathemas in reverse, howled by the Solitaire—that "evil genius" of Pascalian thought—in an effort to purge himself of Faust's all-too-rational presence. This effort also had the opposite effect of purging Faust from the thundering and disharmonious noise of the Solitaire's mad ravings. Thrusting Faust from icy heights of fideism, the Solitaire causes him to fall back on his own ingenuity, onto a scene of seductive *charmes* and passions that Faust's active will, rediscovered by his "lumière naturelle" and his methodical doubt can probe, enjoy, and ultimately refuse to accept.

But by thrusting Faust back entirely on the resourcefulness of his mind, unhindered by existential anguish, the Solitaire has ironically converted from a lycanthropic "beast" into an unwitting "angel" of mercy. His act of violence has paradoxically inverted the Pascalian premise, "qui veut faire l'ange fait la bête," adding one more proof to the morality expressed by Faust's dictum "qu'il n'y a ni haut, ni bas." This latter conjecture itself can actually be traced to Goethe's Mephisto. It is a Faustian adaptation of Mephisto's injunction in *Faust II*, when he sends off his companion to wrest the "moving but lifeless images" of Paris and Helena from the "Mothers," those mythical movers of ancestral memories in the collective unconscious (cf. *Faust II*, 6275 f.; for a complete analysis, see below chapter four). In short, against the Solitaire's fondest expectations, his rude "excommunication" of Faust has the same astonishing effects as the "thunderbolt" in Descartes' second dream: while banishing Faust from the deadly domain of his "evil genius," it ironically casts out the latter from his mind, signaling "l'Esprit de vérité qui descendoit sur luy [on Faust, as it did on Descartes] pour le posséder." We shall see how in *Les Fées* the themes of the Cartesian doubt, Descartes' third dream, and his views on *Les passions de l'âme* intertwine in the charade played on the stage of Faust's mind.

3. Faust's Mind—The Proper Stage for the "Drame Intellectuel"

Everything seems to suggest that Act One and *Les Fées* represent antithetical attitudes of the mind in a drama that might well borrow its title from Victor Hugo's *Une tempête sous un crâne*. If Faust's brain is indeed the stage where these spectacles unfold, the strangely antistrophic symmetry of the Solitaire's and Faust's positions, when we first perceive the former in Act One and the latter in *Les Fées*, can hardly be written off as a matter of chance. "Couché à plat ventre sur une roche plate," the Solitaire agonized in the open, but high above the last traces of life, amidst amorphous masses of ice and snow, and surrounded by precipices, in an atmosphere so rarefied that breathing was practically impeded. In his vain attempts to cross the threshold of transcendence, he had literally and metaphorically "gone out of his mind," without entering Faust's rational soul as little more than a repulsive and perfectly forgettable spectacle.

In *Les Fées*, by contrast, Faust is first seen peacefully asleep, lying on his back. Although unconscious, he seems at ease, and his relaxed posture indicates that no nightmare is haunting his mind. As the curtain rises, a skull-like basalt grotto slowly emerges from darkness. The scene is described as a mixture of "fantastic palace" and groups of very tall trees. In this interior setting, where Nature and Art concur to produce "a closed architectural system which is gradually lit by a silvery light," "enormous tree trunks and their endlessly multiplied branches hold the crystalline masses in their knotty mesh." The scene resembles an oneiric evocation of Descartes' schematic drawings of the human brain during stages of sleep and dream

—with the "silvery light" providing the proper tint for gray matter, while the "endlessly multiplied branches," with their "crystalline masses" of clear and distinct ideas held *in petto*, are not unlike the vast net of arteries that, "se divisant en mille branches fort déliées, tapissent le fond des concavités du cerveau," where they serve as passageways for the weakest of animal spirits (*L'Homme*, AT, XI, 172). Faust is seen resting on "a block covered with a strangely rich carpet which extends far out on the ground." The little Fays are lined up around him, ready to begin their airy round. The two taller Fays are seen at his sides, the Prime Fay holding him by the hand as though to guide and comfort him, the Second Fay bent over his face like Narcissus over his mirror image.

Valéry's essays on Descartes prove that he was thoroughly acquainted with Cartesian speculations on the structure of the human body and soul. Hence it cannot be a mere coincidence that the conjunction of the stage set with the grouping of Faust and the Fays bears a close resemblance to the anatomy of the "fibrous" human brain and to the factors determining its "motions," as seen by Descartes. Faust, indeed, occupies the very spot on stage that, in the Cartesian concept of the brain, would correspond to the pineal gland, where body and soul unite; here the body's "will" is translated into "passions of the soul," and the mind's "thoughts" into the soul's "actions." In this setting, Faust incarnates by analogy the *unity* and simplicity, i.e., the *Oneness* of the intellect's immediate functions, with its seat in the pineal gland, hard pressed and surrounded by the swift motions of *two* groups of little Fays, performing the twofold mechanical tasks of the "animal spirits" and the mind's innate *semina scientiae*, ready to revive the swooning Faust with pricks of sensations and flashes of tantalizing images.[2] The two taller Fays, in turn, allegorize those latent forces of "Imagination" and "Memory"—in Descartes' view, physical faculties too—whose rich stores of "ideas" and "images" will soon lend their aid to the enterprise of luring Faust into a state of self-consciousness and poetic enthusiasm.[3] The "strangely rich carpet" on which Faust is resting, and which "s'étale largement sur le sol," would

[2] My interpretation of the *petites Fées* as representing Cartesian "animal spirits" and *semina scientiae* is borne out in modern psychological and mathematical terms by an entry in the *Cahiers*: "—Quant aux 'harmoniques' (que je représente par le *Solitaire* et par les *Fées*—) ce sont ces valeurs supérieures de la Sensibilité, *qui s'ordonnent en groupes* (au sens quasi mathématique du mot) et qui sont la *structure abstraite* de nos modifications les plus concrètes—les *sensations en soi, au-dessus de toute signification*, et au-dessus *de toute condition accidentelle* de leur production fragmentaire . . ." (Cah. XXVI, 442; 1942; Valéry's italics).

[3] A closer look at Descartes' argument for choosing the pineal gland as the seat of the rational soul would appear to reinforce my hypothesis: "La raison qui me persuade que l'âme ne peut avoir en tout le corps aucun autre lieu que cette glande [pinéale] où elle exerce immédiatement ses fonctions est que je considère que les autres parties de notre cerveau sont toutes doubles, comme aussi nous avons deux yeux, deux mains, deux oreilles, et enfin tous les organes de nos sens extérieurs sont doubles; et que, d'autant que nous n'avons qu'une seule et simple pensée d'une même chose en même temps, il faut nécessairement qu'il y ait quelque lieu où les deux images qui viennent par les deux yeux, ou les deux autres impressions, qui viennent d'un seul objet par les doubles organes des autres sens, se puissent assembler en une avant qu'elles parviennent à l'âme, afin qu'elles ne lui représentent pas deux objets au lieu d'un. Et on peut aisément concevoir que ces images ou autres impressions se réunissent en cette glande par l'entremise des esprits [animaux] qui remplissent les cavités du cerveau, mais il n'y a aucun autre endroit dans le corps où elles puissent ainsi être unies, sinon en suite de ce qu'elles le sont en cette glande." (*Les passions de l'âme*, I, art. 32; AT, XI, 352 f.)

appear to provide the vivid imagery of his dream—a colorful tapestry woven with the resources of imagination and memory.

As though they were bent upon demonstrating the body's impact upon the mind occupied by dream, the little Fays reveal their character as "animal spirits" and "seeds of knowledge" by beginning their swift dance around Faust, while rhythmically chanting in rapid meters, ranging from tetrasyllabic verse to lines of five and seven syllables—their *vers impairs* marking a slightly stinging stimulus, irritating and going counter to the set habits of the mind. The little Fays of the first group start by invoking the transformative powers of sensations on dreams; in Cartesian psychology, they tend to magnify to the point of distortion and total metamorphosis those images which are carried to the sleeping brain by the animal spirits: "Si je lui gratte / Le bout du nez / C'est une mouche / Dans son esprit![4] / Si je lui touche / Un coin de bouche / S'il me sourit, / Il vit, il vit!" (P.ɪɪ, 392). Formally, the tonal plunge from the extreme treble heights of *ee* (S*i*) to the dark depths of *oo* (t*ou*che, b*ou*che) seems to imitate the airy and vivid forces of animal spirits diving into Faust's unconscious, while their vocalic upward sweep in "s*ou*rit," followed by the swift vitality and total brightness of their joyful outcry: "Il vit, il vit!" indicate the anticipation of success in their efforts to resurrect Faust from his sleep. Faust's purely mechanical reaction (his smile) to their entirely physical stimulus (touching the

[4] Cf. Descartes, *L'Homme*: "(. . .) s'il arrive que l'action de quelque objet qui touche les sens puisse passer jusqu'au cerveau pendant le sommeil, elle n'y formera pas la même idée qu'elle ferait pendant la veille, mais quelque autre plus remarquable et plus sensible: comme quelquefois, quand nous dormons, si nous sommes piqués par une mouche, nous songeons qu'on nous donne un coup d'épée (. . .)" etc. (AT, xɪ, 198.)

corner of his mouth) confirms their role within the
scheme of Cartesian psychology. Their conjectures on his
reaction are a disarming commentary on the human
condition, on the dependence of the intellect's freedom of
action on the mechanical functions of the body, which,
though separate from the mind, is united to it, determining its "passions." The little Fays—both as "animal spirits"
and unreleased "seeds of knowledge"—focus on the errors
inflicted upon the soaring mind by its body's earthly and
earthy nature. They whimsically reflect (as does the whole
"interlude") on the paradox of *la panse. qui pense*—a scan-
dal for the devil Bélial (P.II, 337), and for Faust the wel-
come pretext for a projected work on *Le Corps de l'esprit.*

When the little Fays of the second group notice that
Faust is moving his little finger, they admonish each
other: "Pince-le, fais le souffrir / Et les yeux vont se
rouvrir / Et la langue revenir; / Tout vaut mieux que de
mourir!" (P.II, 392 f.). Their continuing efforts to pull
Faust out of his swoon are echoed by the greater insistence
on the *oo-ee* sound sequence; like a magic spell or a liturgical invocation, it is thrice repeated, its repetition occurring at climactic intervals in the rhyme pattern (*souffrir,
ouvrir,* m*ourir*). The imperative "fais le souffrir" suggests
that things will look up when Faust, the rational soul
fettered to its body, is aroused by *les passions de l'âme*—
the sufferings inflicted upon the soul by its lifelong companion, the body, and its volitions. It is the opinion of the
little Fays—the animal spirits in action—that even these
sufferings are preferable to death ("Tout vaut mieux que
de mourir"), while Faust, the rational soul, is dormant,
and awaiting the recovery of language, the very vehicle of
reason and methodical doubt ("Et la langue [va] revenir").

The Cartesian concept of *conservation* is now introduced by the first group of little Fays. "Maintes mailles à reprendre, / L'âme ne s'en ira pas! / Tout s'arrange et se reprise, / La chair comme une chemise . . ." (P.II, 393). The body's mechanism and the life of the mind are restored and preserved through the mending motions of the animal spirits in their restless and uneven flow through the "pores" of the brain. The little Fays invite Memory, the Second Fay, "Baise-le pour ses beaux yeux, / Il ira de mieux en mieux" (*ibid.*). She leans over Faust and gives him a long kiss on his mouth. This gesture is interpreted by Blüher as the traditional kiss of the Muses (Blüher, 102), and the Muses' kiss it is insofar as it is Memory's kiss reviving, once more, the undying myth of the legendary Faust, assisting in midwife fashion the birth of a new Faustian fable. But it is primarily Memory's first kiss, presiding over Faust's awakening, a physical process involving factors and faculties of the body in their combined action upon the mind. It is a Memory still without memories, mechanically set in motion. Its function is to release "seeds of knowledge," and to help unlock the gates of Faust's present amnesia.

The second group of little Fays, taking up the theme of *conservation* through motion, add to it the dimension of time: "Tout s'arrange et se reprise, / S'il n'est pas de temps perdu"—the second line ambiguously hinting, with existential and anti-Proustian irony, at Memory as a force that may assist in the recovery of consciousness but should not be wasted *A la recherche du temps perdu*, i.e., in the vain recovery of a past that is lost forever, and useless in the discovery of the mind's future unexplored possibilities. The little Fays now more clearly allude to the mind's *semina scientiae*, which are latent, like the flame in the flintstone. Simultaneously they hint at their own nature as animal spirits, a fiery substance that carries emotions, i.e., the quintessence of humors heated in various degrees, from the heart to the brain's pineal gland, quite literally *inclining* it toward the "flame" of a given passion: "Et s'il reste un peu de flamme, / Tout va bien pour vous, Madame, / Le baiser sera rendu" (P.II, 393). And indeed, raising himself ever so slightly, Faust returns Memory's kiss "comme en songe, ou les yeux fermés" (*ibid.*), a response that leaps over his present condition like the hyperbaton which describes it:

Premier Groupe: *Il a* | le baiser | *rendu*! (*ibid.*)

They rejoice that the human machine—the "puppet" they endow with the motions of both physical "will" and mental "passions"—is not broken: "Le pantin n'est pas brisé . . ." (*ibid.*). The second group now exults over the success of the combined efforts of animal spirits (the little Fays) and Memory (the Second Fay): "Si la mort cède / Au souvenir, / Si ton remède / Le fait frémir, / Tout va renaître / D'entre les morts, / L'âme et son maître / L'âme et son corps." *Souvenir*, from Latin *subvenire*, means literally "a coming back to the mind."[5] The repetitive pattern of recurrent memories alone verifies and reconstitutes the continuity of the Self, fractured by sleep, dreams, reveries, and distractions. Or, as Valéry puts it more tentatively, in "Une Vue de Descartes," "Notre propre identité est une probabilité de restitution" (P.I, 834). If Memory's kiss will cause Faust to "quiver," he will instantly return from the realm of the dead, from his swoon, from his absence. And so will his intellectual possibilities, stored in *semina scientiae*. His re-entry into the world of the living will be total, in the paradoxical duality

[5] In Valéry's terms: "La mémoire particulière est comprise dans la mémoire générale qui consiste dans la propriété de redevenir soi-même. 'Revenir à soi'—redevenir soi." (Cah. XII, 486.)

of body and soul, here seen from the physiological angle of the animal spirits, as "the soul and its master, / the soul and its body." In an amusing reversal of the Cartesian view, these "incarnations" of the body's mechanical functions try to establish the primacy of the flesh over the soul, of *Le Corps de l'esprit*, of *la panse qui pense* over *la pensée qui pense la panse.*

4. *To Be or Not To Be . . .*

All the Fays now concur in guaranteeing the full recovery of Faust's possibilities, actions, experience, and visions. The rhythmical prestissimo of their tetrasyllabic lines indicates that their resurrecting qualities have reached their peak: *"Toutes les Fées (prestissimo, très rhythmé). Tout ce qu'il put, / Tout ce qu'il sut, / Tout ce qu'il fit, / Tout ce qu'il vit, / Si je le veux, / Pas un cheveu / Ne manquera! . . ."* (P.II, 394). The fourfold anaphora *"Tout ce qu'il . . ."* prolongs the vocalic echo of *"souvenir,"* while repeating the upsweeping sound pattern of the little Fays' first reviving motions, the *oo-ee* of *sourit, souffrir, ouvrir,* etc. In their totality, these tonal and rhetorical devices evoke Faust's restoration to the integrity of his consciousness by the combined pressures of Memory, Imagination, animal spirits, and awakening "seeds of knowledge" in restless and rapid motion.

Now that their physical functions have manifested the body's "will," by reviving the mind through its "passions," the Fays "withdraw into the setting"—in a manner reminiscent of Descartes' description of sensory and intellectual faculties, occupying the concavities of the brain in its waking state. The lighting has become softer. Faust begins to stir; he rises and feels his body. His gestures indicate the awakening of the rational soul at the very point of its

junction with the body. Although it becomes gradually
aware of the body's motions, it is still unconvinced of its
own existence. The first groping steps of Faust's consciousness are heard as antithetical monosyllables, hesitations between "Non? . . . Ou Oui? . . . Mort? Mort ou
vif? . . . Oui? Ou non? ." They are the first tentative
efforts of doubt on its way to becoming methodical, still
resounding with echoes of Hamlet's soliloquy, as it is
evoked in Valéry's discussion of Descartes' antecedents in
Shakespeare and Montaigne—"il y avait du doute dans
l'air de ce temps tout remué de controverses, et que ce
doute, réfléchi dans une certaine tête à tendances et habi-
tudes mathématiques avait des chances de prendre forme
de système, et enfin de trouver sa limite dans la constata-
tion de l'acte même qui l'exprime" (P.i, 818).

But Faust's first words also reflect the essence of the
Ausonius poem on the Pythagorean "Est et Non" (*Eclogue
IV*), which played so decisive a role in Descartes' third
dream, and which he interpreted to mean "la Vérité et la
Fausseté dans les connoissances humaines, et les sciences
profanes" (Baillet, i, 84). Faust's inarticulate question
concerning his own existence is answered by the Fays
with a muted, "Oui, oui, oui, . . ."—a triple incantation,
airy as the wind-like Cartesian animal spirits "blown
through the brain's arteries as though by the bellows of an
organ." They arouse "seeds of knowledge," whose first
stirrings become manifest when Faust begins to speak in
complete sentences. He interrogates himself, probing for
evidence that might prove his existence: "Est-ce que je
souffre? Tout est là. C'est la seule et positive question:
Souffrir, ne pas souffrir. Tout le reste est philosophie"
(P.ii, 394). Again it is Hamlet's question, "To be or not to
be," modulated in a Cartesian key, where the consciousness of "suffering" (i.e., *les passions de l'âme*), is an as-

sertion of "thought," the proof of existence; or, in the words of the *Seconde Méditation*: "Mais qu'est-ce donc que je suis? Une chose qui pense. Qu'est-ce qu'une chose qui pense? C'est-à-dire une chose qui doute, qui conçoit, qui affirme, qui nie, qui veut, qui ne veut pas, qui imagine aussi, et qui sent" (AT, ix, 22).

In this descending order of levels of "thought," sensations occupy the lowest place. They are perceived only mechanically as pain or pleasure, once they have entered consciousness; and they are felt, without being first defined by the intellect. It is not surprising that the awakening Faust, after his fall from the Solitaire's metaphysical heights, should start out on the road to lucidity from this lowest level of "thought": "Je me sens quelque chose par là; et par ici. Un peu dans la tête; et assez dans les reins" (P.II, 394). From the pure passivity (= passion) of experiencing mere sensations, the next (still passive) step leads to *le sens commun*, "la puissance imaginative" (AT, ix, 25). Here imagination prompts the mind to look for favorable signs and portents. "Bon . . . Ce mal est plutôt signe de bon. Signe de vie. Bon. Si vivre est bon" (P.II, 394). But such speculations on signs of life are based on superstition, on the mere passivity of the soul, submitting to the body's "will." The mind must rise against this new attack by "passion," which blocks out clear and distinct notions: "Debout! On n'y voit pas clair, ici" (*ibid.*). This imperative to rise above confused sensations marks the next step upward by the "chose qui pense," the thought *qu'elle ne veut pas*, i.e., negative will, the mind's will to resist the passions. If, as yet, there are no clear and distinct ideas about the present, there are none of the past either: "Mais je n'y vois pas davantage en arrière: le passé est aussi absent que le présent" (*ibid.*). But the past *is* present; if not in clear and distinct notions (as actions of the mind), it makes its presence known in a passive way, affecting the head with suffering. In short, it is a headache: memory without memories, plagued by amorphous feelings about lost *souvenirs* which elude memory's efforts to bring them into focus: "Je me trouve des débris de pensée, des esquilles dans une plaie de l'entendement. La tête a souffert. Mais de quoi?" (*ibid.*).

Goaded by dramatic irony, the reader begins to suspect a connection between Faust's encounter with the Solitaire, and this dull assault by vague memories that fail to come into focus. The reference to "debris" and "splinters of thought," which are stuck in Faust's "plaie de l'entendement" as so many causes of his headache—this reference seems to crystallize into faint reminiscences of the Solitaire's scrambled Pascalian *Pensées*. They are noticeable to Faust only as mere sensations, as the vague rumblings of an irrational "passion" of his soul: "C'est drôle que la pensée puisse être mise en morceaux. Des morceaux de pensée, et brouillés ensemble" (*ibid.*). Indistinct, the Pascalian argument on the wager, "le pari" (*Pensée* 233) flashes through Faust's consciousness. But instead of focusing on the idea of salvation through the acceptance of blind faith, Faust's mind assimilates it to the Cartesian search of the intellect for its own nature: "J'ai dans la tête plusieurs jeux battus et mêlés . . . En somme, je pourrais bien tirer au sort qui je suis ou plutôt qui je fus . . . C'est la même chose. Après tout, je ne suis que la personne qui parle" (P.ii, 394). We have seen Faust gradually climbing the ladder to the *cogito*. Starting from the lowest rung (sensation), he has proceeded to those of "imagination" and "negative will." Steadily gaining momentum, he is moving up in rapid succession to intellectual acts of "volition," "negation," "affirmation," "conception," and "doubt." "Mais qui parle à qui?" (*ibid.*). Against the Soli-

taire's fractured and deceptive *Pensées,* he invokes the
Cartesian notion of the unity and simplicity of thought
and its object, truth: "Il y a pourtant une vérité et une
seule" (*ibid.*). To find it, the mind must start out afresh,
get rid of the rubbish of scholastic learning and become
tabula rasa; consciousness must sound this void in search
of its own truth: "Je me penche sur mon vide . . . (. . .)
Ma vérité se démêle bien lentement de ce hachis, hachis,
hachis . . . J'ai peut-être mangé hier soir quelque chose de
lourd?" (P.ii, 395). The indigestible hash of the Solitaire's
fragmented thoughts weighs as heavily on *la panse qui
pense,* on Faust's intellectual stomach, as Descartes' first
two dreams had oppressed him—though the second dream
had brought with it the descent of the "spirit of Truth."

5. *The Spirit of Truth Invoked Against a Metaphysical
Indigestion*

Faust's feeling that, the previous night, he might have
eaten something indigestible, occurred right after he himself had invoked the spirit of truth and expressed his firm
faith in its uniqueness: "Surgissez, Vérité! J'espère, je crois
fermement que vous existez et êtes unique . . ." (*ibid.*).
There are other hints at Descartes' three dreams in Faust's
remark about his potential indigestion, and in his short,
but somewhat suspect, outburst of enthusiasm. Baillet
speaks of Descartes' "enthusiasm" when he thought the
Spirit of Truth was taking possession of his soul. He suggests that, the night of his dreams, Descartes might have
drunk a little too much, while celebrating the eve of Saint
Martin's—the feast of the patron saint of good eating and
drinking. But he ultimately rejects this situation, on the
grounds of Descartes' own assertion that he had gone to
bed sober:

Cette dernière imagination tenoit assurément quelque
chose de l'Enthousiasme: et elle nous porteroit volon-
tiers à croire que M. Descartes auroit bû le soir avant
que de se coucher. En effet | c'étoit la veille de saint
Martin, au soir de laquelle on avoit coûtume de faire la
débauche au lieu où il étoit, comme en France. Mais | il
nous assure qu'il avoit passé le soir et toute la journée
dans une grande sobriété, et qu'il y avoit trois mois
entiers qu'il n'avoit bû de vin. Il ajoûte que le Génie
qui excitoit en luy l'enthousiasme dont il se sentoit le
cerveau échauffé depuis quelques jours, luy avoit prédit
ces songes avant que de se mettre au lit, et que l'esprit
humain n'y avoit aucune part. (Baillet 1, 85)

In spirit, if not in substance, so close to the Illuminism
of Louis-Claude de Saint-Martin (while unrelated to the
Feast of Saint Martin), the Solitaire's mystical débauche
of last night has totally failed to inebriate Faust, although
it may have thrown him off balance. *Enthousiasme* is described in the *Dictionnaire de l'Académie Françoise* (1694)
as a "Mouvement extraordinaire d'esprit, par lequel un
Poëte, un Orateur, ou un homme qui travaille de génie
s'esleve en quelque sorte au-dessus de luy-mesme."[6] While
literally meaning "possession by the god"—a dementia like
that of the Pythia, possessed by Apollo—"enthusiasm"
normally refers to a subjective state of creative excitement,
as Descartes experienced it during his three dreams, and as
Faust will gradually discover it in the mythologizing
qualities of imagination and memory. "Travailler de
génie," according to the same *Dictionnaire de l'Académie
Françoise* (1694), denotes "Faire quelque chose de sa
propre invention et d'une manière aisée et naturelle"—a
definition that, applied to the young Descartes' specula-

---

[6] Cf. Aristotle, *Politica*, 1340a, 11, 1342a, 7.

tions in *Olympica*, could easily embrace the stirrings of *semina scientiae*, awakened by imagination and memory, and sparking *la lumière naturelle*, which by itself can guide *le bon sens* in its search for a truth that wholly derives from its diligence. In this sense, Faust can fully disregard the previous night's version of his Self, including the monstrous encounter with his evil genius, the Solitaire ("Hier? Quoi, hier? Connais pas" [P.II, 395]). His existence depends, in Cartesian terms, on his ability to rethink himself; or, in the words of the *Seconde Méditation*: "*Je suis, j'existe*: cela est certain; mais combien de temps? A savoir, autant de temps que je pense" (AT, IX, 21). "Travaillant de génie," Faust concludes that he can invent for himself, with ease and quite naturally (i.e., in accordance with his innate "seeds of knowledge," sparked by enthusiasm), "un passé convenable, correct, décemment historique" (P.II, 395). His resolve to derive his own past and his universe from the poetic (= myth-making) faculty of his mind coincides with the Cartesian method which "invents" (= finds) all knowledge of the Self, God, and the World "par la lumière naturelle," from the postulation of subjective thought focusing on its own functions. It is a poetic act in the literal sense of a "making," by which Faust reinvents himself, i.e., "finds again" the path that leads to self-knowledge, whence he had so carelessly strayed onto the Solitaire's inhospitable heights.

6. *Preterit—the Past Historic, a Definite Past*

The act of reinventing himself begins with the invention of an appropriate past: "Affaire d'imagination, en somme" (P.II, 395). Since a man's past attaches to his name, what he needs above all is a name. Promptly, Imagination (rather than Memory) comes to his aid. For it is the Prime

Fay, now standing behind him, who whispers: "Faust!" into his ear. "Faust? Faust . . . Pourquoi pas? Ce mot me vient. C'est un nom" (*ibid.*). The indifference with which Faust accepts a name that may or may not be his own may be a result of the mind's natural laziness. But then again, his indifference may suggest that he embodies the Cartesian *bon sens*, which indifferently inhabits every sane human mind, since it is "la chose du monde la mieux partagée" (*Discours* I, AT, VI, 1). At the same time, his preoccupation with finding himself through naming himself once again stresses the importance of the *cogito* for existence, since one exists only as often as one thinks himself (*Seconde Méditation*, AT, IX, 21, see above). Accepting his name is the first step toward the recovery of "*un passé défini*" (P.II, 395)—as a verbal tense (preterit) signifying a unique past that will never repeat itself, and as a statement about his forgotten past, a clearly defined prehistory. Assured of his continuity, Faust now asks himself what "mauvaise affaire" has happened to him? Memory, the Second Fay, prompts: "Le Fou, Le Seul, là-haut . . . ," revealing last night's evil genius "on high," le Solitaire, as an idol on the order of the seemingly omnipotent *malin génie* whom Descartes had tentatively postulated in the *Première Méditation*, in order to explain the deceptions to which both the mind and the senses are prone:

> Je supposerai donc qu'il y a, non point un vrai Dieu, qui est la souveraine source de vérité, mais un certain mauvais génie, non moins rusé et trompeur que puissant, qui a employé toute son industrie à me tromper. (AT, IX, 17)

When Faust had encountered his own *malin génie* in the person of the Solitaire, he had acted like Descartes:

C'est pourquoi je prendrai garde soigneusement de ne point recevoir en ma croyance aucune fausseté, et préparerai si bien mon esprit à toutes les ruses de ce grand trompeur, que, pour puissant et rusé qu'il soit, il ne me pourra jamais rien imposer. (AT, IX, 18)

Cartesian precepts may also explain why, thrust back onto the *tabula rasa* of his mind's wondrous palace, Faust lies in a swoon, when the curtain rises on *Les Fées*; we find him in a state where he has abandoned all reliance on sense perceptions, in apparent compliance with Descartes' decision:

Je me considérerai moi-même comme n'ayant point de mains, point d'yeux, point de chair, point de sang, comme n'ayant point de sens mais croyant faussement toutes ces choses. (*ibid.*)

Guided by Memory's prompting, Faust recovers his memories of the previous night's incident. But simultaneously he fails again, by straying once more from the laborious path of methodical doubt, in accordance with Descartes' own experience: "Mais ce dessein est pénible et laborieux, et une certaine paresse m'entraîne insensiblement dans le train de ma vie ordinaire" (*ibid.*). A certain laziness causes Faust to fall back on the deeply ingrained habits of daily life, which find their reflection in reliance on Memory, the deceptive mother of the Self's continuity: "Tu es ma mère, Mémoire! Tu m'enfantes . . ." (P.II, 395). But Memory, as a positive force serving the active mind, can also deliver from evil, for Faust now fully remembers "le Fou d'En-Haut; il était fort comme la mort, ce monstre! Il m'a poussé. Il criait. J'ai glissé, roulé . . . Il s'était entouré de précipices" (P.II, 396). Faust's paraphrase for the Cartesian *malin génie* of the *Première Méditation* seems to fuse with recollections of the evil genius who, determining the course of Descartes' first dream, in the end assumes the form of "le Vent qui le poussoit vers l'Eglise du collège"—in Faust's case: Port-Royal and its Jansenist theology—"lorsqu'il avoit mal au côté droit" (Baillet I, 85). The Descartes of the first dream had interpreted this evil force as "le mauvois Génie qui tâchoit de le jetter par force dans un lieu, où son dessein étoit d'aller volontairement" (*ibid*.).

At first, Faust is inclined to think that the Solitaire had indeed succeeded in throwing him into the bottom of one of his abysses. He now suddenly recalls the Second Fay's "very fresh" and "very potent" kiss, which fills him with lyrical enthusiasm. But, chronologically, he places it before his fall. This lapse, unknown to him, testifies to Memory's deceptions, which latently exist prior to any particular reminiscence, and whose refracted images tend to distort individual memories. Upon the Solitaire's temptations—which were intertwined with the deceptions of sense perceptions assaulting the mind from without— follow the more subtle and seductive temptations held out to the mind from within. Faust is ready to enter his own domain, his intellectual "reality," leaving behind his dubious "prehistory," together with all myths of a "truth" outside his mind's intensive efforts to observe its own functioning. Still uncertain whether he is dead or alive, dreaming or waking, Faust begins to wonder about the nature of the abyss into which he was plunged by the Solitaire. Is it the "hated Self" ("Le moi est haïssable"), as seen from the Solitaire's Pascalian heights, self-love and egotistical self-analysis as the very precipice of eternal death? If this be so, it is a most unenlightened abyss: "Si c'est ici l'abîme de la mort, la mort est trop mal éclairée . . ." (P.II, 396).

7. The Mind's Natural Light Enlightens Symbols

Hardly has Faust uttered these words when "la lumière se fait, dorée." The golden light, which so suddenly prevails throughout the magic palace of Faust's brain, heralds a *prise de conscience* where, enlightened by more distinct memories, "l'humanité faustienne fait des progrès immenses: le passé, le présent, tout lui vient, tout s'éclaire" (*ibid.*). Faust speaks of himself in the third person singular. Like the experimentalist observing his experiment, he has turned into consciousness watching the very processes of its own enlightenment. Now at last he fully understands that the void into which he has fallen is the *tabula rasa* of his mind, freed from the nightmare of the Solitaire's deceptions. He stands ready to discover his inner truth, the functioning of his consciousness, identical to his very existence. He finds his inner truth by his "natural light," unimpeded by the errors of the senses, unimpeded, too, by obscurantism and superstitions assaulting the mind from without. Reflecting upon its own nature, Faust's consciousness considers the very stage set where its "passions" and "actions" take place—i.e., the conformation of his brain: "C'est beau ici. Qu'est-ce que c'est?"

The first probing question: "Caverne?" alludes to Plato's cave, a hidden reference to the Cartesian skepticism with regard to the truth of sense perceptions. The next testing step moves in the direction of the mind's poeticizing powers, its ability to decipher Nature's mysteries by way of analogies: "Temple? Non. Forêt? Non . . . C'est au fond de la mer . . . C'est absurde. Il n'y a point d'eau. Temple vivant? Forêt pétrifiée? . . . La nature parfois s'amuse à faire l'artiste, à faire croire qu'elle peut travailler avec les mains, d'après une idée . . ." (*ibid.*). The mind's transformative powers become manifest through mathematics and language, its unique instruments in the dynamic conversion of reality into abstractions, analogies, and metaphors. As though to anticipate the Prime Fay's concluding axiom, "La Parole a pouvoir sur la Métamorphose" (P.II, 402), language is shown *in actu*, metamorphosing the first quatrain of Baudelaire's sonnet "Correspondances" into a product of Faust's own mind:

> La Nature est un temple où de vivants piliers
> Laissent parfois sortir de confuses paroles;
> L'homme y passe à travers des forêts de symboles
> Qui l'observent avec des regards familiers . . .

Faust assimilates the essence of Baudelaire's lines to the nature of the intellect's modes of fabrication, different in kind from those of both Nature and human mechanical skills, and dependent on the special logic of those symbolizing idioms of mathematics and speech, which serve to express the human experience of the Self and the Universe. Language is scientifically flawed but also aesthetically enhanced by its metaphorical leaps, limited as it is to accounting for intellectual phenomena only by analogies with the mechanical aspects of physical processes. Intellectual modes of fabrication involve all mental functions, including sensations, recollections, reverie, and dream—phenomena that are largely effected by the intervention of imagination and memory, as they are represented on the theatre of Faust's mind by the Prime and the Second Fays. Faust's suggestions on the figurative character of language, which serves to describe operations of the mind, reflect much of Valéry's own thought, but also some of Descartes' earliest observations in the so-called *Olympica* fragment, which was supposedly conceived after his three decisive dreams in the November night of 1619:

Vt imaginatio vtitur figuris ad corpora concipienda, ita intellectus vtitur quibusdam corporibus sensibilibus ad spiritualia figuranda, vt vento, lumine: undè altiùs philosophantes mentem cognitione possumus in sublime tollere. (AT, x, 217)

(In the same way in which imagination uses figures to conceive bodies, intelligence uses certain sensitive bodies, like wind, light, to symbolize spiritual matters. Consequently, we can lead the mind through knowledge towards higher things.)

It was this insight into the primarily figurative quality of language which had led the young Descartes to place greater faith in truths expressed by poets possessed with enthusiasm, than in the laborious speculations of philosophers guided only by Reason, deaf to the associative overtones of simile and blind to metaphorical imagery. Since I have repeatedly referred to this passage, its wording may be of interest:

Mirum videri possit, quare graves sententiae in scriptis poetarum, magis quam philosophorum. Ratio est quòd poetae per enthusiasmum et vim imaginationis scripsêre: sunt in nobis semina scientiae, vt in silice, quae per rationem à philosophis educuntur, per imaginationem à poetis excutiuntur magisque elucent. (*ibid.*)

(It may seem astonishing that weighty thoughts are found in the writings of poets rather than in those of the philosophers. The reason for this is that the poets wrote under the impact of enthusiasm and the force of imagination. There are seeds of knowledge in us, as there are seeds of fire in a flint; the philosophers bring them forth from reason; the poets extract them through imagination; therefore [their seeds of knowledge] shine more brightly.)[7]

8. The "Cogito" and the Temptation of Poetry

"Je raisonne. Donc . . ."—half the *cogito* is spun out by Faust, when the Prime Fay (Imagination) sings on two distinct notes: "Faust, Faust!" With her prompting, Faust gropes for a certainty which suddenly enlightens his mind: "Faust? C'est moi, je crois? . . . C'est moi qui pense et moi qui suis. Voilà une vérité générale" (P.II, 396). At long last, the universal truth of the *cogito* is engendered and brought to the mind's light of day. But the proof of its universality will come only when it is found applicable to the particular case: "Et, comme l'application particulière hypothétique—qui suis peut-être Faust" (P.II, 396 f.). The repeated test of self-consciousness, i.e., of Faust rethinking Faust, will guarantee the working hypothesis of Faust's continuous existence. It is predicated on the momentum derived from the metaphorical presence of language, incarnate in the refinements suggested to it by Imagination and Memory, which are subject to acts of denial by the methodically doubting intellect itself. All truth begins with self-consciousness, the intellect's act of contemplating its own functioning, and observing the

[7] Baillet ascribes this thought to Descartes' interpretation of the two Ausonius poems and the *Corpus poetarum* in his third dream, the meaning of which came to him while he was still asleep. With regard to the greater wisdom of the poets over that of the philosophers, Baillet explains: "Il [Descartes] attribuoit cette merveille à la divinité de l'Enthousiasme, et à la force de l'Imagination, qui fait sortir les semences de la sagesse (qui se trouvent dans l'esprit de tous les hommes comme les étincelles de feu dans les cailloux) avec beaucoup plus de facilité et beaucoup plus de brillant même, que ne peut faire la Raison dans les Philosophes." (Baillet I, 84.)

modifications it undergoes through the "passions" inflicted upon it by faculties and sense perceptions. Self-consciousness takes on more concrete dimensions for Faust when he notices the approach of the two taller Fays who are calling him by his name. He is overwhelmed by their loveliness: "Oh! . . . Qu'elles sont jolies! Que vous êtes aimables! (. . . .) Dames inattendues!" He seems to recognize, though only vaguely, those generating powers of ideas and myth which are inherent in the similes of language, and set in motion by associative and mythologizing powers of Imagination and Memory. Faust's apostrophe, "Dames inattendues," appears indeed to hint at their ability to endow language with those analogizing ambiguities which are invoked in "Aurore" (P.I, 111), Valéry's *charme* on the first gropings of the awakening mind: "Similitudes amies / Qui brillez parmi les mots!"

And indeed, Faust's "Dames inattendues" have awakened his latent poetic impulses. For now, inadvertently, he produces the unexpected *trouvaille*, his first alexandrine which is still barely discernible in the context of his prose:

Un certain goût de vivre apparaît avec vous. (P.II, 397)

His imperceptible progress from prose to verse was discreetly incited by the Fays' appeal. It darkly recalls Mephisto's remark to the disciple: "La prose n'est jamais qu'un pis-aller, mon cher" (P.II, 355)—a hidden warning about the Mephistophelian potential of their *charmes* (*carmina*, incantatory poetry). But Faust's first steps in poetry also mark that early stage in Cartesian thought where the temptation of poetry fills the awakening mind with reverence for the wisdom that poets were believed to derive from their divinely inspired "enthusiasm." But Faust is as yet at a loss by what name to call the graceful Fays who, to his surprise, seem to know or recognize him.

The Prime Fay throws out a tentative hemistiche: it suggests an acquaintance of long standing: "Je t'ai connu
enfant" (P.II, 397). Faust answers in kind with a second
hemistiche, thus completing by stichomythia the alexandrine she began, but expressing disbelief: "Toi, Jeune
Fille? Non" (*ibid.*). He fails to understand the Fay's
eternal youth, i.e., Imagination's fatal gift of conserving
infantile memories intact, guaranteeing their resistance to
the body's aging, and their vivacious and haunting recur-
rences.

As though to renew her spell on Faust's mature mind,
the Prime Fay recites a litany of fairyland fantasies, reaching far back into his first childhood dreams. Her *vers libres*
consist mainly of octosyllables—the ideal meter for narrative verse, since it has no fixed caesura, and is flexible
enough for the sinuosities of fable and myth. The octosyllables are embraced by alexandrines that lend some
gravity to the Fay's recital. Her verse lulls Faust into a
dreamlike state of which, however, he remains fully
aware: "Je suis sûr que je dors, si je crois mes oreilles"
(P.II, 398). His single alexandrine again intimates gravity.
He senses a *caveat* in the air. Together, his dreamlike
passivity and the nursery tales invoked by the Prime Fay
suggest those educational flaws which Descartes ascribed
to "des sens imparfaits, un instinct aveugle, et des nourrices
impertinentes" (Epistémon in *La Recherche de la vérité*
[AT, x, 507].). Noxious influences of the lowest order,
they are seen as inclining the mind toward error and
superstition. The Prime Fay now paints a delusive picture
of dream as a more intense form of life, which she opposes to the mechanical functions of a humdrum everyday
existence; suggesting that "les merveilles éveillent," she
concludes that shattered images of the past's resemblances
are needed to permit the intellect to sparkle (*ibid.*). Her
presentation, though deceptive, is not necessarily meant to

delude, since it discreetly identifies the Prime Fay as an allegory of the Cartesian concept of Imagination, a faculty more powerful during dream and rêverie where "images" are thought to be more vivacious than "sensations." The latter, Descartes thought, are more vivid, and dominate the mind, during the state of waking (*L'Homme*, AT, XI, 197 f.).

Against Faust's objection that he has left his childhood far behind, the Prime Fay uses the rhetorical device of *reflexio*, holding up to him the proposed mirror image of a childhood never lost: "Elle [l'enfance de Faust] n'a point cessé" (P.II, 398). But Faust remains unconvinced, protesting that he has "more than lived," survived numerous crises, consumed all imaginable wealth, lost all hopes, and tasted the full mixture of virtues and vices. In a whimsical reversal of all she has said, Imagination demonstrates her ability to evoke and to erase the past, in efforts to explore the future: "Ce qui fut n'est plus rien. Tu n'as jamais vécu" (*ibid.*). Her existential appeal goes to Faust's unrealized possibilities. Hyperbaton, the rhetorical device of "stepping over" the logical order of words, is used to persuade Faust to break the thread of recent memories by leaping over the dead body of the past he has lived:

Sache | *du souvenir* | rompre le fil de soie
Et | *des temps accomplis* | cesse d'être la proie. (My italics)

The Fays' power can undo the fabric of duration and open up the untold possibilities of Faust's existence (*ibid.*). Anacoluthon now denotes Faust's confusion and his heightened emotions, as well as a vague recollection of his fall: "Dans quel enchantement . . . Où donc suis-je tombé?" (P.II, 399). The Prime Fay now stresses the medicinal virtues of her sisters; their magic activity of reweaving the threads of Faust's life is underscored by the reduplicating effect of anadiplosis—her "tel, tel" imitating the sound and motions of the weaver's shuttle;

> Dans un abîme | *tel, tel* | autre eût succombé (*ibid.*; my italics).

The suggestion that Faust alone was able to survive his fall into an abyss where any other person would have "succumbed," i.e., died, or surrendered to the Fays' enchantment, tacitly raises the question whether Faust, who had withstood the assault by the Solitaire's Pascalian "thoughts," will be equally strong in holding his own against the seductive charms of these new incarnations of the Pascalian *puissances trompeuses*. They are indeed represented by the amiable Fays, whose sirens' song is now wooing the rational soul in this profoundest abyss of Faust's consciousness. Their persuasive powers are awesome. They skillfully avail themselves of rhetorical tricks and subtleties. A flattering anaphora lays the snares meant to entrap their intended victim:

> *La Prime Fée: Mais* tous ne sont pas toi . . . *Mais* il est des abîmes
> Où la Fortune guette et *comble* ses victimes (*ibid.*; my italics)

But Faust is on his guard. He knows all about the fallacies of dreams and delusions; and since he is no mean rhetorician himself, he can outdo the Prime Fay by opposing two anadiploses to her single one:

> *Faust*: Je suis *comblé* de | *Vous, Belles* | qui m'avez pris,
> Et fîtes par un sortilège
> Du fond d' | *un précipice un abîme* | sans prix
> Dont je dois craindre ou le songe ou le piège. (*ibid.*; my italics)

His first anadiplosis (*"Vous, Belles"*) indicates his awareness of the dual temptation by the deceptive powers of imagination and memory; the second one stresses the preciosity of this "precipice," whose poetic enchantments threaten to swallow up reason, paralyzed under the spell of dreams, and in the snares of delusions. He parries by thrusting back at the Prime Fay the essence of the predicate "combler"—an ambiguous term, which means "to gratify," as well as "to fill in." In this latter sense, Faust's abyss, "filled in" with dreams and fantasies, would turn into a grave for his rational soul. On the other hand, Faust's reply, by way of *reflexio*, demonstrates his awareness that "la Fortune," which promises to "gratify" him by "burying" his rational faculties, is identical with the two Fays ("Je suis *comblé* de Vous, Belles . . ."), the Fates, truly fatal forces who are preying on his reason in these precipitous depths of his mind.

Memory, the Second Fay, intervenes, as though she were anticipating Faust's fears:

> *La Seconde Fée*: Faust qui devais périr, il n'est rien de
> *fatal*
> Qui ne le cède à quelque *charme*. (*ibid.*, my italics)

Memory guarantees Faust's rather precarious continuity. She is the warranter of his genius, holding out the promise of salvation through lyrical incantation (*charme*); its spell (*charme*) promises to cast out fatal threats, metamorphosing Faust's potentially threatening Fate into harmless fantasies and myths. In this sense, she is indeed his Muse who does not fail to remind him of a kiss he had fervently returned while he was still in a swoon. What she offers him is the equivalent of a bath in Lethe: rebirth in pristine oblivion of past and present. Hyperbaton—the rhetorical device of "leaping over" the regular order of words—underscores her proposal to help him overcome his habitual distastes:

> *La Seconde Fée*: Je puis | *de tes dégoûts* | fondre une
> âme nouvelle . . . (*ibid.*, my italics)

She allows him to lift the veil of her mystery by reminding him that, without her reviving and conserving powers, he would be dead; her kiss brought him back to the light of consciousness:

> *La Seconde Fée*: Tu n'offrais déjà plus qu'un visage de
> cendre,
> *Ame ivre de néant sur les rives du rien,*
> Ta chair et toi n'aviez qu'un souffle pour lien . . .
> Je vins baiser ta bouche sans défense.
> (*ibid.*, my italics)

9. *The Pathetic Treasures of This World*

Far from defining Faust as a nihilist, "Ame ivre de néant sur les rives du rien," credits him with Valéry's own lifelong search for precision, his *morale de la mort*, a brutal resolve to pursue his ends to the bitter end, as he expressed it as early as 1894 in a letter to Gide: "Tout ce que j'ai bien voulu, je l'ai voulu en fixant le mot: Fin . . . . La médiocrité m'empoisonne et le vague me tue" (Corr. AG-PV, 217 f.). But "Ame ivre de néant sur les rives du rien" also captures the phenomenon of the Cartesian *cogito* hovering over its own operation in an effort to draw out of it the proofs of existence, certitude about the Self, God, and the Universe. Moreover, it represents Descartes' methodical doubt and its radical attempts to make *tabula rasa*, to clear the house of the intellect of all accumulated rubbish and spider webs. Even more than that, the Second

Fay's magnificent line constitutes a formal profession of faith by Faust's Memory (his Muse), in Mallarmé's poetic principles, so close to Valéry's idea of the necessary and irresolvable union of *le son et le sens*, as it is embodied in a famous line by Mallarmé that could stand as a definition of "pure poetry" and of Mallarmé's and Valéry's poetics altogether: "Aboli bibelot d'inanité sonore"—a line exemplifying the essence of verse itself. Its sonorous sinuosities and its ironic meaning, which establishes itself by abolishing itself, are successfully imitated by Valéry's "Ame ivre de néant sur les rives du rien."

Faust vaguely remembers Memory's kiss and his own, but he opposes his rational will to her present temptation: ". . . j'ai repris la force d'être Moi" (*ibid.*). She changes her strategy, dangling before him possibilities of his unrealized self, and vaguely hinting at her own role by depicting "Un Faust, dont les excès n'auront fait que l'instruire" (P.II, 400). Pointing to his past *personae*, she hints at potential repeat performances:

> *La Seconde Fée*: Veux-tu redevenir et reparaître roi,
> Roi du temps, roi des coeurs, fait pour vaincre et
> séduire? (*ibid.*)

It is a new variation on the temptation of Christ by the Devil, as Goethe had imitated it in *Faust II*, Act IV, where Mephistopheles shows Faust the treasures of this world (see Chapter Four). Valéry's Faust, though enchanted by visions of "thrones" endowed with splendor by the Fay's "beaux regards," knows that this magnificence does not exist outside the myths fabricated by language. It is a fabric of poetry, and the Fay's "beaux regards" are those of his "MUSE" and his "GRACE." For those whom they fascinate, they mirror a beauty fatal like that of Baudelaire's "La Beauté," whose warning they might very well echo: "Car, j'ai, pour fasciner ces dociles amants, / De purs miroirs qui font toutes choses plus belles: / Mes yeux, mes larges yeux aux clartés éternelles!" Enchanted by the Fay's "pure voix, / Si transparente et profonde," Faust, nonetheless, recognizes its essentially diabolical appeal which stirs ancient daydreams in his heart:

> *Faust*: Mais chacun de tes mots, *qui sont des pierreries Idéales*, riant sur le seuil le plus beau,
> Irritent dans mon coeur de vieilles rêveries . . . (P.ɪɪ, 400; my italics)

The diabolical nature of these "pierreries idéales" comes to light by comparison with four lines in *Ebauche d'un serpent*: "O Chanteur, ô secret buveur / *Des plus profondes pierreries*, / Berceau du reptile rêveur / Qui jeta l'Eve en rêveries" (P.ɪ, 145; my italics). Faust's temptation by the Second Fay takes us back to the young Valéry's formula that sees the Devil's hand in all art: "All art gives *form* to the famous words *Et eritis sicut Dii*. . . . It may well be the Devil, but all that strays from its path is but amorphous and chaotic" (letter to Gide, dated December 5, 1891; see above, chapter one). Faust's immediate reaction is a resounding "Non." His "laurels" are wilted, his "roses" faded, his ambitions and lust are dead and buried. Memory is scorned for throwing new light onto their shadows:

> *Faust*: Et tu viens dans cette ombre agiter ton flambeau!
> (P.ɪɪ, 400)

On second thought, he likes the idea of living again, but only in an aura of absolute certainty, his accumulated knowledge protecting him against disorder, trials, and errors. Omniscient, omnipotent, infallible, fully armed like Pallas-Athena, his mind could plunge into the very heart of the universe,

> Une puissance vierge, et de tout informée,
> [plonger] Au coeur même du monde . . . Et de mes fiers mains,
> Vaincre l'homme et la femme, et tous les dieux humains . . . (*ibid.*)

It is the eternal archetype of the serpent's *Et eritis sicut Dii* . . . , forever preserved by Memory, and forever rising again in the human mind, in the form of the Cartesian ideal of an universal language, similar to the signs and symbols of mathematics,

> . . . qui aiderait au jugement, lui représentant si distinctement toutes choses, qu'il lui serait presque impossible de se tromper; au lieu que, tout au rebours, les mots que nous avons n'ont quasi que des significations confuses, auxquelles l'esprit des hommes s'étant accoutumé de longue main, cela est cause qu'il n'entend presque rien parfaitement. (Descartes' letter to Mersenne, dated November 20, 1629 [Alquié I, 231 f.])

In alexandrines worthy of Racine, the Second Fay now appeals to Faust's self-love, depicting the glory of absolute power. *Aposiopesis* marks her breathless excitement, her impatience to hear his reply, the intensity of her emotional appeal and, above all, the seductive urgency of her diabolical prodding: "Parle . . . Un mot . . . Même pas . . . *Ton silence consent?*" (P.II, 400; my italics). Faust's silent consent would signify his willingness to speak her language, to become the passive vehicle of passions inspired by her prompting. But he incarnates the mind's active side, its "will," which manifests itself in Cartesian methodical doubt. *Reflexio* serves to refract his hesitations: *"Mon silence interroge*: il attend qu'on l'instruise" (P.II, 401; my italics). Faust is not in the habit of blindly accepting blessings that are showered upon him. The Second Fay attempts once again to define herself and her sisters: they are captives of a fate that prohibits their acquiescence to human tenderness—an allusion to their purely aesthetic essence. They are abstract powers unleashing the Cartesian "passions de l'âme" and, as such, assimilated to Valéry's poetics, they become the deceptive and enchanting forces of the poetic imagination and memory, fashioning myth and fable out of the stuff of which the passionate reality of dream is made.

10. *Fleshless Temptations and Verbal Alchemy*

The Fays' nature is supernatural: they are fleshless temptations of the enchanted mind.

La Seconde Fée: L'incorruptible honneur d'une chair
     enchantée
     Nous refusant l'émoi de toute chair tentée (P.II, 401),
—vivid images for the immortal language of poetry; the incarnate word, in Valéry's poetics: inspiring emotions but uninspired by them—

Trop heureuses sans joie, indignes de périr,
Nos grâces comblent ceux que nous pensons chérir
     (*ibid.*).

"Trop heureuses sans joie," lucky *trouvailles* but unmoved by joy, unworthy to perish (distinct in that from Valéry's concept of prose that abolishes itself in the process of reading by clearly revealing its meaning), the imperishable grace of poetry overwhelms those cherished by the

Muses, the poet, and the ideal reader alike. The Second
Fay now refers to her *charmes*, her *carmina* and their
"strange energy," asking Faust to "believe" and "trust"
her, for, as she explains parenthetically, neither art nor
magic can exist without some amount of faith in their
reality. Her parenthesis permits inferences as to the decep-
tiveness of her offerings, in the light of Valéry's axiom
that faith always presupposes some bad faith: "Il n'y a
point de foi sans quelque mauvaise foi" (Cah. IV, 670).
In the end, the Second Fay reveals herself as the *language*
of Memory, embellishing the past and purifying it—a
transformative power on the order of Rimbaud's *Al-
chémie du Verbe*:

> *La Seconde Fée*: Je sais rendre au plomb vil la lueur
> de l'or pur. (P.II, 401)

11. *An Anti-Proustian View of Memory*

In this capacity, the Second Fay proves to be the very
opposite of the Proustian concept of Memory. If Proust
sees in Memory a subjective but totally reliable force that,
under favorable conditions, can resurrect privileged moments of the past, Valéry's Second Fay represents an
equally subjective but wholly unreliable faculty, whose
verbal and always fallacious arrangements infallibly distort the past. She has nothing in common with that sub-
conscious duration which allows blocks of the past to
surface intact when the sensual experiences of the original
event are duplicated (Proust's *petite madeleine*, the *dalle
de Venise*, etc.). Instead, she accommodates the present
with mythical evocations of an irretrievable past that are
meant to awaken ambitions for future exploits: "Je recon-
nais l'enfant dans le visage dur (. . .) / Je défais, fil à fil,

la trame des vieux jours (. . .) / Je songe avec tendresse à ton adolescence (. . .) / J'y distingue celui que tu pourrais renaître, / Faust, si tu veux me croire et te fier à moi. / Veux-tu redevenir et reparaître en roi?" (P.II, 401). Here Memory is not acting as a midwife assisting the rebirth of a Proustian past "lost" and "regained." Instead she reveals herself as the deceptive power that transforms leaden fragments of a past forever gone into golden dreams of concupiscence and glory, i.e., "passions of the mind." Distracting the mind from the vitality of the instant present (in which life is incarnate), she entices it into verbal fictions that, by virtue of their refraction in Memory, endow the things they are meant to signify with the dreamlike and unreal aura of myth. Her subtle deception strangely coincides with Descartes's critique of language as a function of memory which both distorts reality and memories themselves:

> Au reste, parce que nous attachons nos conceptions à certaines paroles afin de les exprimer de bouche, et que nous nous souvenons plutôt des paroles que des choses, à peine saurions-nous concevoir aucune chose si distinctement que nous séparions entièrement ce que nous concevons d'avec les paroles qui avaient été choisies pour l'exprimer. Ainsi tous les hommes donnent leur attention aux paroles plutôt qu'aux choses; ce qui est cause qu'ils donnent bien souvent leur consentement à des termes qu'ils n'entendent point, et qu'ils ne se soucient pas beaucoup d'entendre, ou parce qu'ils croient les avoir entendus autrefois, ou parce qu'il leur a semblé que ceux qui les leur ont enseignés en connaissaient la signification, et qu'ils l'ont apprise par même moyen.
> . . .
>
> (*Les Principes de la philosophie* I, 74; AT, IX, ii, 60 f.)

Faust contemptuously rejects the Fay's tempting offer to "undo, thread by thread, the woof" of his past and of his old age. His reply is Cartesian: the past cannot be sounded, it is forever lost in the linguistic web of legendary history: "Si tu sais tout de moi, tu ne sais qu'une fable" (P.II, 401). The truth of existence, as the *cogito* brings it to light, remains forever ineffable: "Le véritable vrai n'est jamais qu'ineffable" (*ibid.*). What language can tell accounts for very little: "Ce que l'on peut conter ne compte que fort peu!" (P.II, 402). The double paranomasia "peut-peu" and "conter-compter" underscores the ultimate weakness of any idiom—its practical nullity ("peut . . . peu")—when confronted with the mysterious truth of life itself, which flows through the veins without accounting for itself or for the fiery passions it carries to the mind: both *conter* and *compter* are derived from *computare* "to sum up," "to reckon"—*conter* representing language as verbalization, while *compter* hints at its more precise, quantifying aspects in the signs and symbols of mathematics. It would seem that Faust has no illusions left about the potentialities of any idiom to express the universal truth of life, which can be sensed only as a subjective experience of passions and actions of the intellect. His skepticism can be likened to that of Descartes, who ultimately rejects as fallacious the dream of a "universal language" that might transcend subjectivity:

Mais n'espérez pas de la [i.e., la langue universelle] voir jamais en usage; cela présuppose de grands changements en l'ordre des choses, et il faudrait que tout le Monde ne fût qu'un paradis terrestre, ce qui n'est bon à proposer que dans le pays des romans. (Letter to Mersenne, dated November 20, 1629 [Alquié I, 232])

Whatever Imagination and Memory, the Muses and Graces presiding over language, can cast into words, are propositions for a return to the state of innocence; they are magical mirages of "a terrestrial Paradise" that can be found only in fiction—"dans le pays des romans."

12. The Pascalian "Wager" and the "Cogito"

Their temptations, though graceful and, in their lyrical stance, infinitely enchanting, are not different in kind from the Solitaire's much cruder Pascalian temptation of the gambler's "wager" against death and for eternal life. They all hinge on a gesture of blind faith in uncertainties, unacceptable to Faust as it was to Descartes:

> *Faust*: Le joueur garde au coeur le secret de son jeu,
>   Mais la perte et le gain lui sont des passes vaines:
>   Il ne sait que le feu qui lui court dans les veines:
>   Sa violente vie est le seul bien qu'il veut,
>   Lui qui ne voit d'objet qu'il ne jette à ce feu! . . .
>   (P.II, 402)

The fire in his veins, heated by his heart, literally coincides with the Cartesian metaphor for life's mechanical pulsations, the carriers of the body's passions, the "animal spirits." Is it merely a matter of coincidence that this "fire" constitutes both the ends and the means of Faust's "gamble"? The extended metaphor of the "fire running through his veins to consume itself" is a bold simile for the *cogito*'s *sum*, for the "I am" of the "I think," i.e., for the solipsism of thought probing the very operations of thought as the only true *raison d'être* of thought, regardless of all "losses" or "gains" that its egocentric functions may engender in the process of its self-reflective gamble. It is a process where container and contents have reciprocal appurtenances on the order of Valéry's perception: "je suis *dans* un monde qui est *en* moi, enfermé dans ce que j'enferme, produit de ce que je forme et entretiens,—comme mes deux Serpents dont chacun est finalement *dans* l'autre" (Cah. xxv, 702).

This text is accompanied by three drawings of two serpents, each one swallowing the other's tail and both of them forming circles containing the letter M. These dual representations of Ouroboros eating Ouroboros (the mythical serpent biting its tail as the hieroglyph for eternity) could stand for the vicious circle of the Cartesian *cogito, ergo sum,* to Valéry's mind a tautology, since "le petit verbe *être* ne possède aucune vertu particulière, que sa fonction n'est que de joindre; et que, de dire que l'on n'est pas est dire la même chose que de dire que l'on est" (P.ı, 806). In short, the *cogito* is meant to express something else, "*que l'on ne sait pas précisément exprimer,* et qui est de l'ordre des sensations" (Cah. ıx, 53; Valéry's italics). Sensations, however, in Valéry as in Descartes' physio-psychology, "ne servent que par la mémoire. Sensations sans souvenir ne sont qu'un langage inconnu" (Cah. ııı, 498). But since sensations must be related to definite sensuous experiences, it would seem that they cannot accompany the purely intellectual act of the *cogito.* A methodical self-assertion of man's thinking essence, the *cogito* would represent a Faustian "moment of eternity," an instant of total detachment and freedom from the bondage of the body's passions, its sensations, and of the faculties imprinting the mind with physical images and sensations, i.e., imagination and memory. It is a supreme and quixotic expression of *a superior intellect's egotism,* of the mind's proud contention that its thought can proceed from its own essence, without being *sustained* by any tangible *substance,* in short: independent of the body and the physical universe to which its creative (and self-creative) activity alone lends existence.

In this sense, Valéry can declare that "le *Cogito* me fait l'effet d'un appel sonné par Descartes à ses puissances égotistes" (P.ɪ, 807), an appeal that ultimately results in the paradox of an intellectual sensation, "le sentiment du Moi," producing a consciousness and "cette maîtrise centrale de nos pouvoirs," where the Self "feeling" its existence "se fait délibérément système de référence du monde, foyer des réformes créatrices qu'il oppose à l'incohérence" (*ibid.*). Under these circumstances, which fully apply to Faust's present situation, the Fays' appeal to incoherent physical desires and to passions of political concupiscence can hardly overwhelm Faust, the Cartesian "rational soul," sustaining itself on the *cogito*. By fanning the fire of the *passions de l'âme*, they instead inflame *semina scientiae*, "seeds of knowledge" rebelling against their dominance. The lines of battle are drawn between the mind's passions, stirred by Memory and Imagination, and the intellect's will to stand on the merit of its own actions that, in the end, outweighs the body's seductive resources:

> *Faust*: Tu [la Seconde Fée] m'as rendu le souffle et crois que je soupire
> Après tous ces trésors, et les coeurs et l'empire,
> Et que j'espère au monde un suprême plaisir . . .
> Mais mon esprit superbe a défait le désir. (P.ɪɪ, 402)

In the light of the intellect's supreme effort to "feel" its existence and to explore its unsoundable mysteries, all the "crimes," "fervors," "strangled virtues," and "carnal triumphs" that the world has surrendered to Faust's "diverse demons" seem trivial and wasted. He cares even less for any temptations the future may hold in store for him. He gathers the full strength of his self-consciousness, which is probing the depths of its own precipices, in one doubly self-asserting anaphora ("Moi, . . . , Moi . . ."). Its parallel isocola—as though imitating the Ouroboroi fettering Valéry's *Moi* in their vicious circles (see above, Cah. xxv, 702)—lump together his contempt for human concepts of glory; and, reinforced by a polysyndeton of negation, extending beyond the anaphora, they stress his present indifference to the temptations of Hell, Heaven, and the earthy pleasures of the flesh:

> *Faust: Moi,* toujours plus rebelle à ce qui les enivre,
> [i.e., les hommes]
> *Moi,* que *n*'ont pu gagner *ni* l'Enfer *ni* les Cieux,
> *Ni* fondre la tiédeur des corps délicieux. (. . .) (P.II, 402; my italics)

13. *The Mind Abhors Repetition*

Whatever temptations the Fays may dangle before him, will leave Faust indifferent for reasons that are identical in Descartes' and in Valéry's thought: "La mémoire est d'essence corporelle," Valéry asserts (in full agreement with Descartes), "(en tant que le corps est organisation) car elle est liée à la *forme*" (Cah. xix, 145). In Cartesian terms, Memory's dependence on "form" is Memory's dependence on "ideas" and "images" imprinted by Imagination. Memory is repetition, and, inasmuch as "la mémoire est l'avenir du passé" (Cah. xix, 163), its fantasies on future delights can only project into the future, repetitions of similar past events. But "l'esprit abhorre la répétition," and "en tant que l'on se répète, *il n'y a pas esprit*" (Cah. xix, 145; Valéry's italics). Since the intellect *is* what does *not* repeat itself—a delight outside Memory's realm—

there are no established points of reference for the cognition of its activity, except this activity *beyond* cognition which *leads* to knowledge but *cannot know* its own essence, although its own essence can be *experienced in actu.* This self-realization of the intellect is a heightened instant of eternity, exceeding in intensity all potential gratifications of the flesh and of ambitions. The intellect's ultimate climax, it marks nonetheless the mind's failure to understand and define in clear and distinct notions the nature of its solipsistic experience. But this failure will paradoxically reveal itself as a ringing success of Valéry's *morale de la mort,* the total refusal of uncertainty and illusions. For, in a superb hyperbaton, Faust "leaps over" hope, ridding himself of the last (and most lasting) of human passions and deceptive powers. At the same time, a litotes reminiscent of Chimène's "Va, je ne te hais point," discreetly hints at Faust's love for "the immense bitterness" he feels for not having found the fire that consumes him; i.e., his love for intellectual drives, whose nature he cannot probe while he intuitively knows that their fire, flowing through his veins and consuming him, is the vital essence by virtue of which he is "une chose qui pense":

> *Faust*: Je ne hais pas en moi cette immense amertume
> De n'avoir pu trouver le feu qui me consume,
> Et | de tous les espoirs | je me sens délié
> Comme de ce passé dont j'ai tout oublié (. . .) (P.ɪɪ,
> 402)

Oblivion of the past frees Faust from the fetters of Memory—this repetitive faculty of the body, which proves to be so repulsive to the mind in its progression toward knowledge and certainty. Epanalepsis underscores his emphatic rejection of the body's faculties and their fallacious gifts—sensations and confused desires, the lures of Memory and Imagination:

> *Faust: Non, non* . . . N'égarez point vos complaisances,
>   Fées . . .
>   Si grand soient les pouvoirs que l'on m'a découverts,
>   Ils ne me rendront pas le goût de l'Univers. (*ibid.*;
>   my italics)

14. *Faust, "Uomo Universale," and "Les Malédictions d'univers"*

Lust had called Faust "cet être d'Univers" (P.ɪɪ, 374), "this universal being"—a tacit reference to Leonardo, *uomo universale*, for whom Valéry invents a method ("Introduction à la méthode de Léonard de Vinci" [P.ɪ, 1153 ff.]) worthy of Descartes—a reference, too (implied at least), to *Monsieur Teste*. Throughout *Le Solitaire*, Faust, *cet être d'Univers*,[8] is exposed to those "universal curses" that lurk in the subtitle of the play, *les malédictions d'univers*. They befall the mind's sensitivity in the form of *idées reçues*, irrational monsters, confused notions, or enchanted visions of sexual and political power, reminding the intellect of its irresolvable union with the body and its "passionate" demands. It is a marriage be-

---

[8] In a literal sense, *être d'univers*, suggests "integral man," or a being turned toward the integral (*Universum = versus* "turned to" *unus* "a whole"). Faust's nostalgia for *totality*, for an integral unattainable to man, unleashes those *malédictions d'univers* which afflict his mind, in Act One, with the shattered view of the Solitaire's Pascalian attempt to capture the integral; and, in *Les Fées*, with the beckoning of deceptive powers enticing him into the solipsistic egotism of the *cogito*, a subjective absolute of self-deception.

tween the sublime and the grotesque, which haunts the
grotto of the mind in an intellectual drama of liturgical
dimensions, with demonic forces assaulting the intellect
from within, true to Valéry's professed experience, "puisque je suis *dans* un monde qui est *en* moi, enfermé dans
ce que j'enferme . . ." (Cah. xxv, 702).

On this unique stage, all possible combinations have
apparently been played, proving over and over again
reason's failure to free itself from the "passions" inflicted
on it by its irrational companion, the body. Nor will any
new adventure abolish the uncertainties of the purely
subjective world of the *Moi* that the mind incarcerates in
its depths and that, in turn, imprisons the *Moi*. Neither
Imagination, the Prime Fay with her Fata Morgana mirages, nor Memory, the Second Fay, *le re-présent*, "the represent," which comes back from the past without ever
tracing back its road (Cah. xvi, 249), can renew Faust's
lost "taste for the world," *le goût de l'Univers*. It is a
world so inextricably intertwined with the imprecisions
projected into it by the paradoxical troubles of *la panse
qui pense* that the equally subjective perception of the
cogito is the only certainty on which the mind can fall
back. But in a final gesture of rebellion, which exceeds his
victory over "the angel" and his betrayal of "the Demon,"
Faust shakes off the ontological trap of the *cogito*. Transcending Descartes, he refuses to be the dupe of his subjective experience of reason, just as he had rejected the
enchantment of the passions, inherent in the Fays' sirens'
song.

15. *The Vicious Circle of Creatureliness*

Both the "passions of the mind" and its "actions" build
the invisible prison walls of Faust's exasperating creatureliness, from which there is no escape:

Faust: Le souci ne m'est point de quelque autre aventure,
   Moi qui sus | *l'ange* | vaincre et | *le démon* | trahir,
   J'en sais trop pour aimer, j'en sais trop pour haïr,
   Et je suis excédé d'être une créature. (P.II, 402; my
   italics)

The double hyperbaton in "Moi qui sus | *l'ange* | vaincre
et | *le démon* | trahir" marks Faust's victory over the
mythologizing powers of pure reason (*l'ange*), and his
betrayal of its humble companion, the flesh, with its temptations of lust and power (*le démon*). It represents a "leap
over" the incantations of the intellect's *cogito* and fantasies
inspired by the body's passions. In short, it is Faust's wishful thinking, his eagerness to leap out of body and mind
into the one absolute certainty that remains—a plunge
into total oblivion, true to Valéry's *morale de la mort*.
Knowledge establishes a perfect balance of indifference to
all human passions; this equilibrium is maintained in the
antithesis of the parallel isocola "J'en sais trop pour aimer,
j'en sais trop pour haïr."

   The intellect cannot create its own world *ex nihilo*. To a
humiliating extent, its creation depends on a fallacious
idiom, dominated by sense perception, memory, and imagination. The mind is as much a creature of physical
organs and faculties as the body is a vicarious creature of
the intellect. Creatureliness is indeed the vicious circle
that encloses the Self in the Ouroboros of its "universal
curses," its *malédictions d'Univers*. They lead back to the
serpent's frustrating lure "Et eritis sicut Dii," and forward
onto a delusive world, created by the Self, and that serves
as the Self's lifelong prison. Up to this point, *Les Fées*
reflects the moral of "Quod vitae sectabor iter . . . ," the
Ausonius poem (*Eclogue II*) in Descartes' third dream,
which discusses the path one should pursue in life—interpreted by him as the advice "of a wise person, or of Moral

Theology" (Baillet 1, 84). This eclogue reflects Faust's dilemma in more general terms:

> dissidit ambiguis semper mens obvia votis,
> nec voluisse homini satis est: optata recusat.

> (Our mind is forever beset by conflicting wishes;
> Nor is man satisfied with wishes fulfilled: what he
> opted for, he rejects.)

Like Faust's words, this eclogue climaxes in the only certitudes man can attain: the certainty of uncertainty, and the painful knowledge that all paths in life end as impasses; that, indeed, they are those *malédictions d'Univers*, those universal curses which plague the human condition:

> cuncta tibi adversis contraria casibus. ergo
> optima Graiorum sententia: quippe homini aiunt
> non nasci esse bonum aut natum cito morte potiri.

> (All paths face you with adverse hazards. Hence
> the Greeks' axiom is best: surely, they say, it is good
> for Man not to be born, or if he be born, to die
> quickly.)

Faust's dilemma is the mutual dependence of intellect and body, which seals the mind's inescapable fate as a "creature," even where it acts as *creator spiritus*. It is godlike only in appearance, a dilemma hardly assuaged by the Second Fay, when she exclaims: "Hélas! . . . Nous ne pouvons enfin que t'obéir . . ." (P.II, 402).

16. *Solipsism*

Prima facie, the Fay asserts the primacy of the intellect. But her words also confirm Faust's suspicion that the Cartesian freedom of the mind does not transcend the

solipsism of the *cogito*, of consciousness mirrored in its
own reflective processes and in a world of its own creation
whose prisoner it is. Simultaneously, the lures of the body's
passions and sensations, invading the brain from without,
can instantly distract "thought" and destroy its precious
fabrics by confirming the mind's awareness of the body's
omnipresence. This awareness remains as a painful reminder of the intellect's purely human limitations, even
when the body's faculties admit that, in the end, they must
always obey the dictates of reason. But is it human reason,
bound by its union to a finite body, or absolute reason,
the mysterious freedom of the creative word, a tantalizing
fiction that Imagination has imprinted on Memory?

> *La Prime Fée*: Que si nous disposons de toute la nature
>   C'est esclaves de mots pour nous mystérieux:
>   Qui les possède règne et commande à nos jeux. (P.ii,
>   402)

The Fays dispose of *toute la nature*: they purvey impressions of natural phenomena that the mind assimilates to
its speculations on "universal laws," under whose do-
minion it then proceeds to envisage its own functioning.

But if the Fays' enchantment suggests images of external
Nature to the mind, they in turn also dispose of *toute la
nature de Faust,* of his *naturel,* i.e., of his character, his
native (and *naïve*) instincts and dispositions. They do so
in blind obedience to the creative word, a supernatural
force, above and outside the physical world, although
shaped by physical organs and phenomena, and necessary
for the expression of thought, perceptions, and the mind's
will. Its essence eludes the Fays' comprehension, for as
faculties of the body they are without intelligence (understanding), though it is their primary task to purvey intelligence (information). Yet, Imagination, the Prime Fay,

knows about the Protean qualities of the creative word
that transforms reality into irrational dreams, reveries and
poetry, but also into the rational stuff of which the intellect's cogitations are made:

> La Prime Fée: La Parole a pouvoir sur la Métamorphose,
>   Tu devrais le savoir, toi qui sais toute chose. (*ibid.*)

The polyptoton, which moves from the conditional "you
should know it" to the mocking assertion "you who know
everything," actually stresses what is being questioned
here: Faust's access to the mysterious word that could set
him free from the ironies of his paradoxical duality, the
cause of uncertainty and unclear, indistinct ideas. Does
Faust, the allegory of human wit, understand the language that Memory and Imagination fail to apprehend
while it governs and commands their "jeu," i.e., both
their "gamble" for dominance and the "play" they perform in the theatre of his brain? But here, reason with
all its inventive powers is as much at a loss as are the
faculties that convey passions and sensations to the mind;
for Faust now asks Montaigne's question, the "Que sais-
je?" that underlies Cartesian doubt and the method of the
cogito positing the subjective *sentiment du Moi* as the
very foundation of God and the world:

> Faust: Sais-je l'un de ces mots? (P.II, 403)

As a creature proceeding from Valéry's mind, he seems
to be aware that "l'acte *conscient peut être irréfléchi*"
(Cah. XXVIII, 477). Indeed, tired of the solipsistic self-
deception involved in the *cogito*'s self-reflection, Faust,
the uncompromising "rational soul," looks to the physical
faculties for a potential answer. But they throw the mind
back on its own purely negative resources, Memory recalling his lifelong rejections of deceptive solutions:

La Seconde Fée: Tu ne sais que nier (P.ɪɪ, 403),

and Imagination reflecting the imprint of the reawakening Faust's first word in their presence:

La Prime Fée: Ton premier mot fut NON. . . . (*ibid.*)

17. *Life's Cycles of Reality and Dream*

Faust's return to life and lucidity had indeed begun
with the groping monosyllables: "Non? . . . Ou oui? . . .
Mort? Mort ou vif? . . . Oui? Ou non?" (P.ɪɪ, 394)—as
though they were meant to echo the other Ausonius poem
(*Eclogue IV*) in Descartes' third dream which considers
the Pythagorean "Yes" and "No":

> Est et Non cuncti monosyllaba nota frequentant.
> his demptis nil est, hominum quod sermo volutet, etc.

> ("Yes" and "No," forever everyone uses these well-
> known monosyllables. If you take them away, human
> speech will have nothing left to toss about, etc.)

Baillet recounts the interpretation given by Descartes to
the occurrence of this poem in his dream: "Par la pièce
de Vers *Est et Non*, qui est le Oui et le Non de Pythagore,
il comprenoit la Vérité et la Fausseté dans les connoissances humaines, et les sciences profanes" (Baillet ɪ, 84).
Baillet concludes, "il fut assez hardy pour se persuader,
que c'étoit l'Esprit de Vérité qui avoit voulu lui ouvrir
les trésors de toutes les sciences par ce songe" (*ibid.*).
Descartes' encounter with the "Spirit of Truth" led to
the proud acceptance of the *cogito*'s purely subjective
reality as the source of all certainty. Faust's own moment
of truth comes when his mind consults the physical faculties that inform his perception of his needs and of the
outside world that confronts him. It is an anguishing

moment where the irreconcilable duality of body and mind determines their final dissension, which was existent from the very beginning, in the spirit of Ausonius' fourth eclogue:

> sin controversum, dissensio subiciet "Non."

> (If their [the discussants'] controversy persists, dissension throws in its "No.")

The Prime Fay had prompted: "Ton premier mot fut NON"; now the Second Fay decrees: "Qui sera le / dernier" (P.II, 403). *Reflexio* closes the cycle of negation. It forms the figure of Valéry's concentric Ouroboroi, encircling the "Ame ivre de néant sur les rives du rien" (P.II, 399), with Imagination tracing the subjective *néant* of Faust's *cogito* back to his first word, and Memory, Faust's unreliable continuity, thrusting it back onto the refracting and distorting mirror of consciousness. (See Figure I.)

FIGURE I

It thus becomes an emblem and hieroglyph for the mind's ultimate nostalgia, prompted by the serpent's original "Et eritis sicut Dii"—the radical desire to transcend the human

condition, and to reduce to a point zero (o) the agony of
"the Self *in* a world which is *in* the Self." But, in the
serpent's spirit of total negation, "Et eritis sicut Dii,"
equals an "Et eritis sicut nihilum." The serpent's advice
is circular like the path of birth, death, and rebirth.[9] The
only certainty that lies ahead is that of annihilation, be it
total (in death) or temporal (in the false death of sleep).
Faust's struggle on the labyrinthine stage of his brain
comes to an end when the curtain falls on the Fays' dual
"No." Unrelieved, the continuing paradox of *la panse qui
pense* only seemingly *ends* at the very point where it is
destined to *begin* again, every dawn, when the reawakening intellect takes its first groping steps in forever vain
attempts to disentangle itself from the mingled properties
of body and mind. The uncertain "Yes" of the waking
mind, and the less uncertain "No" of its eventual sub-
mergence in relative or absolute oblivion, are the head
and the tail of the Ouroboros, encircling its fragile existence. It is an image that corresponds to the climax of the
Ausonius poem on the Pythagorean *Est et Non*, evoked
(but not quoted) in Descartes' third dream:

> Qualis vita hominum, duo quam monosyllaba versant!

> (What is the nature of human life, tossed about as it
> is by two monosyllables!)

18. *Conclusion*

We have accompanied Valéry's Cartesian Faust in his
hazardous and imperfect pursuit of certainty. *Lust, la
demoiselle de cristal*, had presented him as an actor on an
external stage, where *Eros energoumenos*, Love possessed

---

[9] In 1940, Valéry expresses this cyclical concern in purely
Nietzschean terms: "Je ferais un F en victime du Retour éternel;
châtié d'avoir voulu Recommencer—" (Cah. xxiii, 894).

by the Devil, and the heart's distracting passions had troubled the intellect's search for clear and distinct notions. The liturgical comedy, *Lust*, was followed by the Gothic melodrama of Faust's encounter with the Solitaire (*Le Solitaire, ou les malédictions d'Univers*, Act I). Here the scene abruptly changed from the external stage of Faust's domestic and scholarly life to the inside of his skull, where we saw him as a reluctant *spectator* of unleashed Pascalian *pensées* and their final lycanthropic effect. In *Les Fées*, Faust performs as an *actor* on the labyrinthine stage of the brain, where he is tempted by the poetic seductions of deceptive powers, Memory and Imagination, once again demonstrating the frustrating interdependence of body and mind, the grandeur and the humiliating ironies of *la panse qui pense*. *Lust* as well as *Le Solitaire* represent by way of charade the misfortunes of the Cartesian *cogito*. Faust, "the thing that thinks" and aspires to the exclusiveness of thought, in the end is always caught in the impasse of the body's passionate demands, or in the self-annihilating solipsism of thought thinking itself in terms of existence.

With its strange air of finality, *Les Fées* gives the impression of not being what it purports to be, an interlude between two acts. Its strongly operatic overtones are rather those of a *finale*. It represents one possibility among numerous other conclusions that, rather than putting an end to Faust's dilemma, suggests irresolvable tensions. It remains as tentative and provisional as Descartes' moral precepts, while he tries to work out his system. Valéry's preface "Au lecteur de bonne foi et de mauvaise volonté" had explained his intention to write an unspecified amount of *Faust* plays, each one in a different mood and genre. The subtitle, "Ebauches," is as tentative as the *Mon Faust* fragments (and their endings) are provisional—a problem which I shall examine at length below, in Chapter Four.

It is true, there are Cahier entries that hint at possibilities for a third, and even a fourth act of *Le Solitaire:* "*Solitaire III* et peut-être *IV*? Ici essayer d'opposer les Harmoniques aux choses et idées. (. . .) Le 3e acte devrait être de scène en scène, (. . .) un reveil de degré en degré—Les choses et les perspectives, mort, vie, *personnalités*, pensée se transformant en valeur selon la connaissance croissante (Méphistophélès d'échange). Final: Harmoniques" (Cah. XXIII, 913 f.). The mathematical term "harmoniques" with its musical connotations approaches the vision of both Descartes and Pythagoras, in a manner reminiscent of the Ausonius poem *Est et Non*, which plays such a decisive role in Descartes' third dream. The concept of "thought transforming itself in value according to increasing knowledge" is one of Descartes' most persistent ideas, the very foundation of his method. In the context where it occurs, it lends substance to my argument that *Mon Faust* represents Valéry's attempt to rectify the Romantic flaws of Goethe's hero by endowing Faust with a Cartesian mind. In doing so, Valéry added the dimension of the *cogito*'s ontological trap, a solipsism as inescapable as the Romantic self-deceptions of Goethe's hero, but on a level of abstraction and refinement that competes with the more brutal ironies that beleaguer the mind of the latter.

Four.

POETIC SEMI-REALITIES: SELF-PERCEPTION AND SELF-DECEPTION IN GOETHE'S AND VALÉRY'S FAUST

1. *The Shattered Theatre Metaphor in Goethe's "Faust"*

The moment has come to compare Valéry's Faust with his primary model, the protagonist of Goethe's "tragedy" —a tragedy in name only, it would seem, since the hero in the end is saved by Angelic intervention. It is a tragedy all the same, in purely human terms, since it illuminates Faust's impotence vis-à-vis the human condition that he is forever unable to transcend, and it brings into sharp focus the ironies of self-deception that accompany all human self-perception: the discrepencies between lofty ideals and their inevitable perversion through the insufficiencies of human knowledge and human means applied to their realization. Whatever "ideal" solutions Goethe's Faust contemplates are degraded, wither, and come to naught under the impact of his human, all too human, weaknesses. He is doomed, again and again, to exemplify the Pascalian "qui veut faire l'ange fait la bête."

A serious flaw in Faust's character is revealed in the very first scene of *Faust I*. It is expressed in the theatre and alchemic imagery that conforms to the "historical" Faust's Renaissance and Baroque world: Faust refuses to content himself with that unmediated knowledge which Hermetics were deemed to derive from the mere contemplation of "hieroglyphs," i.e., emblems that were thought to be analogies or symbols for Nature's mysterious forces and for a type of hermetic truth, accessible only to the initiate's intuition. Gazing at the "sign of the macrocosm," Faust despairs of his human lot, which confines him to the role of a mere spectator of Nature's "fine show":

> *Faust*: Welch Schauspiel! Aber ach! ein Schauspiel nur!
> Wo fass' ich dich, unendliche Natur?
> Euch Brüste, wo? Ihr Quellen alles Lebens (. . .)
> (*Faust I*, 454)

> (*Faust*: What a fine show! Alas! it's but a show!
> Where can I grasp you, infinite Nature?
> Grasp you, breasts, where? You sources of all life . . .)

A mixture of stage and carnal imagery, this extended metaphor expresses Faust's impatience with the mere spectacle of Nature, and his Romantic longing for union with the infinite. It finds its rhetorical expression in a paradoxical refusal of knowledge by way of deciphering Nature's analogies in hermetic emblems, "hieroglyphs" or symbols. He fervently desires fusion, identity with Nature, whose elusive powers he wants to subjugate in an act of quasi physical and mental copulation. Seen in this light, his passionate outburst, lamenting his impotence, would seem to satirize (from Goethe's perspective) the erroneous reading that the *Sturm und Drang* admirers of Shakespeare gave to the Baroque image of "All the World's a Stage." They had introduced a strange misconception by interpreting this metaphor in a literal sense, unaware as they were that in Shakespeare as in Calderón's *El gran teatro del Mundo*, the theatre functions as the stage for an allegory where *personae*, from beggar to king, perform as best they can the roles incumbent upon their souls during their short pilgrimage on earth.

Faust accepts no such finite persona, nor does he look upon his this-worldly life as a period of tests and trials. He is modern to the extent that life on earth is the only existence that matters to him. He seeks the infinite and eternity in the incessant renewal of insatiable aspirations, the sum total of which will afford him as many metamorphoses and diverse experiences as can be crammed into his earthly lifespan. His lamentation on Nature's mere "show," and the inviolability of her mysteries, expresses the Romantic hero's discontent with the limitations imposed upon him by a persona, a character and social mask, which constrains his Protean desire to partake of *all* possible personae, of all natural and supernatural phenomena that happen to strike his fancy. Like the hero (or author) of a *Sturm und Drang* drama, he mistakes the theatrical illusion for a reality that invites audience participation. Striving to be godlike[1] in his idealism, and desirous to assume any role, he is always struck down while embracing phantasms that have arisen from his feverish

[1] His human limitations become clear to him at least twice: once in a nocturnal Nordic environment, when, likening himself to the *Erdgeist*, the elemental spirit of earth whom he conjured, Faust is put in his place by the Spirit's words:

Du gleichst dem Geist, den Du begreifst,
Nicht mir! (*Faust I*, 512 f.)

(You resemble the Spirit that you can grasp,
Not me!)

The second time, in the "classical Walpurgisnacht," on the rocky shores of the Aegean Sea, Nereus informs Homunculus about man's vain aspirations to become godlike:

Gebilde, strebsam, Götter zu erreichen,
Und doch verdammt, sich immer selbst zu gleichen.
(*Faust II*, 8096 f.)

(Creatures that strive to become godlike
But who are damned, forever to be like unto themselves.)

imagination that he never learns to distrust. Nor does he ever learn from the experiences of his ever-soaring mind, whose lofty aspirations are always brought to a fall, since it is wedded to an earthbound and finite body that cannot partake of its flight. Yet, mental aspirations are translated into images of physical passions that tend to destroy their object, or their purpose. Thus, the sign of the macrocosm is meant to provide intuitive insights into the mysterious life and death cycles of Nature. It even allows the personification of Nature's abstract forces. But Faust, the Romantic hero who absurdly attempts to "grasp" the delusive allegory of Nature by her "breasts," is misguided by his all-too-literal interpretation of a metaphorical catachresis: his libidinous fervor seems to blind him to the irreality of an ideal vision, conjured up by a rather simple rhetorical device that he fails to recognize as such.

Faust's character is already fully reflected in the theatre metaphor of the "fine show" which, alas! is "but a show." It is a theatre metaphor that Faust instantly shatters by his impetuous but vain efforts to break through the confines of the theatrical illusion. His frustrations are those of a mere spectator, dissatisfied with his passive role, and anxious to leap onto the stage to rape the leading lady—be she Helena's phantom conjured from the shadowy Hades of archetypal memories, or the allegory of Nature herself.

Faust's lines about Nature's "fine show" date back to the *Urfaust*. They demonstrate the aesthetic distance the young Goethe establishes between himself and his hero, although he still empathizes with Faust's Titanism. Faust's impatience with the mere "show" of natural truth and supernatural beauty exposes his tragicomic flaw; it will manifest itself throughout the play by the consistency with which he always confuses the actress with her role, the symbol with the thing symbolized, or, in Goethe's

terms, the *Gleichnis*, the allegory, with *dem Vergäng-
lichen*, its passing or evanescent embodiment (appropri-
ately expressed by a substantivized attribute). The Italian
voyage of 1786-1787 had been a turning point in Goethe's
life. It had opened his eyes to the depth of beauty and
truth to be found *in* (rather than *behind*) the colorful
reflection of objects, but also had kept him from identify-
ing reflected color with the object that reflects it or with
life itself—a distinction that, as we shall see below, escapes
Faust's understanding.

As a delayed reaction, in the late 1790s, the Italian
voyage had hardened Goethe's position vis-à-vis German
idealism, and its introspective way of abstracting the
quintessence of aesthetics from *a priori* principles, rather
than empirically deriving it from the contemplation and
analysis of works of art. His sensitivity is offended by
the *nordische Barbarei*, with its abstract notions of beauty,
its misty mysticism, its exaltation of *Geist* to the detri-
ment of the senses, and its coarseness in matters of taste
and good manners.[2] The sensuous, urbane, cosmopolitan
author of an *Iphigenie*, the coiner of the term *Weltliter-
atur* now feels a kinship for the Hellenistic paganism and
sensuality that, after Winckelmann, he sought to dis-

---

[2] His ambiguity toward his compatriots is constantly growing.
He is alert to "German pettiness," which affects his own writing:
"Es kostet mich Aufpassens, bis ich meine kleinliche deutsche Art
abschaffe," he wrote to Charlotte von Stein as early as 1787
(Goethe XIX, 65 f.). He castigates the Germans' Philistine charac-
ter, their lacking sense of humor: "Dafür [Humor] hat der
Deutsche so selten Sinn, weil ihn seine Philisterhaftigkeit jede
Albernheit nur ästimieren lässt, die einen Schein von Empfindung
oder Menschenverstand vor sich trägt" (To Schiller, Jan. 31, 1798,
Goethe XX, 513; ["The Germans have so seldom a sense of humour,
because their Philistine character has them only show esteem for
silliness with some appearance of sensibility or intelligence"]).

cover in Italy. As the gulf begins to widen between those who will soon represent the new school of German Romantics and, on the other hand, his own and Schiller's professed *Klassik*, Goethe comes gradually to identify *Faust* with the rigors and gloom of the "Nordic winter" and a "nebulous world of symbols and ideas."[3] With Apollonian detachment, he comes to look upon the "Nordic phantoms"[4] and "Nordic Barbarity"[5] of the Faustian ambiance as corresponding to "a monstrous Nordic audience,"[6] worthy of what he now characterizes as an altogether "Barbarian production."[7] In "Abschied," a "Farewell" to Faust, prematurely written in the Spring of 1822 (Goethe v, 529), Goethe tries to distance himself from that Barbarian chaos of sentimentality and magic humbug that essentially characterizes the Romantic qualities of his all-too-Germanic personae dramatis:

> Wer schildert gern den Wirrwarr des Gefühles,
> Wenn ihn der Weg zur Klarheit aufgeführt?
> Und so geschlossen sei der Barbareien
> Beschränkter Kreis mit seinen Zaubereien, etc.
> (Vv. 12-15)

[3] "(. . .) da ich bei Meyers Gesundheitsumständen noch immer erwarten muss einen *nordischen Winter* zuzubringen, (. . .) und bereite mir einen Rückzug in *diese Symbol-, Ideen- und Nebelwelt* (. . .) vor" (To Schiller, June 24, 1797).

[4] "(. . .) die *nordischen Phantome* sind durch die südlichen Reminiscenzen (. . .) zurückgedrängt (. . .)" (To Schiller, July 1, 1797).

[5] "(. . .) indem ich meinen 'Faust' zu endigen, *mich aber auch zugleich von aller nordischen Barbarei loszusagen wünsche*" (To Schiller, December 25, 1797).

[6] "Ebenso will ich meinen 'Faust' auch fertig machen, *der seiner nordischen Natur nach ein ungeheures nordisches Publikum finden muss*" (To Schiller, April 28, 1798).

[7] "Freund Meyer wird es auch für einen Raub achten, zu dieser *barbarischen Production* Zeichnungen zu verfertigen" (*ibid.*).

(Who likes to show the chaos of feelings,
When his path leads him upward towards clarity?
And thus be closed the narrow circle of barbarities
    with its magic humbug.)

No wonder then that Faust is not the only victim of
the shattered theatre metaphor on the "fine show" that
is "but a show." It is indeed central to all quid pro quo
situations in *Faust II*, where nebulous ideas or symbols
are mistaken for reality; and it affects all those "Northern
Barbarians," regardless of their station in life, to whom
Goethe so often refers in his early letters to Schiller, when
he evokes with good-humored irony the composition of
his *Faust* that, in the late 1790s, had pretty much ground
to a halt. With their nebulous Fichtean idealism,[8] their
refusal of Cartesian "clarity," and their mixed-up emotions, Goethe's "Northern Barbarians" are ideally suited
to commit the categorical mistake implicit in Faust's
shattered theatre metaphor: the temptation to confuse the
world *of* the stage with the World *as* a stage; to mistake
the comical illusion for the elusive comedy of life itself.
And in fact, the shattered theatre metaphor of Nature's

---

[8] Goethe had read Fichte's *Wissenschaftslehre* with feverish excitement, in the early 1790s. It had at first strongly influenced his
work on the Theory of Colors. In the late 1790s, Schiller had
caused him to break with transcendental philosophy, for the sake
of scientific clearheadedness. Schiller's distich, *Naturforscher und
Transcendental-Philosophen*, is said to have had a decisive impact
on Goethe's changing attitude:

Feindschaft sei zwischen euch! Noch kommt das Bündnis zu
    frühe:
    Wenn ihr im Suchen euch trennt, wird erst die Wahrheit
    erkannt.

(May there be enmity between you! It is too early for an
    alliance, as yet:
    Only if you separate in your search, will truth be found.)

"fine show" that is "but a show" holds the key in Act I
(*Mummenschanz*) to the Emperor's and his courtiers'
unceremonious way of helping themselves to the pseudo-
treasures of Faust-Plutus. In vain, *Knabe Lenker*, Faust's
putto-charioteer, had revealed the illusory nature of this
opulence, by hinting at his own role. While incarnating
Poetry as Prodigality, he simultaneously symbolizes Eros
who speaks with the mythologizing voice of Logos:

> *Knabe Lenker*: Bin die Verschwendung, bin die Poesie;
> Bin der Poet, der sich vollendet,
> Wenn er sein eigenst Gut verschwendet
> (*Faust II*, 5573 ff.)

> (*Youth Charioteer*: I am Prodigality, am Poetry;
> I am the poet perfecting himself
> By lavishly wasting his very own wealth).

The warning has gone unheeded, that these treasures are
but imagery, a poetic illusion, a magic show that goes up
in flames in the Emperor's greedy hands, singeing his
mask—ironically the mask of Pan, the god to whom
panic fear is ascribed (*Faust II*, 5715 ff.; 5920 ff.).

The shattered theatre metaphor, too, presides over the
bankrupt Emperor's hasty approval of Mephisto's invention: paper money as legal tender, covered by imaginary
treasures and precious metal ore still buried in the ground
and as yet undiscovered (*Faust II*, 6057 ff.). Mephisto's
paper currency is a transposition of the theatre metaphor
onto the abstract stage of economics: the banknote as
"signifier" is vicariously identified with the "signified,"
the precious metal meant to cover it, but that so far is little
more than a fiction. It is perhaps no mere coincidence
that Mephisto's paper currency is introduced in the very
center of a play (verses 6057 ff.) with 12,111 lines. Mephisto's paper money holds a mirror to the major truth

of *Faust*, reflecting what is central to the play: the theme
that illusory treasures of poetic magic tend to deceive the
illusionist and his audience alike. This apparent structural
secret becomes all the more manifest in the light of
Goethe's own views on the dangers of paper currency: in
a figurative sense, he sees it as a type of counterfeit money,
exemplifying the confusion of symbolic values with a
reality of which they partake without coinciding with it:
"Alles Ideelle, sobald es vom Realen gefordert wird, zehrt
endlich dieses und sich selbst auf. So der Kredit das
Silber und sich selbst" (*Maximen und Reflexionen* 315,
IX, 532). ("All symbols, as soon as they are exchanged
for the real things they symbolize, in the end consume
these real things and themselves. Thus paper money [con-
sumes] [its] silver [cover] and itself.") Planted in the
play's very center, Mephisto's paper money seems to stand
as a symbol for all of Faust's and Mephisto's magic doings,
which throughout the play create the delusive semblance
of values that glitter but are not gold, and ultimately
vanish into thin air.

2. *Romantic Excessiveness, Classical Restraints, and the Human Condition*

Like his phantasmagoric son Euphorion and the By-
ronic spirit he allegorizes, Faust touches upon the outer
limits of Romantic *démesure*. His impatient desire to
violate Nature's innermost secrets stands in sharp contrast to Goethe's averred reverence for mysteries that, he
feels, one must carefully shield by cloaking them in silence: "Gewissen Geheimnissen, und wenn sie offenbar
wären, muss man durch Verhüllen und Schweigen
Achtung erweisen. . . ," is a major lesson in *Wilhelm
Meisters Wanderjahre* II, 1; Goethe VIII, 165. ("For cer-

tain mysteries, even if they were manifest, one must show reverence by veiling them in silence. . . .") Erich Heller [*The Disinherited Mind*, p. 99 ff.] has brilliantly discussed Goethe's reasons for refusing to use complex instruments that extend the reach of the human senses. Thus Goethe confides to Eckermann his abstention from studying astronomy, "weil hiebei die Sinne nicht mehr ausreichen, sondern weil man hier schon zu Instrumenten, Berechnungen und Mechanik seine Zuflucht nehmen muss, . . . die nicht meine Sache sind" (Eckermann, Feb. 1, 1827; Goethe xxiv, 238; ["because here our senses no longer suffice for here one must have recourse to instruments, calculations and mechanics, . . . that are not my cup of tea"]). "Die Nature verstummt auf der Folter" (*Maximen und Reflexionen* 115; Goethe ix, 510; ["Nature becomes silent when put to the rack"]) is the aged Goethe's somewhat inadequate answer to the physicists, the Newtonian "*Messkünstler*" ("measuring artists"), who fail to warm up to his anti-Newtonian theory of colors. These are the words of a poet and an ecologist *avant la lettre*.

Goethe, the natural scientist, declines the aid of optical instruments for reasons quite similar to those which prompt him to go to extremes of mystification, e.g., to keep intact the occult rites of Freemasonry. In both instances, the gesture is a symbol for the protection of secrets that are meant to remain inviolate, and intelligible only to the initiate. While Goethe recognizes the importance of mathematical symbols for the translation of natural phenomena, he himself abstains from using them, thereby making his rather formal bow to the limits that, to his thinking, are set to man's initiation into Nature's mysteries. These limits are dictated by what he considers the boundaries of human nature (*Grenzen der Menschheit*), i.e., the limitations of our natural senses, imperfect and faulty as they are. Faust's constant attempts to break through these limits, his irreverence toward all social, natural, and supernatural hierarchies, are a type of *sansculotisme*, which, on Goethe's scale of values, corresponds to a similar disrespect for universal mysteries as he finds it expressed in Newton's quantifying physics.[9]

To the abstract quantification of Nature, and to human attempts to manipulate and change her order, Goethe opposes *das Anschauen*, a type of intuitive speculation, based on direct observation, unmediated, i.e., as much as possible unaided by instruments or complex apparatus. It suggests the intellect's intuitive grasp or "seeing," as implicit in *intueri*. In the preface to his major anti-Newtonian work, *Zur Farbenlehre* ("Regarding the Theory of Colors"), he explains the successive steps involved in methodical *Anschauen*: "Jedes Ansehen geht über in ein Betrachten, jedes Betrachten in ein Sinnen, jedes Sinnen in ein Verknüpfen, und so kann man sagen, dass wir schon bei jedem aufmerksamen Blick in die Welt theoretisieren" (*Zur Farbenlehre*, "Vorwort," Goethe xvi, 11; ["Any first glance changes into an observation, every observation into a meditation, every meditation into the logical connexion of associations, so that it can be said that we theorize whenever we look attentively at the world"]). *Speculation* and *theory*, in the literal sense of their etymologies (Latin *specto, speculo* and Greek

[9] ". . . die höhere Mathematik (war) ihm (Newton) als das eigentliche Organ gegeben, durch das er seine innere Welt aufzubauen und die äussere zu gewältigen suchte" (*Geschichte der Farbenlehre, 6. Abt.* "Newtons Persönlichkeit," Goethe xvi, 574; [". . . higher mathematics (was) given to him (Newton) as his proper organ, through which he attempted to build his inner world and to violate the external universe"]). This is one of Goethe's milder definitions of what William Blake was to call "Newton's night."

θεάομαι, "to observe," "to watch," "to gaze at with wonderment," etc.) are both the foundation and the exercise of Goethe's method. It is a method that, in his *Anthropology*, Goethe's contemporary Heinroth had characterized as *gegenständliches Denken*, a simultaneous and mutual penetration of thought and the very object of thought, so that, in Goethe's paraphrase of Heinroth's remarks, "mein Anschauen selbst ein Denken, mein Denken ein Anschauen sei" (*Bedeutende Fördernis durch ein einziges geistreiches Wort*; Goethe xvi, 879; ["my perceptions are themselves a way of thinking, and my thought a way of perceiving"]). *Gegenständliches Denken*—i.e., thought arising simultaneously *with* observation, rather than deriving *from* it, resembles the Renaissance practice of contemplating "truth" in emblems and hieroglyphs. It is intuitive and qualitative but not quantifying; it has its poetic equivalent in *gegenständlichem Dichten* (*ibid.*, Goethe xvi, 880).

Goethe's method allows the scientist to benefit from the poet's intuition, and the poet to bring to his vision the precision of the experimental scientist, excerpting from the physical world and human nature such epitomes as provide insights into universal principles, without violating their mystery. Goethe's *gegenständliches Dichten* and *Denken* search for a primitive model that, reduced to primal simplicity, exemplifies the universality of an entire category of phenomena. They lead, e.g., to theories about the *Urpflanze*, a universal prototype, in which the unity of vegetative metamorphoses can be observed, as they apply to the vast diversity of all plant life. *Urpflanze* (the primal plant) and *Urphänomen* (the primal phenomenon) straddle the borderline between intuition and perception. "Urphänomen / ideal als das letzte Erkennbare, / real als erkannt, / symbolisch, weil es alle Fälle begreift, / identisch mit allen Fällen" (*Maximen und Reflexionen* 1360; Goethe IX, 672; ["*Urphänomen*, the primal phenomenon: *ideal* as the very limit of what *can be known; real* as what *is known; symbolic* since it embraces all phenomena; identical with all phenomena"]). It is the ultimate, the irreducible, the only phenomenon, where the polarity of analogy and identity meet.

Goethe's theories on the *Urphänomen* as the unifying point of mental and physical phenomena is not unlike Descartes' attempt to unify the separate entities of mind and body by locating their "meeting place" in the pineal gland. *Anschauen, gegenständliches Dichten* and *Denken* are those midwife qualities which preside over its birth, its intelligibility to the human mind. They are facets of one and the same method, the true pivot of Goethe's lifelong endeavors as a poet, as a drawer, and as a scientist opposed to quantification. They are tools in Goethe's systematic efforts to epitomize the manifold strands of his experience. He might, in fact, have defined himself as an *Epitomator*, an epitomist, of universal and human nature—the term he applied to all poets in *Shakespeare und kein Ende* (Goethe XIV, 766), and, with some irony, to himself as a *Lebenskünstler* in a letter to Sulpiz Boisserée (Jan. 27, 1823; Goethe XXI, 530). As early as July 7, 1778, he had written to Merck: "Aber Du weisst, wie ich im Anschaun lebe . . ." ("But you know, how totally I live in intuitive seeing"); and as late as one year before his death, on March 22, 1831, he again asserted to Sulpiz Boisserée: "Das unmittelbare Anschauen der Dinge ist mir alles" ("The unmediated observation of things means everything to me").

Anschauen, schauen ("to divine," "to intuit," as well as "to observe," "to watch," "to perceive," etc.) and *Schau* ("view," "show," "spectacle") are so closely related to

Schauspiel ("play," "show," "drama") that by their very associations they partake of the theatre metaphor. These close connections between ideas related to the theatre and concepts of intuition, perception, observation, and theorizing were etymologically present in ancient Greek. In terms of metaphor and semantics, *Anschauen* (θέαομαι) can choose as its theatre (θέατρον) the stage, as well as all of Nature, Society, Art, and the supernatural spectacles of the Divine and the Demonic. The spectators (οἱ θεαταί) may watch (θέαομαι) the show (θέαμα) but, of course, they may not "play on stage" (θεάτρειον). Their vantage point is the audience, θεωριὸν, a noun closely related to θεωρία, the term corresponding to *Anschauen*. Simultaneously, it characterizes their condition as spectators, and the benefits they may derive from this condition: the dramatic discovery of "intuitive insights," "ideas" and "theories." Whatever the show, its performance combines ideas with appearances, or in Goethe's words: "Nur im Höchsten und im Gemeinsten trifft Idee und Erscheinung zusammen; auf allen mittleren Stufen des Betrachtens und Erfahrens trennen sie sich. Das Höchste ist das Anschauen des Verschiedenen als identisch; das Gemeinste ist die Tat, das aktive Verbinden des Getrennten zur Identität" (*Maximen und Reflexionen*, 1137; Goethe IX, 643; ["Only on the sublime and on the lowest level do idea and appearance coincide; on all intermediate levels of contemplation and experience, they are separate. The sublime state opens vistas (*das Anschauen*) onto identity in diversity; its lowest manifestation is action, the act of combining into a (false) identity what is separated, diverse"]). The theoretician and his model, the audience and the performers on stage constitute such separate entities without a common identity.

On most every occasion, Faust commits the categorical

mistake of confusing "ideas" with "appearances," the objects of contemplation with those of action. Faust the scientist is impatient with mere theory ($\theta\epsilon\omega\rho\acute{\iota}\alpha$) based on empirical observation; he would scorn Goethe's temperate concept of the "experiment as the mediator between object and subject" (*Der Versuch als Vermittler von Object und Subject*, 1793). Faust the magician is dissatisfied with the illusion of a vaporous phantom world he conjures up with the aid of Mephisto's prompting. His ardor for the objects of his contemplation gives the lie to any pretense of detachment, although we see him occasionally pay lip service to the theorizing charms of *das Anschauen*. At such rare intervals, it would almost seem as though he might momentarily accept his humble place in Nature's scheme. Thus, for instance, when he addresses for a second time the Earth Spirit, in the scene *Wald und Höhle* ("Forest and Cavern"):

> *Faust*: Du führst die Reihe der Lebendigen
>   Vor mir vorbei, und lehrst mich meine Brüder
>   Im stillen Busch, in Luft und Wasser kennen. (*Faust I*, 3225 ff.)

> (*Faust*: Aye, you parade the ranks of living things
>   Before me and you teach me to know my brothers
>   In the quiet copse, in the water, in the air.) (MacNeice, p. 104)

But Faust's fraternal recognition of his fellow creatures in three elements (earth, air, and water) is promptly upset by his sudden awareness of the fourth element, the fire of his Titanic appetites and its infernal equivalent, the flames of uncontrollable passions, which Mephisto's ministrations keep burning in his veins. But his consciousness of this situation does not alter his innate character. Confusing once again the picture with the reality it feigns to represent, in the very next moment he is burning, not for Margarete but significantly for her "beauteous image" (*Faust I*, 3248) while he defines himself in terms of a Petrarchist conceit, which shows him chiastically crucified on a cross formed by desires and fulfillment forever unsatisfied:

> *Faust*: So tauml' ich von Begierde zu Genuss,
> Und im Genuss verschmacht' ich nach Begierde.
> (*Faust I*, 3249 f.)

> (*Faust*: And so I stagger from desire to enjoyment
> And in enjoyment languish for desire.) (MacNeice,
> p. 105)

If dispassionate *Anschauen* is not Faust's forte, he finds it equally hard to sort out the mind's passions from those of the libido. He may temporarily lapse into respecting the *noli me tangere* of ideal beauty and truth, but such rare flashes of aesthetic delight have no lasting effect on his behavior. They tend to vanish at the very moment of their manifestation.

3. *Reawakening to Life in "Faust II" and in "Les Fées"*

The critics have duly noted the similarities between *Les Fées*, the opening scene of *Faust II*, and, of course, Berlioz' ballet of the Sylphides in *La Damnation de Faust*. The poetic enchantment in the Fays' magic palace marks the purgation of Valéry's Faust and his disengagement from the irrational snares of the Solitaire's Pascalian apologetics, and from Faust's equally fatal entrapment in the solipsism of the *cogito*. It is a temporary purgation that, on the surface, resembles the purification and revival of Goethe's Faust by Ariel and his chorus of elves. This cleansing process takes place in terms of Renaissance notions of alchemy and mythology (both classical and Nordic).[10] The elves proceed to revive Goethe's hero in four stages: first bedding him down, then bathing him in "dew from Lethe's stream," granting him refreshing sleep, and finally returning him to "holy light" (*Faust II*, 4628 ff.). When Faust is awakening from his stupor, he greets Nature's elemental forces in this order: air (*ibid.*, 4680), earth (*ibid.*, 4681 ff.), fire (*ibid.*, 4708 ff.), and water (*ibid.*, 4716 ff.). The conjunction of fire and water, the polarity of Vulcanism and Neptunism, are needed to bring about his full recovery;[11] just as their union alone can bring life to Wagner's test-tube baby, Homunculus (*Faust II*, Act II, 8466), whose dim vital flame must first shipwreck on Galatea's shell carriage, and die in the ocean, ultimately to be reborn in life's evolutionary cycles.

Sweet Nature ("Anmutige Gegend"—"A pleasant Landscape") is the external force from which Goethe's Faust draws new strength. Ariel and his elves represent Nature's healing powers that revive him from without. By contrast, the closed crypt of the brain, where the *petites Fées* play

[10] On Shakespearean reminiscences (Ariel = Puck, etc.) and Dantesque models in this and other scenes, see Paul Friedländer, *Rhythmen und Landschaften im zweiten Teil des Faust*, Hermann Böhlaus Nachf., Weimar, 1953, passim.

[11] The *Zendavesta* myth of life originating from a union of water and fire is borrowed, no doubt, from Friedrich Georg Creuzer's *Symbolik und Mythologie der alten Völker*, a work Goethe had read and distrusted as much as he did its author. Yet, he borrowed from Creuzer material that suited his poetic purposes, as certain poems clearly indicate (*Urworte* "Orphisch"; "Gingko biloba," *West-Oestlicher Divan*). Our passage derives from Creuzer's *Symbolik* I, 211: "Alles Gedeihen in der Natur entspringt aus Feuer und Wasser [gemäss der persischen *Zendavesta*]; jenes ist männlich, dieses weiblich, und aus beiden ist das Licht entstanden." ("All fertility in Nature springs from fire and water [according to the Persian Zendavesta]; the former is male, the latter is female, and light was engendered from both.")

their part in bringing Valéry's Faust back to life from within, indicates their kinship with Descartes' "animal spirits"[12] and innate "seeds of knowledge."[13]

In the first scene of *Faust II*, the lifeless hero is seen in the silvery light of the Moon ("Tiefsten Ruhens Glück besiegelnd / Herrscht des Mondes volle Pracht"—"Bearing witness to the delight of deepest rest / The Moon's full splendor exerts its rule" (*Faust II*, 4648 f.). The alchemist wedding of Luna, the feminine and "passive" power of the Moon, with Apollo, the male and "active" force of the Sun, this portentous fusion of Silver and Gold, symbol of purification, presides over the reawakening of Goethe's Faust to life, while an "immense clamor announces the approach of the Sun" ("Ungeheures Getöse verkündet das Herannahen der Sonne"—scenic direction after *Faust II*, 4665). The fantasy palace, too, where Valéry's Faust lies unconscious, at first "s'éclaire peu à peu d'une lumière argentée" (P.II, 392), to give way to a deep "golden" lighting, when he regains full possession of his consciousness ("La lumière se fait, dorée"—scenic direction, P.II, 396). Yet, we have seen that the circumstances of Faust's awakening in *Les Fées* are considerably more ambiguous than those which accompany the revival of Goethe's protagonist.

4. *Ideal Beauty and Its Unreality*

With "dew from Lethe's stream," the elves had deleted the Gretchen tragedy from the memory of Goethe's Faust. Together with his guilt feelings, all traces of his culpability seem erased by these pagan sprites embodying natural forces; they represent Nature's indifference in

---

[12] Cf. *L'Homme*, AT, XI, 165 ff.; *Discours* V; AT, VI, 54 ff.; *Les Passions de l'âme*, AT, XI, 237 ff., *passim*.
[13] Cf. *Cogitationes privatae*, AT, X, 327.

matters of good and evil. Ariel voices their sympathetic
healing powers:

> *Ariel*: Ob er heilig, ob er böse,
>   Jammert sie der Unglücksmann. (*Faust II*, 4619 f.)

> (*Ariel*: Be he holy, be he evil,
>   They [the elves] pity the star-crossed man.)

We experienced Faust's rebirth through his own narrative, which rolls on in majestic iambic pentameters and
Dantesque *terza rima*. He looks at first straight into the
blinding light of the rising sun. Then, turning his back
to the "sea of flames," he feasts his eyes on a rainbow
which—now clearly defined, now fading again—bridges
a waterfall. He has recovered full consciousness. Meditat-
ing on the rainbow and on inferences to be drawn from
this phenomenon, he utters some of his most beautiful
lines:

> *Faust*: Allein wie herrlich, diesem Sturm entspriessend,
>   Wölbt sich des bunten Bogens Wechseldauer,
>   Bald rein gezeichnet, bald in Luft zerfliessend,
>   Umher verbreitend duftig kühle Schauer.
>   *Der* spiegelt ab das menschliche Bestreben.
>   Ihm sinne nach, und du begreifst genauer:
>   Am farbigen Abglanz haben wir das Leben. (*Faust
>   II*, 4721 ff.)

> (*Faust*: And yet how nobly from this splash and pelting
>   The changing permanence of the rainbow flowers,
>   Now clearly drawn, now into vapor melting,
>   Spreading around it cool and fragrant showers.
>   This bow will serve to image man's endeavor.
>   Think on it and you grasp what lot is ours:
>   Reflected color forms our life forever.) (MacNeice,
>   p. 157)

On the surface, these majestic iambic pentameters seem to culminate in a moment of Goethean *Anschauen*. There is certainly something Goethean about Faust's unwillingness to concur with Newton; what he sees in the rainbow is not the solar spectrum but a mysterious phenomenon compounded by both refraction and reflection. Faust's existential equation of "man's endeavor" with the totality of his life—a constant struggle for growth and beauty—is not so far off the mark either, although he seems to give little thought to the fiascoes and errors in the human pursuit of the forever elusive meaning of life and beauty. Goethe himself expresses this ineffable and ironic process in Platonist terms: "Das Schöne ist ein Urphänomen, das zwar nie selber zur Erscheinung kommt, dessen *Abglanz* aber in tausend verschiedenen Äusserungen des schaffenden Geistes sichtbar wird und so mannigfaltig und so verschiedenartig ist als die Natur selber" (Eckermann, 18.iv.1827; Goethe xxiv, 617; ["Beauty is a primal phenomenon, which itself never becomes overt, whose reflection, however, is manifest in a thousand diverse expressions of the creative spirit; it is as manifold and as heterogeneous as Nature herself"]).

To understand how much Faust's views are here at variance with Goethe's Platonist (and even Platonic) aesthetics and epistemology, we must render as literal a translation as possible of "Am farbigen Abglanz haben wir das Leben." In observing that "In colorful reflection we have life," Faust commits the same categorical mistake of confusing the phenomenal with the ontal world, which we saw him make in the very first scene of *Faust I* ("Where do I grasp you, infinite Nature?" *Faust I*, 455), an error he will commit again in the Mother scenes of *Faust II*, where he will blunder by taking "life's pictures, moving, without life" (6430) for Paris and Helena in the flesh. The polarity Goethe-Faust is evident in Goethe's own insights on the symbolic rather than existential meaning of all "colorful reflections." They illuminate the ever-passing show of life's metamorphoses, while pointing beyond their temporal embodiments to the permanence of an ideal archetype of beauty that, divine in essence, permeates all earthly forms while simultaneously transcending them.[14] Faust fails to see the dual anthropomorphism of beauty that, on the one hand, is an artifice projected by human sensitivity into Nature, and, on the other, an excitement provoked in the creative mind by Nature's fleeting impressions. Anthropomorphic in their origins, both types of beauty are symbolic of a higher order—mysterious, unintelligible but darkly accessible to intuition and divination by way of poetic analogies. Although beauty can be seen, loved, and desired, as an Idea it escapes the human embrace. Whatsoever one embraces as "beauty" is an evanescent phenomenon, reflecting those values which, in a given culture and period, human conventions perceive as "beauty." It is admissible to lust for the "reflection" of beauty, as long as one is aware that this reflection is not identical to the ineffable essence of beauty:

> Nur im Widerschein das Schöne
> Sehen, lieben und begehren,
> Ist denn das so grosse Schuld?
> (Gedichte, "Paralipomena"; Goethe II, 556)

("To see, to love and to desire Beauty in its mere reflec-

---

[14] "Das Wahre, mit dem Göttlichen identisch, lässt sich niemals von uns direkt erkennen: wir schauen es nur im *Abglanz*, im Beispiel, Symbol, in einzelnen und verwandten Erscheinungen; wir werden es gewahr als unbegreifliches Leben und können dem Wunsch nicht entsagen, es dennoch zu begreifen." *Versuch einer Witterungslehre*; Goethe XVII, 639. (My italics.)

tion, is that so great a crime?") While Faust's short temper has him rush into adventures where he fails to distinguish between idea and reality, between the highly subjective perception of beauty and the object it endows with beauty, Goethe tries to derive from the interpenetration of subjective and objective experience the irreducible phenomenon of beauty *per se*. He knows that the elusive essence of beauty may excite and attract the beholder; but he also knows that it escapes the sensuous embrace that touches (and only *can* touch) the mere *object* of beauty's passing incarnation. "Ja wir sollen das Schöne kennen," exclaims the Werther-like fictitious letter writer of Goethe's *Briefe aus der Schweiz*, "wir sollen es mit Entzücken betrachten und uns zu ihm, zu seiner Natur zu erheben suchen; und um das zu vermögen, sollen wir uns uneigennützig erhalten, wir sollen es uns nicht zueignen . . ." (Goethe IX, 484; ["Yes, we must know beauty, we must look at it with excitement and try to elevate ourselves to it, to its nature; and to be able to do so, we must remain disinterested, abstain from helping ourselves to it . . ."]).

The evanescence of beauty, its metamorphoses and its intangibility, are concepts that hardly change throughout Goethe's long career. As early as 1770 he conceived of beauty as "ein schwimmendes, glänzendes Schattenbild, dessen Umriss keine Definition hascht" (letter to Hetzler the Younger, dated July 14, 1770; Goethe XVIII, 142; ["a hazy, brilliant phantom whose outlines escape definition"]). The transient images of beauty are elusive; they pass only through transient forms:

> Warum bin ich vergänglich, o Zeus? so fragte die
> Schönheit.
> Macht ich doch, sagte der Gott, nur das Vergängliche
> schön. (*Vier Jahreszeiten*, "Sommer" 35; Goethe I,
> 259)

(Why am I mortal, o Zeus? was Beauty's question.
Answered the God: because I only made mortal
    things beautiful.) (*Four Seasons*, "Summer" 35;
    Goethe I, 259)

Faust constantly mistakes life's colorful reflections for life
itself; he confuses the phenomenon of beauty, as it is reflected in Gretchen and Helena, with the very essence of
das *Ewig-Weibliche* (*eternally* feminine qualities). By
contrast, Goethe knows how to intuit the absolutes of life
and beauty from their evanescence in those mortal forms,
which, in their relativity, never cease to excite, to exalt,
and to attract him. For Goethe, there is but one Beauty,
Protean in its endless transmigrations. A Platonist Idea, it
is reflected in ever-changing forms on earth. His concept
of beauty is close to Shelley's perception of Keats, the passing incarnation and lasting ideal of Poetry: "The One remains, the many change and pass" (*Adonais*, st. 52):

Schönheit ist ewig nur eine, doch mannigfach
    wechselt das Schöne,
    Dass es wechselt, das macht eben das Eine nur
    schön. (*Tabulae votivae* 30, "Schönheit"; Goethe
    II, 534)

(There is but one Beauty eternal, yet, Beauty's
    changes are manifold,
    That the One changes is precisely what alone
    makes it beautiful.)

From the beginning to the end of Goethe's *Faust*, the
protagonist is at variance with the play's morality, as it is
expressed by the Chorus mysticus in the cryptic lines
which introduce the closing stanza of *Faust II*:

Alles Vergängliche   (All that is passing
Ist nur ein Gleichnis   Is but a symbol)
            (*Faust II*, 12104 f.)

There exists a secret bond between "all that is passing" and Mephisto's infernal invention, the paper money so greedily seized upon by the Emperor and his entourage. Both are meaningless when taken at their face value. Only with reference to the precious metal, for which it symbolically stands, can the true merit of paper currency come to light—indirectly at that, and provided it be covered by the hidden but real assets it represents. For, palpable as it may be, its worth is abstract and intangible like the Idea of Beauty with its ineffable permanence throughout its ever-changing, ever-passing embodiments.

5. *Formal Hints at Archetypal Patterns*

What the critics have hitherto failed to notice are analogies between the restless activities of the two adult Fays in Valéry's Interlude to *Le Solitaire—Les Fées*—and the tasks ascribed by Goethe's Mephistopheles to the mysterious Mothers (*Faust II*, 6212 ff.), archetypal *matrices*, i.e., motherly wombs for the evolutionary patterns and metamorphoses of all living forms:

> ... Gestaltung, Umgestaltung,
> Des ewigen Sinnes ewige Unterhaltung.
> Umschwebt von Bildern aller Kreatur;
> Sie sehn dich (Faust) nicht, denn Schemen sehn
>   sie nur.
>
>   (... Formation, transformation.
> The eternal Mind's eternal entertainment.
> Surrounded by floating images of all creatures;
> They do not see you, for they only see patterns.)
> (*Faust II*, 6287 ff.)

The fact that it is Mephistopheles who describes these goddesses unknown to mere mortals ("Göttinnen, ungekannt / Euch Sterblichen" [*Faust II*, 6218 f.]), renders them somewhat suspect. Residing outside time and space ("Um sie kein Ort, noch weniger eine Zeit" [*ibid.*, 6214]), some are seated, others standing or pacing ("Die einen sitzen, andre stehn und gehn" [*ibid.*, 6286]) at the very bottom of the innermost depths ("im tiefsten, allertiefsten Grund" [*ibid.*, 6284]). It is evident that they are not mere personae dramatis. Allegories, they move on the mind's intimate stage. There they represent those deceptive powers which control what almost a century after the completion of Goethe's *Faust II*, C. G. Jung called archetypal forms that survive in the "collective unconscious."

Their characterization by Mephistopheles finds an echo in certain alexandrines of the Prime Fée. The Fay's verses transport archetypal imagery from the realm of the collective unconscious to the dreamlike domain of the individual's intellect confronted by the deceptive faculties of memory and imagination. On the threshold of consciousness, where dream borders on wishful thinking, the Mothers' cosmic patterning of archetypal figures runs parallel to those perpetual changes which mark the forever provisional perception that Valéry's Faust gains of his constantly changing Self through the ceaseless transformations of his consciousness. The metamorphoses of his self-perception are affected by Memory and Imagination (the two taller Fays) in their weaving, unraveling, and reweaving of those mysterious threads which produce the tapestry of Chance, that mother and matrix of life's necessity. These threads, leading back to the dead realm of Faust's past belong to his present and to his potential future, as it will be hazardously shaped by his acceptance or refusal of remorse and by the revival of love at its matrix, its maternal source:

> L'art subtil de mes soeurs, Tisseuses du Hasard,
> Sait dénouer les noeuds qu'a formés la durée

Et reprendre au passé ce qu'il a pris pour part.
Le regret, le remords ne sont point sans ressources,
Et le plus doux des sens se ravive à la source. (P.ɪɪ,
398)[15]

[15] The last line, in particular, sounds ambiguous, with (1) its reference to Memory, and (2) its barely muted overtones of incest. Faust, witnessing his intellectual renewal, had already recognized Memory as the source of his rebirth: "Tu es ma mère, Mémoire! Tu m'enfantes. . . ." Sound patterns reinforce the meaning: the chiasma of dazzling *voyelles éclatantes* ("a" and its near equivalent in "oi"), embracing the less brilliant *voyelles claires* "è" and "é" in "m*a* mère, Mém*oi*re!" stresses the inverse movements of engenderment $\genfrac{}{}{0pt}{}{a\!\!-\!\!\grave{e}}{oi\!\!\diagdown\!\!\grave{e}}$ (implicit in "m*a* mère"), and of retrospection, reaching backward into the hidden resources of Memory, explicit in "Mém*oi*re." The mere approximation of quasi-rhyming vowel sounds by itself suggests the erratic tendencies of memories, their subtle distortion of those past experiences they re-present, and always tend to misrepresent. The open vowels of "m*a* mère" bespeak the openness (and opening) of the maternal matrix at the crucial moments of coitus and birth, conception and creation— images underscored by the equally open nasals "en" and "an" and by the intensive and nasal "m'" in "Tu m'en*fan*tes. . . ." By contrast, the closed vowels "é" and "oi" in "Mém*oi*re!" seal in the closed system of Memory, locked as it is within the confines of its own matrix, the individual's mind. The three suspension points after "Tu m'enfantes . . ." and the exclamation mark after "Mémoire!" function as *fermate* that further extend indefinitely the lengthy processes of engenderment and reminiscence. The monotonous continuity of Memory's closed world of duration, this motherly womb for the potential re-emergence of the self's past metamorphoses, is evoked by the perfectly balanced alliteration "m-m-r" which prevails as well in "m*a* mère" as it does in the apposition "Mémoire," its double, or rather, its phonetically reversed Narcissus image. In short, Memory as *mater* and *matrix* of the mind's peregrinations through its own past allegorizes a slightly deceptive mirror for bygone stages of consciousness; simultaneously, it is the womb where are born the mind's images of "les noeuds qu'a formés la durée." These "knots" can be untied. But

As Fays, as Fates, they may "reprendre au passé ce qu'il a pris pour part."

6. *The Fays—The Mothers*

Valéry's Faust, at first lost in the oblivion of dreamless sleep, will awaken in a state of amnesia. By analogy, he seems to approximate the condition of Goethe's Faust *en route* to the archetypal underworld of the "Mothers," a condition that Mephisto's description anticipates in these terms:

> Nichts wirst du sehn in ewig leerer Ferne,
> Den Schritt nicht hören, den du tust,
> Nichts Festes finden, wo du ruhst. (*Faust II*, 6246 ff.)

> (In that empty farness you see nothing,
> The step you make you will not hear,
> And where you stand, no ground is there.) (Mac-
> Neice, p. 176)

No way leads to those unsounded depths:

> *Mephistopheles*:   Kein Weg! Ins Unbetretene,
> Nicht zu Betretende; ein Weg ans Unerbetene,
> Nicht zu Erbittende. (*Faust II*, 6222 ff.)

>   (No way! To the unvisited,
> Not to be visited, to be unsolicited,
> And not to be solicited.) (MacNeice, p. 176)

It is Faust's plunge into his innermost depths, a trip to the wasteland where mysterious forces dwell in solitudes vast-

---

their undoing lies with those very forces which have tied them; Memory and Imagination, those fateful "Weavers of Chance" patterns who, transforming reminiscences into the stuff of which dreams are made, nonetheless determine the precarious course of Necessity.

er and more desolate than those deceptive heights to which Valéry's Solitaire, more than a century after Goethe's death, will claim such exclusive rights:

> *Mephistopheles*: Göttinnen thronen hehr in Einsamkeit.
> Um sie kein Ort, noch weniger eine Zeit. (*Faust II*, 6213 f.)

> (Goddesses throned in solitude, sublime,
> Set in no place, still less in any time.) (MacNeice, p. 175)

The stress is on desolation and solitude:

> *Mephistopheles*: Von Einsamkeiten wirst
> umhergetrieben.
> Hast du Begriff von Öd' und Einsamkeit? (*Faust II*, 6226 f.)

> (*M.*: But loneliness will surround and hound you.
> Can you conceive such desolate loneliness?) (MacNeice, p. 176)

That this desolate solitude is a necessary precondition for the poet's orphic descent had been foreshadowed in a previous scene, the *Mummenschanz*, where Knabe Lenker, the ambivalent charioteer of Faust-Plutus, had characterized himself:

> *Knabe Lenker*: Bin die Verschwendung, bin die Poesie
> (*Faust II*, 5573)

> (I am lavishness, am Poetry!)[16]

___

[16] The image of poetry riding high on a carriage is consistent with the metaphorical tradition of classical antiquity. In the first part of his lectures on the History of Greek Literature (University of Basel, 1874-75), Nietzsche points out that "prose is called πεζὸς λόγος; it is pedestrian, walks on foot; the poet rides high on a carriage. The image of the carriage [is] already known to Homer,

A prefiguration of Euphorion, the ephemeral poet be-
gotten by Faust and Helena in Act III (see below), *Knabe
Lenker* will forthwith indicate that solitude alone is con-
ducive to the creation of poetic beauty and excellence:
"Zur Einsamkeit!—Da schaffe deine Welt!" (*Faust II,*
5696) ("Retire to solitude!—There create your own
world!"). These rebus-like hints clearly point to Faust's
trip to the Mothers as an orphic descent *ad inferos,*[17] a
plunge into his intimate Hell, the preliminary step for
his creative effort. In sum, it is an allegory for his descent
to the very matrix of archetypal forms, to the collective
unconscious. Faust's subsequent re-emergence "in priestly
robes with wreath" ("Im Priesterkleid, bekränzt, ein
Wundermann," [*ibid.*, 6421] ambiguously symbolizes his
return as magus, as the *poeta vates* whose mind can bring
forth archetypal images of classical beauty by conjuring
the shadows of Paris and Helena—"Das Musterbild der
Männer so der Frauen" (*Faust II,* 6185) ("The paradigm
of men and that of women"). I have characterized Faust's
priestly appearance as ambiguous; it is equivocal, to say
the least, considering the Mephistophelian source of his
"inspiration." The whole scene ironizes as much as it
symbolizes the Romantic concept of the *poeta vates*. It is a
concept viewed with skepticism by Goethe, the "Klas-
siker," since it pretends to lend prophetic substance to

according to Bergk; hence the conventional formula in Odyssey
VIII 500 ἔθεν ἑλών, 'to drive out thence (in a carriage)'" (F.
Nietzsche, *Philologika*, Leipzig, 1912; II, 13; my translation).

[17] The assumption is confirmed by one of Goethe's major
sources for mythological symbolism, Georg-Friedrich Creuzer's
Symbolik und Mythologie der alten Völker. Creuzer asserts that
it was "Orphic" to sing of "forces and mixtures," "Homeric," to
sing of "persons and actions." ("Von Kräften und Mischungen
zu singen war *orphisch*, von Personen und Handlungen *homer-
isch*" I, 27.)

the poetic illusion that he regards as an end in itself, a product of rhetoric and poetics rather than a vehicle of divine revelation.[18] In this sense the Mothers allegorize the matrix of an eternal beauty that manifests itself in the truth of the poetic illusion but escapes the embrace of reality. Faust's conjuration of Paris and Helena shows them as allegories for mysterious forces that rule over the mind's irrational reservoir of collective archetypes:

> In eurem Namen, Mütter, die ihr thront
> Im Grenzenlosen, ewig einsam wohnt,
> Und doch gesellig. Euer Haupt umschweben
> Des Lebens Bilder, regsam, ohne Leben.
> Was einmal war, in allem Glanz und Schein,
> Es regt sich dort; denn es will ewig sein.
> Und ihr verteilt es, allgewaltige Mächte,
> Zum Zelt des Tages, zum Gewölb der Nächte
> (*Ibid.*, 6427 ff.)

> (In your name, Mothers, each upon your throne
> In the infinite, eternally alone
> And yet in company! Around you weave

---

[18] The amateurish and sentimental productions of German poets who are his contemporaries are satirized in Venetian Epigram 33:

> Alle Künste lernt und treibt der Deutsche; zu jeder
>   Zeigt er ein schönes Talent, wenn er sie ernstlich ergreift.
> Eine Kunst nur treibt er, und will sie nicht lernen, die
>   Dichtkunst.
>   Darum pfuscht er auch so; Freunde, wir habens erlebt.
>   (Goethe 1, 228)

> The German learns and exercises all arts; for all
>   He demonstrates a beautiful talent, when he earnestly takes
>   it up.
> He dabbles in one art only, without wanting to learn it:
>   poetry.
>   That's why he bungles it so; friends, we have experienced it.

> The forms of life, which move but do not live.
> What once existed in full glow and flame,
> It still moves there, eternity its aim.
> And you, omnipotent Powers, apportion it
> To the tent of day or to the vault of night)
> (MacNeice, 185 f.)

"Des Lebens Bilder, regsam, ohne Leben" (*Faust II*, 6430) ("life's pictures, moving, without life") become manifest in the artifice of poetry. Just as the Mothers are metaphors for the creative imagination, and just as Faust's trip to the Mothers is metaphorical in nature—Mephisto's verbal creation—so the delusive images of Paris and Helena will reveal themselves as a poetic vision, created by Faust, and verbally projected before the audience by the Herald and the court astrologer, who take their cue from Mephistopheles, the prompter.

The erotic connotations of Faust's metaphorical descent to the Mothers were prefigured in the *Mummenschanz* scene. There, the creative power of Eros was represented by way of a charade, when Mephistopheles, in the mask of Avarice (*Geiz*), shaped gold into a phallus (*ibid.*, 5781 ff.). Faust's erotic and Orphic descent to the Mothers is as discreetly oedipal and incestuous as the Prime Fée's supplication to "le plus doux des sens" of Valéry's Faust, to revive its strength "à la source," at the maternal well-head of all birth and rebirth. Mephistopheles provides Goethe's Faust with a "key" that, though at first insignificant, will "glow" "sparkle," as did the golden phallus in the hands of Mephistopheles-Avarice. With the libido's animal instinct, Faust's glowing and extended "key" will instantly find its way to a metaphorical partner in heat, a "red-hot tripod," "in the deepest, very deepest depths":

Meph.: Hier diesen Schlüssel nimm.
Faust: Das kleine Ding!
Meph.: Erst fass ihn an[19] und schätz ihn nicht gering.
Faust: Er wächst in meiner Hand! er leuchtet, blitzt!
Meph.: Merkst du nun bald, was man an ihm besitzt?
   Der Schlüssel wird die rechte Stelle wittern,
   Folg ihm hinab, er führt dich zu den Müttern.
   (*Faust II*, 6259 ff.)

(*Meph.*: Here, take this key.
Faust: That little thing! But why?
Meph.: First seize it; it is nothing to decry.
Faust: It grows within my hand! A glow! A spark!
Meph.: Ah, now you see: a possession worth remark!
   It will find out the place among all others;
   Follow it down, it leads you to the Mothers!)
   (MacNeice, p. 177)

Meph.: Ein glühnder Dreifuss tut dir endlich kund,
   Du seist im tiefsten, allertiefsten Grund. (*Faust II*,
   6283 f.)

(*Meph.*: A glowing tripod tells you in the end
   You have descended whence no souls descend.)
   (MacNeice, p. 178)

Key and tripod will act out the charade of *partus*, the ancient Roman marriage rite during which the house key is handed to the bride as a symbol for that other meaning of *partus*, "parturition," "engenderment," "pregnancy," a consequence of *vulvam aperire*, the opening of the womb's gates. No wonder then the delusive images of Paris and Helena are engendered (if not immediately born), as soon

---

[19] *anfassen*, in colloquial German, a euphemism for masturbation.

as Faust's Mephistophelian "key" touches the womblike "tripod":

> *Meph.*: Da fass ein Herz, denn die Gefahr ist gross,
> Und gehe grad' auf jenen Dreifuss los,
> Berühr ihn mit dem Schlüssel! (*ibid.*, 6291 ff.)

> (*Meph.*: Then pluck up heart, the danger is so great,
> Approach that tripod, do not hesitate,
> And touch it with the key.) (MacNeice, p. 178)

Mephisto's description fills Faust with enthusiasm ("Faust begeistert")—a metaphor for the poetic *furere* that has always been associated with the Pythia's tripod at Delphi.[20]

---

[20] The Astrologer's words twice define the "tripod" as "Schale" (vessel): "Schon ahn' ich aus der *Schale* Weihrauchduft" (*Faust II*, 6424) ("That censer will soon function, I surmise" [MacNeice, p. 185]), and "Der glühnde Schlüssel rührt die *Schale* kaum" (*ibid.*, 6439) ("The glowing key has hardly touched the censer" [MacNeice, p. 186]).

"Key" and "tripod" may well stand, too, as symbols that hint at *Faust II* itself as a work where the author has consciously concealed mysteries that forever exact bold and continuous efforts of interpretation. It is conceivable that, in "serious jest," the "key" for decoding Faust is combined with the "tripod" (seat of oracular and ironic poetry) to form a rebus for two of the aged Goethe's favorite oxymora: "offenbares Geheimnis" ("manifest mystery") and "offenbares Rätsel" ("manifest enigma"). They signify as much the poet's working method, e.g., about *Faust II*: "Da habe ich viel hineingeheimnisst" (Conversation with J. v. Pappenheim, May 4, 1828) ("I intentionally concealed in it a lot of mysteries"); or in a letter to Zelter where he says in jest that he would like to finish *Faust II* in a monastery garden: "(. . .) auch wohl dem fertig Hingestellten noch einige Mantelfalten zuschlagen, damit alles zusammen ein offenbares Rätsel bleibe, die Menschen fort und fort ergötze und ihnen zu schaffen mache" (letter of Mid-May 1831). ("(. . .) [I should also like to] add to the finished portions a few closed folds of the coat, so that the whole altogether may remain a manifest puzzle, amusing generations to come and forever keeping them busy.") As a rule of conduct,

The symbolic rape of the tripod, matrix of archetypes and seat of "enthusiastic" (i.e., "inspired") poetry (i.e., "the making of fiction") is explained as the preliminary step for the conjuration of the prototypes of Hellenic beauty. Once the key has penetrated the tripod-womb, the latter will fasten on to it; the matrix of poetic imagery will rise together with Faust from the night of the unconscious to the daylight of consciousness, where the hero and heroine can then be brought forth:

> *Meph.*: Er (der Dreifuss) schliesst sich an, er folgt als
>   treuer Knecht;
> Gelassen steigst du, dich erhebt das Glück,
> Und eh' sie's merken, bist mit ihm zurück.
> Und hast du ihn einmal hierher gebracht,
> So rufst du Held und Heldin aus der Nacht (. . .)
> (*Faust II*, 6294 ff.)

> (*Meph.*:   A true
> Servant, the tripod then will follow you.
> Fortune will help you climb, you calmly rise,
> Are back—before they notice—with your prize.
> And once you have brought it here, brought it to light,
> You call that heroic pair out of the night . . .)
> (MacNeice, p. 178)

"manifest mysteries" must be respected, e.g.: "Gewissen Geheimnissen, und wenn sie offenbar wären, muss man durch Verhüllen und Schweigen Achtung erweisen, denn dieses wirkt auf Scham und gute Sitten" ("Certain mysteries, even if they were manifest, must be respected by concealment and through silence, for this favorably affects modesty and mores.") (*Wilhelm Meisters Wanderjahre* ii, 1). It is a rule of conduct which Faust fails to observe; hence catastrophe results, when he tries to rape Helena, the "manifest mystery" he has brought back from his terrifying descent *ad inferos* ("Mein Schreckensgang bringt seligsten Gewinn" [*Faust II*, 6489]).

Faust's enthusiasm does not augur well for the outcome. It is the curse of his relationship with Mephistopheles that communications always break down, since both he and his partner can think and act only according to the limitations of their nature. There exists an unbridgeable gulf between their respective habits of thought and style. While Faust moves on the level of the sublime, rationalizing his impatience, his insatiable curiosity, greed, and carnal desires in terms of ideal ends that, to his mind, justify the means, Mephistopheles, the pragmatist and Realpolitiker, while apparently coming closer to the mark, is equally erroneous in interpreting both Faust's means and Faust's ends from his own base perspective of the banality of evil. Thus, Faust may dream of possessing Helena, the prototype of classical beauty and of "das Ewig-Weibliche" (the evanescence of the Eternally Feminine); or he may dream of freedom arising from technocratic tyranny, even if his vision of freedom be predicated on illegitimate acquisitions, murder, and arson committed in his, Faust's, name.

But Mephistopheles is no dreamer, by any stretch of the imagination. He gets things done. Yet, the things that get done are seldom what they ought to be; least of all, when the doer is Mephistopheles. Seen from Mephisto's point of view, his dirty tricks are good public relations. He considers them legitimate, as long as they serve Faust's ends. The idealistic interpretation that a rationalizing Faust chooses to place on his own self-interested pursuits would be deemed quixotic and unrealistic by Mephistopheles, the Master of this World, whose reasoning conforms, after all, to that of his human colleagues, the politicians, fundraisers, and administrators on earth. Later, we shall see how little Goethe thinks of demagogical *Freiheitsapostel* (apostles of freedom) and of Faust's libertine fervor for the evanescent phenomena of feminine beauty.

It would be unfair, however, to accuse Mephisto of being intent on deceiving his companion. He and Faust just speak different languages. Hence, Faust is totally deaf to Mephisto's reminder that the ensuing act of conjuring phantoms out of thin (but heavily incensed) air is little more than quackery:

> *Meph.*: Dann muss fortan, nach magischem Behandeln,
>   Der Weihrauchsnebel sich in Götter wandeln
>   (*Faust II*, 6301 f.)

> (*Meph.*: Henceforward, as magic custom has bespoke,
>   Gods must appear out of that incense smoke)
>   (MacNeice, p. 178)[21]

Almost a hundred lines and two scenes later, Faust's magic act will be performed in a "deep theatre," which "seems to erect itself" from the suddenly fissured and upturned walls (*Faust II*, 6395 f.) forming the dimly lit "Rittersaal" ("Hall of the Knights"), where the Emperor and his entourage are assembled. The show itself takes place under dazzling lighting. That it is little more than an optical illusion, on the order of the show in Plato's cave, is suggested by the fact that its commentator, the court astrologer (himself a charlatan), is prompted by Mephistopheles. The latter, "emerging from the prompter's box," painstakingly explains his own role:

> *Meph.*: Von hier aus (i.e., from the prompter's box)
>   hoff' ich allgemeine Gunst,
>   Einbläsereien sind des Teufels Redekunst.
>   (*Faust II*, 6399 f.)

> (*Meph.*: As prompter all, I trust, will find me slick
>   Since promptings are the devil's rhetoric.)
>   (MacNeice, p. 184)

---

[21] Literally: ". . . subjected to magical treatment, / The incense smoke must change into Gods."

Helena's image, conjured up by Mephisto's rhetoric, is a ghost of pagan Beauty that ironically affects the Astrologer, a false apostle, in a manner not so different from the divine inspiration brought to Christ's apostles by the Pentecostal descent of the Holy Ghost: ". . . und hätt' ich Feuerzungen!" (*Faust II*, 6483) (". . . and had I tongues of fire!"). Mephisto's infernal pyrotechnics prove convincing enough to invite comparison with the divine and apostolic *linguae tanquam ignis* (Acts 2:3). Goethe's satire on the queer interplay of faith and quackery is enhanced by the Astrologer's earlier variation on a theme by Tertulian, "*credo quia absurdum*"—"Unmöglich ist's, drum eben glaubenswert" (*Faust II*, 6420) ("It is impossible, hence worthy of belief").

There are curious affinities between the "deep theatre" of Faust's magic show and the "dark gallery" where Mephistopheles, its prompter and director, had briefed Faust for his "trip" to the Mothers, and rehearsed (in spirit, at least) the events leading up to the present performance. For it is conceivable that Goethe, the author of these "very serious jests,"[22] plays on a pun concealed in

---

[22] Looking at the facetious aspects of Goethe's *Faust II* has seldom appealed to German scholars, who are generally awed by the "Olympian" image of Goethe they themselves have created, taking their cue from Eckermann, Goethe's rather humorless, dull, and mythologizing Boswell. Only recently has attention been paid to Goethe's own hints at the *serio ludere* that presided over the composition of *Faust II*. Not long before his death, Goethe referred to *Faust II* as "diese ernst gemeinten Scherze" ("these jests which are meant to be serious," [letter of November 24, 1831, to Sulpiz Boisserée]), and again as "diese sehr ernsten Scherze" ("these very serious jests," in his last letter, to Wilhelm von Humboldt, dated March 17, 1832). Ehrhard Bahr was the first urbane scholar to trace Goethe's irony throughout the symbolism in the writings of his last period (cf., *Die Ironie im Spätwerk Goethes*. ". . . diese sehr ernsten Scherze . . . ," [Erich Schmidt

the etymology of "Galerie"—a charade that I believe has hitherto escaped detection. The seventeenth-century German "Galerie" is derived from "Galiläa" (Galilee), a Hebrew word that means "circle," the ideal figure for eternity, and, coincidentally, the name of the province where Jesus was born. The site where Mephistopheles initiates Faust into the magic rites that will enable him to surface at the Emperor's court with the likenesses of Paris and Helena evokes like the "deep theatre," where this show will be performed, a *circle* not unlike the second circle of Dante's Hell, Helena's locale among the *Lussoriosi*, the Lustful (*Inferno* v, 64 f.). Its cyclical form reinforces the figure that dominates Mephisto's myth of the Mothers, the circular image of matrix, tripod, and womb, whence Memory and Imagination can conjure up long defunct and fictitious shadows to surface again. They are resurrected, it is true, in a spirit quite different from that of the Galilean.

Mephisto's prompting then, would suggest the production of a poetic illusion. But the grandiose Helena act (*Faust II*, Act iii), where Faust and Helen of Troy are seen consummating their union, was also conceived as nothing more than merely a poetic illusion. As we learn from *Paralipomenon 70* (Goethe v, 560), it was meant to

---

Verlag, Berlin, 1972]). Goethe, it seems, looked upon *Faust II* with a sense of humor that few of his critics were able to muster. Witness these lines to Zelter, dated January 4, 1831, which go far beyond *captatio benevolentiae*: "The first two acts of 'Faust' [II] are ready. Cardinal Este's exclamation, with which he thought he was honoring Ariosto, seems to be in order. . . ." The cardinal's compliment was indeed a strange one: "Messer Lodovico, dove trovaste mai tante coglionerie?" Goethe's source for this anecdote was C. L. Fernow, *Leben Lodovico Ariosto's des Göttlichen*, Zürich, 1809, p. 97.

represent, and does indeed show, the "half-truth" of Faust's imaginary communion with the essence of classical beauty. His ephemeral union with Helena, whom he has himself magically "drawn into life" (*Faust II*, 7439), again takes place inside a *circle*: it is fulfilled in the "Inner Court" and the "Shadowy Woods" of a castle "surrounded by a magic circle, inside which alone these semi-realities can come to fruition" ("dass das Schloss von einer Zaubergrenze umzogen ist innerhalb welcher allein diese Halbwirklichkeiten gedeihen können").[23] "Finstere Galerie," the implicit circle in Act I, where the conjuration of Helena is planned, the arena or "deep theatre" where it is executed, and, finally, the "magic circle" surrounding the castle where, in Act III, Faust and Helena appear to beget Euphorion, before son and mother forever return to the realm of shadows: these enchanted scenes have in common that they symbolize the ever-repeated and forever delusive truth of the illusionist *par excellence,* the poet and his magic art of animating life's lifeless images with the deceptive appearance of life. Inspired by the all-pervasive inventor of the "Et eritis sicut dii," his persuasive rhetoric creates the enchanting illusions of "semi-realities." They compete with the creation of the Divine Logos, and with that equally almighty daemon, Eros—the *Eros energoumenos* of Mephisto's prompting in *Lust.* For in one of Goethe's most deadly serious ironies, Eros is allowed to usurp that place "in the beginning" which the Gospel according to John (1:1) had assigned to the Creative Word: "So herrsche denn Eros, der alles begonnen" (*Faust II*, 8479) ("Let Eros rule, who was in the beginning") is the sirens' seductive song that accompanies the death-plunge of Wagner's flaming test-tube Homunculus into the

---

[23] *Paralipomenon 70*, dated December 16, 1816, summarizing the planned plot for *Faust II*, Acts I to IV (Goethe v, 557 ff.).

sea, where he is destined to be reborn in the cycles of life's evolution.

The audience never sees Faust's descent to the Mothers. This scene is witnessed through the nebulous veil of Mephisto's and Faust's creative Word. Eros, rather than Logos, is revealed as the mysterious force that draws the shadows of Paris and Helena out of mist and clouds ("Ein dunstiger Nebel . . . / . . . er wogt nach Wolkenart") (*Faust II*, 6440 f.). When the stage set, a Greek temple, seems suddenly animated by music, and Paris *dances* onto the scene in the measured steps of iambic pentameters, it becomes evident that he and Helena are little more than images, poetry set in motion by the concurrence of melodious rhythms:

> "Ein schöner Jüngling tritt im Takt hervor."
> (*ibid.*, 6450)

> ("There steps a comely youth with a dancer's tread.")
> (MacNeice, p. 186)

The spectacle must be viewed as phantasmagoria, not to be confused with reality. It may show the archetypal truth of classical beauty, but it remains deceptive, on the order of the phantom show watched by the prisoners in Plato's Cave.

The metaphor of Eros engendering the poetic harmonies of a verbal creation is darkly mirrored in the settings for Faust's imaginary trip to the Mothers and his hieratic return. Both "Finstere Galerie" and "ein tief Theater" emblematize the poetic process that brings forth fiction and its delusively realistic imagery by the poet's perilous descent into the appropriate Dantesque "dark circle" (or "gallery," or "Zaubergrenze") of the mind's infernal depths, where madness hovers as *furor poeticus*, and by Faust's re-emergence in the "deep" but brightly lit "theater" of consciousness. As Mephistopheles sends Faust off to the Mothers, his parting words hold a key to the poetic nature of this orphic descent: "Versinke stampfend, stampfend steigst du wieder" (*Faust II*, 6304) ("Sink by stamping, by stamping you will rise again"). The epanalepsis "stampfend, stampfend" *literally* suggests the poet counting his iambic pentameters by rhythmically stamping his foot, while it *figuratively* conveys the magic effect of his poetic production. For "aus dem Boden stampfen" is a metaphor for "conjuring up." What emerges from the dark descent *ad inferos*, a hybrid half truth, half illusion, "(. . .) neither light nor night. Twilight; a production of truth and untruth. A thing intermediate" (Letter to Friederike Oeser, Feb. 13, 1769; Goethe xviii, 121).[24] The purely poetic beauty and mythical unreality of Paris and Helena is ambiguously evoked by the astrologer's description of the "deep theatre" and its mysterious illumination within the twilight ambiance of the *Rittersaal* scene; it suggests the beam of a magic lantern:

> *Astrolog*: Ein tief Theater scheint sich aufzustellen.
> Geheimnisvoll ein Schein uns zu erhellen, (. . .)
> (*Faust II*, 6396 f.)

> (A deep theatre appears to rise,
> Mysteriously, a light [also: illusion] to enlighten us.)

[24] ". . . was ist Schönheit? Sie ist nicht Licht und nicht Nacht. Dämmerung; eine Geburt von Wahrheit und Unwahrheit. Ein Mittelding." (To Friederike Oeser, February 13, 1769; Goethe xviii, 121.) The same holds true for the principle of evil and its apparent metamorphoses:

> *Faust*: Ist es Schatten? ist's Wirklichkeit? (*Faust I*, 1249)
> (*Faust*: Is it a shadow? is it reality?)

asks Faust in the presence of the Protean poodle who is undergoing rapid and manifold changes, before he manifests himself as Mephistopheles.

"Scheint" and "Schein" are the key words in this couplet. They insistently hammer away at the theme of "appearance" and "illusion" ("scheinen," "Schein"), as both action (the verb "scheinen") and substance (the substantive "Schein") of the show about to begin. "Geheimnisvoll ein Schein uns zu erhellen" points both to the "mysterious lighting" on a stage (which is, itself, illusory), and to the very meaning of a fictitious performance that promises "mysteriously to enlighten us through an illusion," while simultaneously throwing light on "mysteries" by way of appearances that transcend reality but whose truth lies in their beauty. For, Goethe's linguistic instinct clearly detects the semantic link between the glittering shining splendors of "Schönheit" and "Schein," which is manifest in their common etymology: "Schönheit kommt von Schein (...)" ("Beauty is derived from appearance, illusion; it is an appearance, an illusion . . .") (*Schriften zur Kunst. Der Sammler und die Seinigen. 5. Brief*; Goethe XIII, 286).

7. Cyclical Symbols

In the complex charade of the *Finstere Galerie* and the *Rittersaal* scenes, the cyclical arena of this "deep theater" and the "magic circle" (*Zaubergrenze*) traced around the castle in Act III, where Faust will once again bring back to life, and embrace Helena's delusive image, symbolize the locale where the poetic illusion originates, the mind's Hades—an ironic matrix, womb and gate to the storehouse for archetypal phantoms. On the other hand, Mephisto's epic description of the Mothers personifies mysterious forces of Memory and Imagination; they weave the imagery of fiction into the seductive fabric that surfaces in the poeticizing artifice of the footlights. The dangerous descent *ad inferos* must be followed, we have seen, by an equally perilous return to lucidity that calls the poetic illusion into existence, calling it simultaneously into question. For it must be stressed again: whatever is brought back from the Orphic journey below can survive only on condition that it be not confused with reality. Faust's experience comes to naught when he fails to maintain the ironic distance separating the magician from the phantoms his act engenders, and the poet from the visions he structures.

From his prompter's box in the *Rittersaal* scene, Mephistopheles tries in vain to sound a warning: "So fasst Euch doch, und fallt nicht aus der Rolle!" (*Faust II*, 6501 ["Take hold of yourself, and don't fall out of character."])[25] Faust is as deaf to Mephisto's warning as he is blind to the irreality of the shadows he has brought back to light from the limbo of the collective unconscious—though, ironically, we have heard him accurately describe this sort of magic lantern show as "Des Lebens Bilder, regsam, ohne Leben" (*Faust II*, 6430 ["Life's pictures, moving, without life"]). He hopelessly confuses the illusion of Paris and Helena, which he has created, with reality; mistaking art for Nature, myth for truth, and Logos for Eros. In short, he behaves not unlike the crude spectator who shoots the villain on stage,[26] engaging, as he does, in shadow-boxing

[25] Ironically, Helena will have to address the same words to Mephistopheles, in the Helena act, where Mephisto burns with desire for Paris, much like Faust lusting for Helena in the *Rittersaal* theatre: "*Helena*: Du fällst / Ganz aus der Rolle" (*Faust II*, 9047f. ["Helena: You are falling / out of character"]).

[26] Every once in a while there is a clear hint at the discrepancies between the *illusion comique*, the "Halbwirklichkeiten" (semi-realities) of *Faust II* and the tangible world of reality: *e.g.*, when Homunculus "experiences" the geological revolutions of "Vulcanism," Thales warns: "Sei ruhig! Es war nur gedacht!" (*Faust II*, 7946 ["Calm down, It was only *thought*."]), i.e., fantasy, not reality.

with the phantom of Paris for Helena's ghost—all the while remaining impervious to Mephisto's sober remark that the images of Paris and Helena are of his, Faust's, own making, set in motion by Faust's own overheated imagination, and lifelessly moving across the stage as ghostly caricatures: "Machst du's doch selbst, das Fratzengeisterspiel" (*Faust II*, 6546 ["Yourself alone put on this grotesque phantom play"]).

Faust's uncontrolled lust for Helena seems indeed to imply that her image has arisen from a *bolgia* of his fantasy life that closely corresponds to the second circle of Dante's *Inferno*, where Helena's shadow is seen dwelling among the *Lussoriosi*, the Lustful. His attempted "Rape of Helena" (*Faust II*, 6548) ends with an explosion that strikes him down, while the conjured ghosts of Paris and Helena dissolve into thin air. The experience sours, not so much because Faust tried to rape the beauty that his own fantasies have created, for in this he acts pretty much as everyone else on earth. Nor does the attempt go wrong because, violating the code of aesthetics, it threatens to transgress into pornography; for, after all, Pygmalion has succeeded where Faust fails. It ultimately sours for two reasons: the first one founded in problems of semantics, wherever Mephisto's prompting or aid is involved; the second one based on an elementary law of poetics: poetic beauty exists to be contemplated; it cannot be physically embraced. Thus, on the figurative level of poetics, Faust's *échec* serves as a warning to the poet who is heedless that poetry's *substance* resides in its *form* that, engendered by Logos *and* Eros, is meant to delight mind and senses but vanishes when libidinous desire attempts to tear off its mysterious veil woven of myth. On the level of Goethe's secretive ironies, this paradox could hold the key to the concluding lines of *Faust II*: "Das Ewig-Weibliche / Zieht uns hinan" (*Faust II*, 12110 f.). "The eternally feminine / Attracts us," its polar (*and male*) opposite, bringing together both the ends and the means of the creative experience. In other terms, the mater-matrix of all potential beauty—the collective unconscious—attracts Eros and gives birth to Logos, the beauty of all potential verbal forms whose purely formal essence can be savored only from the safe distance that aesthetics and irony must establish between the viewer and the object of his vision, between Faust and his fantasies, between the author and his play, the poem and the reader.[27]

As *personae dramatis* at court and as players in the *Mummenschanz*—a play within the play—the Emperor and his courtiers are multiple mirrors reflecting Faust's own behavior. Like Faust, they are fated to mistake "counterfeit" money for legal tender, glitter for gold, ideas for reality, artifice for Nature, appearances for the substance of life, the stage for the world, and carnal knowledge for intellectual knowledge. As Faust emerges as the archetype of the "Northern Barbarian," he gradually merges with Goethe's idea of Lord Byron, the Romantic poet *par excellence*, greatly admired by the author of *Faust* (which the British poet, in 1820, introduced to the English reading public), but also sharply criticized by Goethe for his vain attempts to "usher the ideal into life," and for his failure to realize that "the ideal must remain rigorously divorced from vulgar reality."[28]

[27] Faust's "enthusiasm" had been his downfall, just as *furere*, the "possession by the God" augurs ill in Valéry's "poietics." Cf. "La Pythie."

[28] "Es ist eben ein Unglück, dass so ideenreiche Geister [wie Byron] ihr Ideal durchaus verwirklichen, ins Leben einführen wollen. Das geht einmal nicht, das Ideal und die gemeine Wirklichkeit müssen streng geschieden bleiben." To F. v. Müller, June

It is only logical that, in the Helena act, Euphorion, the paradoxical and short-lived offspring of Faust and Helena —the *ideal* of beauty—first appears on the scene with a golden lyre, like a young Phoebus (*Faust II*, 9620). He then takes flight and crashes like Icarus (*Faust II*, 9901), only to be revealed in his apotheosis as Lord Byron. Euphorion represents both the ephemeral triumph and the ultimate fiasco ordained by the *mésalliance* of Helena, the elusive embodiment of classical form and formality, and Faust, incarnating the Romantic hero's amorphous nostalgia for the infinite. For a moment, Faust achieves with Helena the illusion of savoring requited love, a state not unlike that "intellectual copulation" which Valéry held in store as the climax for *Lust*, a *moment d'éternité*, the crowning of a Cartesian Faust's relationship with the heroine of the first *Mon Faust* fragment (*Lust IV, Moment II*, P.ii, 1414). While Valéry's Faust dreams of a coitus between consciousness and sensitivity reflected in consciousness, which will engender poetry in the abstract (*ibid.*), Goethe's Faust and Helena physically beget the ambiguous incarnation of the Romantic poet devoted to classical meters and masters: Euphorion-Byron (*Faust II*, 9599 ff.), the formal imitator of Pope, is brought forth by neo-Classicism (i.e., Helena in a Renaissance environment); but by virtue of his poetry's very climate and themes, he is Faust's son, the true child of Romanticism. A flighty product of genius, he briefly incarnates an ideal fusion without hopes for duration—the ephemeral issue of an incompatible union between Classicism and Ro-

---

13, 1824; Goethe xxiii, 350. "Im Idealen kommt alles auf die *élans*, im Realen auf die Beharrlichkeit an." *Max. und Refl.* 926; Goethe ix, 619.

manticism. Thus he may stand as an allegory for the
"interlude to Faust," as the Helena act was first conceived
(about 1800) to represent a "Klassisch-romantische Phan-
tasmagorie" (Ausg. Letzt. Hand, IV, 229 ff.). Euphorion-
Byron's Romantic nostalgia will grow wings too feeble
to carry him on his vain flight toward an unattainable
classical ideal, but also fragile enough to allow him to
share the classically tragic fate of Icarus (*Faust II*, 9901).
His frail body "disappears" in Hades, leaving behind his
gown and his lyre, while his "halo" rises heavenwards,
not, as the hero's reward, to become a constellation, but as
a "comet" bearing ill omens from the aged Goethe to his
contemporary colleagues who, like Friedrich Schlegel and
Hölderlin, attempt to wed the Barbarian Romantic North
to the classical beauty of Greece.

From Hades, Euphorion's voice is heard calling Helena,
his mother: "Lass mich im düstern Reich, / Mutter, mich
nicht allein!" (*ibid.*, 9905 f. ["Do not abandon me,
Mother! me alone in the tenebrous realm!"]). Dissolving
in a cloud, Helena follows her son, asserting the tragic
sense of life inherent in classical beauty: "Dass Glück und
Schönheit dauerhaft sich nicht vereint" (*ibid.*, 9940 ["That
good fortune and beauty form no lasting union"]). Only
Helena's gown and her veil remain in Faust's arms. They
signify, like Euphorion's gown and lyre on the ground,
that poetry's beauty, be it Classical or Romantic, resides
like Maya's splendor in its veil and its symbols. It is a
delicate beauty that escapes the libidinous embrace, speaking only to what Valéry once so aptly called *la sensibilité
de l'intellect* (Cah. XII, 68). The beauty we can grasp is
the beauty created by our fantasies: a phantom conjured
up by our intellectual sensitivity, it vanishes at the touch
of passion, leaving behind a fabric woven by Imagination
and Memory, the two seductive Fays in Valéry's *Les*

Fées. In his repeated attempts to embrace Helena's phantom—the archetype of classical beauty, created by his own demon and his imagination—Faust has acted out a charade expressed in clear and distinct terms by one of his dramatic predecessors, Cipriano, in Calderón's "Prodigious Magician":[29]

Pues sólo fantasmas hallo   (For I only find phantoms,
Adonde hermosuras busco   Where I seek beauty . . .)
    (. . .) (*El mágico prodigioso*, jornada III)[29a]

[29] On October 17, 1812, i.e., during the long period of work on the Helena act (completed in the late 1820s), Goethe wrote to Knebel on Calderón's *El mágico prodigioso*, which he had read in Einsiedel's translation: "Es ist das Sujet vom Dr. Faust mit einer unglaublichen Grossheit behandelt" ("It is the topic of Dr. Faust, transposed with an incredible grandeur").

[29a] Hederich's *Gründliches mythologisches Lexicon* (1724)—one of Goethe's sources for Greek mythology—describes Euphorion as "a son of Achilles and Helena, engendered on the Fortunate Islands [i.e., the Canaries], and born with wings. He owed his name to the fertility of the land. Jupiter fell in love with him, and, since he could not seduce him, he slew him with a thunderbolt on the island of Melos, while his victim was fleeing from him. . . ." Goethe's assimilation of the Euphorion myth to the literary allegory of the Helena act is all the more poignant, since Faust's weaknesses resemble those of the impetuous Achilles. Like Achilles—who burned with passion for Helena ever since he first saw her on the walls of Troy—Faust desired her passionately in the "deep theatre" of the *Rittersaal*. Achilles, obsessed by Helena's image, embraces her first in a dream, without deriving satisfaction from this illusion. Similarly, Faust lusts for Helena in a dream, after the *Rittersaal* incident, resting in his study. His dream is related by Homunculus (*Faust II*, 6904-20). The parallel becomes even more striking when Faust embraces Helena's phantom long after her death, begetting Euphorion. Achilles is said, likewise, to have "wed" Helena after her death on the island of Leuce, where Euphorion was engendered and born (Pausanias, *Laconia*, ch. 19; Ptolemaeus Hephaestionis, *Historia nova ad variam eruditionem*, book VI).

8. *Goethe's Faust: an Apostle of Counterfeit Freedom*

The long series of Faust's overreachings started with
his impatient contemplation of the sign of the Macrocosm.
It ends (or does it really end?)[30] with his beatific vision
of himself as the future liberator of mankind, who, build-
ing a dike against the sea, anticipates "standing on free
soil with free people," while Mephisto's lemures—far
from wresting land from the sea—are in fact digging his
grave.

Much ink has been spilled on the meaning of Faust's
last words with their foreboding of a freedom cautiously
couched in clauses where the subjunctive mood predomi-
nates:

> Solch ein Gewimmel möcht' ich sehn,
> Auf freiem Grund mit freiem Volke stehn.
> Zum Augenblicke dürft' ich sagen:
> Verweile doch, du bist so schön!
> Es kann die Spur von meinen Erdetagen
> Nicht in Äonen untergehn.—
> Im Vorgefühl von solchem hohen Glück
> Geniess' ich jetzt den höchsten Augenblick.
> (*Faust II*, 11579 ff.)

> (Oh to see such activity,
> Treading free ground with people that are free!
> Then could I bid the passing moment:

[30] It would seem that not even Faust's death puts an end to
the results of his overreaching. He had deceived himself as to the
limits of his "freedom" to live up to the terms of his wager with
Mephistopheles, for, a plaything of the same divine grace that
now deprives Mephistopheles of the "freedom" to claim his prey,
he is (and was from the beginning of time) predestined for
salvation, one of the Lord's mysteriously selected "Elect," in the
best Calvinist tradition.

"Linger a while, thou art so fair!"
The traces of my earthly days can never
Sink in the aeons unaware,
And I, who feel ahead such heights of bliss
At last enjoy my highest moment—this.)
(MacNeice, p. 287)

As he stands before us, in the final act, with one foot
in Hades, the blind Faust and his false prophecies—his gift
of delusive treasures—had been anticipated in the *Mummenschanz*, where, under the mask of Plutus, the blind
god of riches and Hades, he had tempted human greed
with the glitter of poetic treasures that went up in flames
and smoke, singeing those who had tried to put their
hands on this counterfeit, purely verbal, wealth. Now,
the dying Faust's last putative clauses seem to indicate
that the hero may at last be willing to content himself
with mere θεωρία, the pure contemplation of an ideal,
no matter how far removed it may be from any possible
(or even probable) reality. It is this semi-resigned acceptance of a contemplative role—Faust's ideal vision of
vita activa transcending the present moment, but eter-
nalizing it through the vicarious enjoyment of a potential
fulfillment in the future—that contributes to the otherwise strangely undeserved salvation of a hero who, on the
threshold of death, is obviously more concerned with *ars
vivendi* than with *ars moriendi*, the dying sinner's pre-
paredness to meet his Maker. On the other hand, Mephistopheles the realist makes his mistake and ultimately loses
his prey to the subtleties of Faust's grammar, one is led
to suspect. For he remains impervious to the distinction
between Faust's idealistic vision, expressed in the subjunctive mood, and a reality markedly removed from his
fantasy about the future.

Finally, it must be pointed out that, in their eagerness
to transform Faust's ultimate self-deception into an apotheosis of social significance, German critics have often
closed their eyes to the mature Goethe's skepticism with
regard to the semantics of "freedom." Nurtured by the
experience of the French Revolution, this notion embraces
the polar aspects of "liberty" as "political freedom," and as
the unbridled debauchery of "libertinism." Both bring
forth particularly unpleasant traits of behavior in the
Germans for whom, to Goethe's mind, politeness and
good taste are not precisely household words, and who
are apt to mistake courtesy for a manifestation of insincerity. Witness the remark of the Baccalaureus: "Im
Deutschen lügt man, wenn man höflich ist" (*Faust II*,
6771 ["The German lies, when he is courteous"]). Where
coarseness and sincerity are posited as equivalents, there
is little room left for good taste and freedom of mind:
"Der Deutsche hat Freiheit der Gesinnung, und daher
merkt er nicht, wenn es ihm an Geschmacks- und Geistes-
freiheit fehlt" (*Max. und Refl.* 80; Goethe ix, 507; ["The
German has freedom of opinions, and hence he does not
notice his lack of freedom of taste and mind"]). Taste and
polite parlance go hand in hand: "Geschmack ist ein Euphemismus. Deutsche haben keinen Geschmack, weil sie
keinen Euphemismus haben und zu derb sind" (To
Riemer, Oct. 26, 1813; Goethe xxii, 697; ["Taste is a euphemism. The Germans have no taste, since they have
no euphemisms, because they are too crude"]). "Euphemisms" are defined as "Schonungen des Ohrs mit Aufre-
gung des Sinnes" (*Max. und Refl.* 1018; Goethe ix, 629)
—they spare the ear from being offended, while they
excite the senses and enhance meaning.

The Germanic sense of "freedom," with all that it implies of brutal license, drunkenness, brawling coarseness,

and invective, reaches a degrading climax in *Auerbachs Keller in Leipzig.* Led on by Mephistopheles, the inebriated *convives* ("Es lebe die Freiheit! Es lebe der Wein!" [*Faust I,* 2244] "Long live liberty! and good wine!") metaphorically turn into the equivalent of Ulysses' companions metamorphosed by Circe into swine: "Uns ist ganz kannibalisch wohl, / Als wie fünfhundert Säuen" (*Faust I,* 2293 f.; ["We feel quite cannibalically well / just like five hundred sows!"]). Their spectacle produces the following exchange between Mephistopheles and Faust (a late addition to the *Urfaust* text):

> *M.*: Das Volk ist frei, seht an, wie wohl's ihm geht!
> *F.*: Ich hätte Lust, nun abzufahren.
> *M.*: Gib nur erst acht, die Bestialität
>   Wird sich gar herrlich offenbaren. (*Faust I,* 2295)

> (*M.*: The people are free, look how well off they are!
> *F.*: I would like to depart now.
> *M.*: Watch them closely, their bestiality
>   Will manifest itself most gloriously.)

There is a note by the aged Goethe that seems tailormade to characterize Faust on the threshold of death, a ruthless tyrant and conqueror who sees himself in the lofty role of a future liberator: "Wie man denn niemals mehr von Freiheit reden hört, als wenn eine Partei die andere unterjochen will und es auf weiter nichts angesehen ist, als dass Gewalt, Einfluss und Vermögen aus einer Hand in die andere gehen sollen." ("One never hears more talk about freedom than in times when one party wants to enslave the other and when actually nothing is involved beyond the changing of supreme power, influence and wealth from one hand to another." *West-Oestlicher Divan,* "Noten und Abhandlungen. Nachtrag," Goethe III, 467.) *Freiheitsapostel,* apostles of freedom, are "wolves in sheep-

skins," who aim only to gain absolute power (*Xenien aus
dem Nachlass* 8, Goethe II, 499). For the contemporary of
Robespierre and Saint-Just, the calls for "political freedom" and universal suffrage are little more than demagogical invitations to participate in universal "suffering": "Ich habe die Tage / Der Freiheit gekannt, / Ich
hab sie die Tage / Der Leiden genannt." ("I have known
the days / Of freedom / I have called them / The days
of suffering" [*Epigrammatisch;* Goethe II, 186]).

> Alle Freiheitsapostel, sie waren mir immer zuwider;
>   Willkür suchte doch nur jeder am Ende für sich.
> Willst du viele befrein, so wag es, vielen zu dienen.
>   Wie gefährlich das sei, willst du es wissen?
>   Versuch's!

> (All apostles of freedom were always repugnant
>   to me;
>   All sought arbitrary power for themselves in the
>   end.
>   If you want to free the masses, dare to serve the
>   masses.
>   You want to know how dangerous this may be?
>   Then try it!)
>   (*Venezianische Epigramme* 50; Goethe I, 233)

These passages, taken at random, may serve to throw
some light on the meaning of Faust's last words. They
can be literally applied to his "apotheosis" of wishful
thinking, which shows him, the self-serving pragmatist,
as an "idealist" who deludes himself into believing that
he is an apostle of freedom, the technocratic servant of the
masses. On the threshold of death, he is physically blinded
by Care, while intellectually and emotionally he blinds
himself to the realities of his role as a reckless usurper,

whose pirate fleet has just returned with treasures plundered on the seven seas. In a last burst of grandiose self-deception, he sees himself reclaiming arable land from the hostile sea that he intends to control through a system of dikes. Yet, iniquitously he stands on land bestowed upon him by an iniquitous Emperor, as a reward for questionable services rendered in worse than questionable ways. His holdings were only recently increased by the humble domain of Philemon and Baucis which, coveted by Faust, had been conquered for him by Mephistopheles and his uncanny helpers, the Three Violent Fellows, through arson and brutal murder: the idyl of rustic life is ruthlessly eradicated to make way for a senseless and all but fallacious concept of growth and progress.

Faust fails to share Goethe's insights on the dangers of ideal visions that are likely to cause men with great ambition to unleash universal misery: "Allgemeine Begriffe und grosser Dünkel sind immer auf dem Wege, entsetzliches Unglück anzurichten" ("Universal notions and great presumption always combine to set in motion horrible misfortunes"). (*Maximen und Reflexionen* 471; Goethe IX, 558.) It would seem fortunate that Goethe puts an end to Faust's pilgrimage on Earth, before his apparently-so-benevolent ambitions can cause any more damage that might further imperil his ultimate redemption. For, in view of the consistent discrepancies between Faust's ideal visions and the disproportionately crude realities they engender, it may well be suspected that his prospective ventures in land reclamation from the sea will work out to be less generous, less humanitarian, and considerably more primitive and tyrannical than his noble rationalizations would lead him (and us) to believe. The Pascalian "qui veut faire l'ange, fait la bête," fully applies to Faust's beatific vision of the technological blessings

growing out of the bestial savagery that reaped the bucolic
lives of Philemon and Baucis. Its truth was anticipated by
Mephistopheles, the realist, impervious to the irrationalist
workings of God's wondrous ways:

> *Meph.*: Der kleine Gott der Welt bleibt stets von
>   gleichem Schlag,
>   Und ist so wunderlich als wie am ersten Tag.
>   Ein wenig besser würd' er leben,
>   Hättst du ihm nicht den Schein des Himmellichts
>   gegeben;
>   Er nennt's Vernunft und braucht's allein,
>   Nur tierischer als jedes Tier zu sein. (*Prologue in
>   Heaven*, 281 ff.)

> (*Meph.*: The little god of the world, one can't reshape,
>   reshade him:
>   He is as strange to-day as that first day you made him.
>   His life would not be so bad, not quite,
>   Had you not granted him a gleam of Heaven's light;
>   He calls it Reason, uses it not the least
>   Except to be more beastly than any beast.) (MacNeice,
>   p. 14)

But if Reason, the Lord's gift to man, is little more than
a mere "semblance" (*Schein*) of Heaven's light, Faust's
fallacious reasoning, his rationalizations, may not be taken
too seriously by the very source of these fallacies, Reason's
supernatural and presumably benevolent Donor. Hence,
in the end, even Faust's monumental self-deceptions and
crimes enter into the mysterious plan of salvation that
(unintelligible to Mephistopheles) the Lord's kindly dis-
position has predestined for his strangely errant servant
Faust.

9. Goethe's Faust: Romantic Genius and Flawed Modern Man

In the final analysis, we have seen Goethe's Faust emerge as the embodiment of the "modern" spirit and the Romantic "genius"—as they were defined in anything but flattering terms in "Shakespeare und kein Ende" (Goethe XIV, 755 ff.). By contrast, the hero of classical tragedy, a plaything of merciless fate, in the end must always submit to "what shall be since it has to be" (*ein Sollen*). His ultimate achievement (*das Vollbringen*) is the knowledge that his predetermined fate is inescapable, that iron necessity has cancelled out all efforts by himself or others (*ein Wollen*) to outwit the Fates. In his erroneous striving, the hero of classical tragedy accepts his human condition, which demonstrates the inadequacy of his "will" when measured against the *force majeure* of a fate that is preordained and will strike him down, regardless of moral values, for it governs beyond good and evil. The saving principle, if there is one, would be the realization of his fate, the consciousness he gains of his condition, which endows him with the greatness of human dignity. The dying Faust, however, deluded by boundless faith in the "freedom" of his "will," remains unaware of his situation. He is incapable of seeing the extent to which his will exceeds his capabilities. He is the "modern" hero par excellence—in Goethe's terminology, a title of dubious distinction. The truly "modern" flaw that Goethe ascribes to Shakespeare's Hamlet, Macbeth, Brutus, and Coriolanus applies with a vengeance to Faust: "genug, ein Wollen, das über die Kräfte eines Individuums hinausgeht, ist modern" (*op.cit.*; Goethe XIV, 763; ["in short, a volition that goes beyond the strength of an individual, is modern"]).

Faust seems indeed to exemplify the "Romantic genius" —not as the German Romantics would visualize him but in Goethe's critical perspective. Half passionate intellectual, half frustrated sentimentalist, intemperate in his sensuality (which, more often than not, he humorlessly confuses with lofty ideals), and always extreme, he never tires of his vain attempts to break out of the human condition. The very antipode of his author, he trades realities for a nebulous fantasy world of "ideals." He fatally mistakes the predetermined patterns of his always-predictable behavior for expressions of his "free will." Faust's wisdom may prevail in matters that do not involve his own passions and ambitions; e.g., when, in a scene modeled on Christ's temptation by the Devil, Mephistopheles shows him the power, the glory, and the treasures of this world, from the summit of a high mountain (*Faust II*, Act iv, 10075 ff.). But his wisdom fails him when his eagerness to clutch the "ideal" again and again abolishes his better judgment, erasing the borderline between intuitive understanding (*Anschauen*) and the desire to blend into one with the object of his passionate, all-too-passionate contemplation.

In his brilliant lecture on Goethe (1932) Valéry calls Faust "l'impatience même" (P.i, 535). His haste to embrace phantasms, mere appearances (*Schein*), without attempting to verify whether they partake of any tangible reality (*Sein*), would make him a poor candidate for *genius* in the classical sense, so modestly depicted in the famous dictum attributed to Buffon, as "no more than a greater aptitude for patience."[31] His restless attitude goes contrary to Goethe's definition of his own genius, whose secret, apparently derived from Buffon's concept, he once

[31] Quoted by Hérault de Séchelles, *Voyage à Montbard*, ed. Aulard, p. 11.

confided to F. von Müller in these terms: "Ich lasse die Gegenstände ruhig auf mich einwirken, beobachte dann diese Wirkung und bemühe mich, sie treu und unverfälscht wiederzugeben; dies ist das ganze Geheimnis, was man Genialität zu nennen beliebt" (*Letzte Lebensjahre*; Goethe xxiii, 824; ["I patiently suffer (. . .) the objects of my observation to act upon me, then I examine this effect and attempt to reproduce it with precision and without falsifying it; this is the whole secret of what one likes to call genius"]).

Nor would Faust fit the formula proposed by Valéry's Mephistophelian Serpent: "Génie! O longue impatience" ("Ebauche d'un serpent," P.i, 144). Rather than reversing Buffon's *bon mot*, it brings precision to its meaning by the introduction of an oxymoron that postulates the tension between impatient expectation and the unexpected chance event of *la trouvaille*, on which all productive activity depends. This "long impatience" paradoxically corresponds to a patient *attente*, the constant readiness and longing for the creative spark that will bring the intuition of truth or beauty, while allowing a clear knowledge of the distinction which exists between art and phenomena of Nature. In this sense, Goethe specifies that genius "begreift, dass Kunst eben darum Kunst heisse, weil sie nicht Natur ist" (*Wilhelm Meisters Wanderjahre* II, 8; Goethe viii, 272; ["(genius) apprehends that art is called art, precisely because it is *not* Nature"]). As the aged Goethe conceives of it, genius respects convention, seeing in its restraints what the best minds have agreed to regard as both necessary and excellent (*ibid.*). But Faust is hardly the man to be awed by convention or bound by formal constraints. He is badly lacking in that "greater aptitude for patience" (the eighteenth-century definition of genius attributed to Buffon). He has neither the paradoxical "longue impatience" ascribed to genius by Valéry's Serpent, nor does he show that quiet expectation of the propitious moment that leads, through repeated "experiments" (*Versuche*) in the observation (*Anschauen*) of phenomena to that intuitive grasp of essentials which Goethe equates with genius. Faust's rare flashes of insight tend to vanish as suddenly as they come. His habitual impatience leaves him ill-equipped for the task of sorting out his mind's passions from his libido's appetites. He seems equally inept when it comes to distinguishing the phenomenal from the ontal world.

10. The Prelude to "Faust II" and Valéry's "Les Fées" Revisited

The attempt to explore the conflicting views of Goethe and his protagonist have led us from the first scene of *Faust I*, over the prelude to *Faust II* (Act One, "Anmutige Gegend"), steeped in the atmosphere of *The Tempest* and *A Mid-Summer Night's Dream*, to the liturgical pastiche of the play's finale, so close to the ending of certain *autos* and *comedias* by Calderón. It remains for us briefly to examine the differences between Goethe's Faust and Valéry's in *Les Fées*, which, as we suggested earlier, is largely modeled on these two scenes. Valéry's variations on "Anmutige Gegend" and on the magnetism of das *Ewig-Weibliche* afford him an opportunity to oppose his Cartesian Faust—skeptical of sense impressions and always bent upon narrowing down experience and thought to utter precision—to Goethe's Faust, whose mind's easy virtue makes him prone to fall for every nebulous delusion of his own day-dreaming and make believe.

As the curtain rises upon *Faust II* and *Les Fées*, Faust is first seen lying unconscious on the ground, surrounded by elves and little Fays. Benevolent and compassionate in "Anmutige Gegend," where they symbolize Nature's healing four elements, they are more mischievous in *Les Fées*. Here they turn out to be part of that intricate medley of now intelligent, then again disappointingly stupid and distracting, flashes that, in their totality, constitute Valéry's concept of the human mind—*Mélange c'est l'esprit* (P.i, 286 et passim). Pertaining to external Nature, Goethe's Shakespearean elves are medicinal powers of paganism; impervious to questions of good and evil, they pour balm on the wound inflicted on Faust by his sickly Christian conscience. Valéry's little Fays, by contrast, are allegories of inner forces—as we have seen—on the order of Descartes' "animal spirits"; their subtle and sanguine fluidity carries the flow of deceptive images, produced by humors and nervous reactions, to the threshold of consciousness, where Imagination and Memory—the two adult Fays—will lead them into lucidity, the daylight world of the mind. To sum up, the whole scene of Valéry's *féerie dramatique* is evocative of *le théâtre dans un cerveau*, or the brain as a theatre, a skull-like dome enclosing the manifold convolutions of elements borrowed from Nature and Art, vegetative life and life of the mind, with Faust's awakening consciousness lying roughly on the spot that, in Descartes' drawings of the brain, is the location of the pineal gland, meeting place of body and mind.

Thus, Goethe's Faust draws his vital strength and revival from the healing powers of external Nature. But Art and Nature, deception and Truth, are uncannily intertwined both in the locale and the seductive artifices of the forces that reawaken Valéry's hero on a stage that reveals itself as the very theatre of his mind. Here he struggles like the Descartes of the *Méditation première* in an effort to distinguish between the irreality of his dream and the realities of his waking existence, unsure whether truth comes to him from a divine source, or whether he is the victim of "un mauvais génie, non moins rusé que trompeur et puissant, qui a employé toute son industrie à [le] tromper." In this sense, Maurice Bémol has rightly intuited that the Fays are "en somme assez méphistophéliques," holding out, as they do, the temptation of absolute rule over "tout l'Univers humain" ("Le jeune Valéry et Goethe," *Revue de littérature comparée* 34:35 [1960]). Although he feels exhilarated by the Fays' "magic" (their poetry), Faust knows how to resist their enchantment. We have seen how he regains consciousness, half succumbing to their charms, half warding them off, and ultimately revolting against their seductive promises of wealth and glory that only bring about the realization of the irremediable hollowness of human pursuits and of life's never-ending wants and delusions. His refusal echoes in a negative vein the wager of Goethe's Faust with Mephistopheles:

> Werd' ich zum Augenblicke sagen:
> Verweile doch! du bist so schön!
> Dann magst du mich in Fesseln schlagen,
> Dann will ich gern zugrunde gehn! (*Faust I*, 1699 ff.)

> (If ever I say to the passing moment
> 'Linger a while! Thou art so fair!'
> Then you may cast me into fetters,
> I will gladly perish then and there!) (MacNeice, p. 59)

But unlike Goethe's Faust, who dies in the delusive preview of a future that will never come, thus vicariously enjoying the unreality of that passing moment, Valéry's Faust, imbued with his author's wisdom that "Vivre est à chaque instant manquer de quelque chose" (P.ɪ, 618), refuses the illusory triumph offered him by the two adult Fays, Imagination and Memory. He is aware that any gifts they may procure will dissolve into dissatisfaction, into the unavoidable taste of ashes that comes with the ever-renewed realization of the inescapable prison of creatureliness. In a sort of Nietzschean *amor fati* and without grandiose postures he accepts his mortality, renouncing the illusions of a godlike glory for a tragic type of lucidity. Thus, his destiny is determined by his Cartesian *bon sens*, and decreed in accordance with his desire for lucid integrity, by the *farior*, the oracular speech of the Fays. The measured rhythms of their poetry echo the counterpoint of his inner voices—the voices of his intimate and ineluctable *Fates*. Imagination and Memory function as his Muses. In their interaction, they create and resurrect the variable selves whose total amounts to the ever-changing dreams and intellectual attitudes of Faust's "constant" self. In the spirit of Rimbaud's "JE est un autre," (Letter to Georges Izambard, dated Charleville, May [13], 1871) they metamorphose the "constant" self into an instrument of *poiesis*, through which pass the instantaneous creations of thought, visions, rhythmical patterns of sound and meaning, reveries.

The colorful tapestry on which Valéry's Faust is seen in a swoon when the curtain rises on *Les Fées*, points back to a literary souvenir and ahead to the very meaning of the Fays. Woven by Memory and Imagination, this colorful carpet is, no doubt, simultaneously meant to be a charade for "Am farbigen Abglanz haben wir das Leben" (*Faust II*, 4727). In a literal sense, this rich fabric is the "underlying ground" for Faust's reawakening to the splendors of the artful yarns the Fays will intertwine into a seductive fabric of poetry, in their enchanting attempts to entice the hero into their fantasy world. Woven by Imagination and Memory, this tapestry is as much of Faust's own making as the images of Helena and Paris brought back by Goethe's Faust from his trip *ad inferos* are creations of his fancy. But unlike Goethe's Faust, whose poetic vision vicariously transforms the rainbow's "colorful reflection," an optical phenomenon without substance, into the very essence of "life"—the awakening hero of *Les Fées* rationally grasps and narrows down the nature of the Fays' *charmes* (*carmina*). While he is willing to delight in their poetic illusion, he refuses to be deluded into confusing art with Nature, fiction with reality. He lucidly faces his deceptive Muses and Fates, confronting them with the acceptance of his human fate, which allows the mind to be exalted by poetry but not to mistake its aesthetic enchantment and extra-temporal symbolism for "life" itself and the promise of immortality. A Cartesian skepticism permeates the Gallic courtesy with which he lends a willing ear to the Fays' incantatory sirens' song. He enjoys their classical alexandrines without showing any willingness to suspend his critical judgment or his polite but insistent disbelief.

By contrast, forever embracing ghostly fantasies of his own (or Mephisto's) making that (like all creations) arise *ex nihilo* to turn again into nothingness, Goethe's Faust never learns from experience when to distrust the promptings of his mephistophelian Muse, or his own visionary impulses. Valéry's Faust, so much closer to his author's mentality, seems to partake of Valéry's wisdom, which elsewhere establishes that "nous sommes par nature condamnés à vivre dans l'imaginaire et dans ce qui ne peut être complété. Et c'est vivre" (P.i, 381). In the end, he will muster his common sense and the Cartesian resources of methodical doubt, in an ever-so-French and courteous effort to resist the temptations of a Beauty forever tantalizing, which Memory and Imagination spread out before his enchanted senses.[32] If he responds to the "traditional Muse's kiss" (Blüher, 102), he does so while still in a swoon, yet, conscious of his response. When he reaches the state of lucidity, he may well succumb to the Fays' *Charmes*, their classical *vers libres* and alexandrines; but he respects the *noli me tangere* of frail poetic Beauty. In this sense, he escapes the ironic crudities that Goethe intentionally built into his Faust, who twice invokes Helena's classical Beauty by magic acts of poetry, and who twice feels her dissolve into thin air under his libidinous embrace. For, as the very stage sets "Finstere Galerie" and "Ein tief Theater" foreshadow the symbolical "meaning" of the Mothers scene in *Faust II*; and as the tapestry on which Valéry Faust is resting forebodes the "farbigen Abglanz," the "colorful reflection" of his dialogue with the Fays—a dialogue evoking "fictions" rather than "facts" of life: so the Mothers scene with Faust's rape *manqué* of Helena's image foreshadows the operatic libretto of his only apparent wish-fulfillment with Helena in Act III, which, in the end, turns out to be (like their first embrace) no more than a poetic illusion—this time, of epic proportions but illusory all the same. It leaves him "holding" the empty cloud into which her delusive shadow

[32] Karl A. Blüher, too, clearly identifies "das Reich der Feen" ("the Fays' realm") with the "Scheinwelt der Poesie" ("the illusory universe of poetry"), while he somewhat simplistically takes Valéry's line at its face value: "Mais, MUSE que j'écoute et GRACE que je vois" (P.II, 400), disregarding the Fays' ironic double duty as Muse and Grace, and as allegories for Faust's Memory and Imagination, the mysterious and undefinable forces that preside over the exercise of poetry. Cf. Blüher, *Strategie des Geistes, Paul Valérys Faust* (*Analecta Romanica*, Heft 10), Frankfurt a.M., o.D., 101.

vanishes to blend, in the beginning of the following act, with the nebulous image of the Romantic and Christian martyr Gretchen (*Faust II*, 10039 ff.). The "Northern Barbarian" exemplar of *das Ewig-Weibliche* and her Hellenic counterpart float away in a cloud that, eventually separating their images, carries each one in the direction of her native clime, while Faust is left behind in the tender care of his companion, Mephistopheles, who tempts him with the glories and riches of this world from the top of "A High Mountainous Area" (*Hochgebirg*).

The equivalent of these incidents is compressed in *Les Fées* with a maximum of economy. The progress of Goethe's Faust leads from his very real copulation with the *Romantic*, petty-bourgeoise Gretchen, to his bold but elusive recovery of the *classical* Ideal, his intellectual vision metamorphosed into a sensuous union with Helena, the tragic Queen of Sparta. This pilgrimage from anticlimax to climax is telescoped in *Les Fées*, to find its parallel in the enchantment experienced by Valéry's hero, when he savors the *classical* poetry of his Northern Fays, who are *Romantic* creations *par excellence*. At the same time, the Fays perform the role of Mephisto, tempting his companion with the treasures of this world. In Goethe's *Faust*, we become aware of Helena succumbing to Faust's love, when she changes from the rhymeless pentameters of Greek antiquity to modern meters and rhymes, thereby decisively moving into Faust's world. Valéry uses a similar device, but he reverses the role of the characters, shifting the powers of seduction from Faust to his female interlocutors. Here it is Faust who responds: enchanted by the Fays' classical verse, he suddenly passes from prose to poetry, imitating their example. But unlike Goethe's Faust, he does not fall victim to the illusion his own mind has staged. Poetry, in Valéry definition, is written "by the ear," and his Faust knows that he is moving in the poet's unreal, or surrealist universe of dreams: "Je suis sûr que je dors, si je crois mes oreilles" (P.II, 398). He is aware of the Fays' true nature: "Tisseuses du Hasard," they embody Imagination—his ingenuity (*ingenium*)—and Memory—the precarious power that provides points of reference for his Cartesian *bon sens* (*iudicium*). Rhetorical devices of invention and imitation, they are his "Muse" and his "Grace" ("Mais MUSE que j'écoute et GRACE que je vois" [P.II, 400]), who weave the Helena veil of classical poetry that, unlike his Goethean model, he is careful not to confuse with the stuff of which reality is made.

11. *Pure Poetry—Forever Unfinished*

Among the technical facets of Goethe's *Faust*, which did not escape Valéry's scrutiny, are its episodic structure, its predominantly lyrical mood, and the slow composition of its scenes, written not in the order of their sequence in the play, but by continuous touches and retouches. In 1916, comparing Shakespeare and Goethe as playwrights, he jotted these observations on *Faust* into his *Cahiers*: "Les personnages tiennent des discours qui visent à la profondeur, au lyrisme. Il y a de l'incohérence, de l'inachevé, du contradictoire, du simili-profond. La pièce se forme par *touches*, ou scènes séparées" (Cah. VI, 319). Much of what Valéry finds incoherent, contradictory, and pseudo-profound in Goethe's *Faust* is due to the insufficiencies of rather bland translations by authors from Nerval to Blaze de Bury and Lichtenberger. But seen in the perspective of Valéry's "poietics," his critique amounts less to a condemnation of structural flaws in Goethe's *Faust* than to an enumeration of criteria, some of which would bring it into the orbit of "pure poetry."

Different from prose, whose essence it is to "perish,"
"c'est-à-dire d'être 'comprise'" (P.ɪ, 1501), pure poetry
can contradict itself (*ibid.*), as does Goethe's *Faust*, and
offer like music "une diversité de variantes ou de solutions
du même sujet" (*ibid.*). Valéry frankly admits to having
been blamed for his practice "d'avoir donné plusieurs
textes du même poème, et même contradictoires" (*ibid.*),
a criticism that might well apply to the various processions
in *Faust II* (*Mummenschanz, Klassische Walpurgisnacht*,
etc.) and to the two conjurations of Helena in Act ɪ and
Act ɪɪɪ. Valéry also confesses to having contracted "ce mal,
ce goût pervers de la reprise indéfinie, et cette complaisance
pour l'état réversible des oeuvres, à l'âge critique où se
forme et se fixe l'homme intellectuel" (P.ɪ, 1497). This
taste for writing in spurts, indefinitely adding to the work,
and little by little, retouching it, is a penchant he shares
with Goethe, with whom he also has in common the gift
of seeing the reversibility of ideas and works. In addition,
he realizes that ". . . un ouvrage n'est jamais *achevé*,
(. . .) mais *abandonné*; et cet abandon, qui le livre aux
flammes ou au public (. . .), est [pour les amateurs d'in-
quiétude et de perfection] une sorte d'*accident*, com-
parable à la rupture d'une réflexion, que la fatigue, le
fâcheux, ou quelque sensation viennent rendre nulle"
(*ibid.*).

Goethe could not have put it better, had he wanted to
explain the strange concatenation of scenes and the episodic structure of *Faust I* and *II* that encompasses all
imaginable types of poetry, from the metaphysical lyric
over operatic and operetta libretti to common doggerel—
all executed with superb virtuosity, while the play takes us
full circle from Heaven to Hell and back to Heaven, on
its travels through all strata of the bourgeois and the
courtly world, including a side trip through time and

space from the fall of Troy to the battle of Missolunghi. Throughout the play, Faust illustrates the mythologizing powers of magic that, verbal in nature, transform reality into dream, and dream into reality, until the myth maker becomes himself inextricably involved in the myth of his own making.

12. *A Cast of the Dice*

More subtle and more Mediterranean in spirit, Valéry's Faust has learned to mystify, without being mystified by myths of his own creation. First among those to be rejected by him is the very fable of Doctor Faustus, the corpus of myths concerning his "person" and his *persona*—illusory fabrics woven by the Fays, Memory and Imagination. They have woven and continue to weave the rich tapestry of his potential visions of glory, on which he may momentarily rest and dream, but that, in the end, he will discard. Wiser than Goethe's Faust, he can lucidly maintain vis-à-vis the Second Fay:

Si tu sais tout de moi, tu ne sais qu'une fable.
Le véritable vrai n'est jamais qu'ineffable. (P.II, 401)

If he seems less a plaything of Divine Grace, his fate is more ominously governed by those occult ironies of demonic forces, intrinsic rather than external, which darkly lurk in the subtitle of *Le Solitaire* as *malédictions d'univers*. Their essence points back to Mallarmé's *Igitur* and *Un Coup de dés jamais n'abolira le hasard*. When their moral is applied to *Mon Faust*, Mallarmé's idea for a Hamlet play, and his great stellar poem, suggest that Valéry's protagonist may depend for his very existence on those ironies of the poetic *trouvaille* whose unpredictable "casts of the dice" determine his lot—his *fortuna*, appearing in both her guises as *chance* and as *fate*. The comedy *Lust, la demoiselle de cristal* represents one *coup de dés*: while it provisionally determines Faust's *fate*, it does not abolish *chance*; i.e., it does not rule out those future chance *coups de dés* which engender quite a different fate for Faust in e.g., *Le Solitaire, ou les malédictions d'univers*.

If Mallarmé's *Igitur* and *Un Coup de dés* afford clues to the fragmentary aspects of Valéry's *Mon Faust*, they may also provide insights into the piecemeal composition of Goethe's grandiose masterpiece that, despite its designation as a "tragedy," seems to burst any mold and genre. What Valéry's and Goethe's plays have in common, beside the name of their protagonist, is their episodic structure and their growth by "touches et scènes séparées." Both Goethe's Faust and Valéry's live as "casts of the dice," as *necessary* constellations created by the demon of *chance*: their essence never changes but their existence could be quite different. In short, both heroes as well as each *Faust* play, each act and each scene in each act, present the paradox of *Un Coup de dés* at once successful and fatal, rolled out of Poetry's cornucopia of potential myths and verbal combinations. In Mallarmé's symbolical dialectics, such *coups de dés* are at once successful and fatal: they are successful, since they cast new verbal "constellations" onto the firmament's *l'azur*, the color symbolizing in theology the eternal Virgin (and, for the layman, the haunting and unattainable ideal); and they are fatal, since as the coagulation of finite poetry on the printed page, they cancel out the infinite possibilities of all unwritten poems that constitute the Platonic Idea of Poetry itself. They represent the triumph of the particular act of creation, and simultaneously the *naufrage*, the shipwreck of the universal of Poetry (or universal Poetry), violated by their very triumph. By the same token, their triumph must ironically signal their failure; for, though as constellations they stand for fate and fatality, they cannot abolish chance, i.e., the possibilities that are dormant in Poetry's horn of plenty. Every act of poetic creation is but an exercise: at once a futile but splendid attempt *at* writing the definitive poem, and a bold and blasphemous attempt *on* the inviolate beauty of the ideal Poem that no written poem can ever approximate.

Applied to *Mon Faust,* the ironic paradox of Mallarmé's *Un Coup de dés* would then establish the existing fragments of plays as exercises in an effort to approximate Valéry's elusive idea of Faust; they would not have precluded future attempts on his part to write any additional number of *Ébauches*—the subtitle of *Mon Faust*—each one (like Mallarmé's poems) an exercise, perfect in itself, and simultaneously an imperfection, a blemish on theatrical poetry with its unlimited possibilities. If Valéry did not complete *Mon Faust,* it was certainly not due to a lack of ideas or material. Under the rubrics *F.* and *F.III,* the *Cahiers* abound in notes and dialogue sketches that were obviously meant to be utilized. If these resources remained largely untapped, the author must have lost interest in further pursuing his *Mon Faust* project. There can hardly be any other reason, since Valéry lived for another five years after the publication of these *Ébauches.* Hence, chance rather than resolve—a premature loss of interest—put an end to the continuation, or even the completion, of *Mon Faust,* a conclusion that fully coincides with Valéry's idea that a work of poetry is never "completed," but "abandoned," so that, in the end, it stands as a monument to chance itself.

Does the same criterion apply, at least in part, to the "completion" of Goethe's *Faust,* which appears so fully rounded a work of art? The alterations and additions for performances of *Faust I*, in Berlin (1814) and Weimar (1815), and 246 extant Paralipomena for *Faust I* and *II*, amply demonstrate that it was not "chance," but Goethe's anticipation of his approaching death that brought about his decision to put an end to his lifelong labors, without adding any further "touches et scènes séparées" to his play. In his famous last letter to Wilhelm von Humboldt (dated March 17, 1832), he admits to having completed on an individual basis "nur die mir gerade interessantesten Stellen" ("only those passages which interested me most"), so that "im zweiten Theile Lücken blieben" ("the second part is shot through with holes"). *Faust II* has indeed been analyzed as consisting largely of processions and *Maskenzüge*, rather than constituting a drama coherent in itself (cf. Emrich, passim). They form a fugal arrangement of exempla for Faust's always excessive desires and the inevitable fiascoes he experiences in rash attempts to fulfill them.

13. *Theatricality Versus Drama*

Like *Les Fées*, the first act of *Faust II* begins—the Helena act and Act v end—in a flurry of lyricism. But while we have seen Goethe's Faust forever trying to draw poetry's fictions into life, Valéry's protagonist accepts their illusions for what they are, poetry for poetry's sake, a delight not intended to arouse the libido but offered as a stimulus to the mind's excitability. The lyrical beginnings and endings of *Faust II* and *Les Fées*, with their metaphysical and liturgical overtones, seem to correspond to *formal* intentions with discreetly hidden images. They may lead to an understanding of that "unfinished" appearance which, in 1916, Valéry had criticized in Goethe's

Faust, and which, to a far greater extent, characterizes the
Mon Faust fragments, as he chose to publish them in 1940.

As dramatic events, neither *Faust II* nor *Le Solitaire*
could possibly satisfy a theatre audience, while both *Faust
I* and *Lust* are plays that can get across. But if *Faust II*
and *Le Solitaire* do not come over as dramas, they can be
considered "theatrical," in the specialized meaning Goethe
confers to this word: "Genau aber genommen, so ist nichts
theatralisch als was für die Augen zugleich symbolisch
ist: eine wichtige Handlung, die auf eine noch wichtigere
deutet" (*Shakespeare und kein Ende*; Goethe xiv, 766; cf.
Maximen und Reflexionen 1053; Goethe ix, 633; ["To be
more precise, nothing is theatrical without simultaneously
being symbolical for the eyes: an important action, hinting at an even more important one"]). This truly symbolist concept of theatricality strangely resembles Valéry's
idea of a liturgical theatre, and his views on Goethe's *Faust*
as a series of enigmatic scenes, pointing beyond their
incidents to other scenes which hold the key to their
riddles.

In Goethe's definition, theatricality is not so much determined by the characteristics of drama (dialogue and
action), as it is rather the product of charades that, by the
device of parallel scenes, focus attention on the repetitive
pattern of the protagonist's progressive deceptions and
self-deception. Goethe's quite secular idea of theatricality
seems to owe as much to his childhood experiences with
Protestant pietism,[33] as an agnostic Valéry's concept of the
liturgical drama is derivative of his Catholic upbringing.
In short, Goethe's notion of theatricality emerges from his
remote Christian past as an *inneres Anschauen* (*Shakespeare und kein Ende*; Goethe xiv, 756)—the urbane crys-

---

[33] About Goethe's childhood contacts with Pietists, Herrnhuter,
etc., see *Dichtung und Wahrheit*, i, i (Goethe x, 50 f.).

tallization of religious meditation in the sense of Loyola's *Exercises*, with the addition of the Illuminists "inner light."

As a technique used by the playwright, theatricality is revealed by the interplay of divine and dramatic irony, which allows the audience to perceive the protagonist's intimate drama of striving in terms of errors he commits and fails to recognize as such, be it forever or until it is too late. Goethe's "inneres Anschauen" is a state of excitement in the spectator's mind, close to *l'état poétique*, Valéry's formula for the effect his poems should awaken in the reader's consciousness. Creative rather than passive, *l'état poétique* stimulates the reader into breathing new life, his own "inspiration," into the poem's seemingly dead letter, a process that revives it with every new reading. The intimate drama of Faust's consciousness struggling with the powers of its own deceptive passions, as we witness it in the Mothers scene and the Helena act, is poetry engendering *l'état poétique*, poetry to be recreated, reinterpreted by the audience. It is poetry, too, giving insights into the dangers of the poetic process: from the safe vantage point of an aesthetic distance, the audience can watch a quixotic Faust getting entangled in myths of his own fabrication. They see Faust, the false "priest," the Romantic *poeta vates*, return from the abstract and archetypal realm of the Mothers, factually intruding into his fiction, and taking literally the purely symbolic mysteries of his hieratic creation.

The same criteria can be applied to the theatrical or liturgical character of *Les Fées*. Although they are worlds apart, Goethe's vast fresco of super-human aspirations, doomed to failure, and Valéry's short interlude in the otherwise relentless *malédictions d'univers* have in common those "theatrical" (or liturgical) aspects which, culminating in the exultation of lyricism rather than in the dynamism of drama, determine their essence as pure poetry; and their poetic purity may well suggest why their unfinished appearance is perhaps a deceptive one. In Mallarmé's and Valéry's view, as it had long before been in Goethe's, the fate of poetry is forever to remain *inachevée*, in a literal sense "infinite," brought at random to a vicarious end, and always open to revision, never "finite," no matter how perfect the poem.

14. *Rhythms and Rebuses*

The paradox of the "perfect" yet forever "unfinished" poem falls, of course, within the range of Valéry's poetic theory and practice, and this particular aspect of Goethe's *Faust* is fully intelligible to him. If he fails to understand most of Goethe's hidden jests and rhythmic ironies, his plays on words, it is due, as we have seen, to the insufficiencies of the French translations through which he came to know this work. At times the translators distort the meaning, although no one approximates the blunder that Goethe imputes to Mme de Staël, when he asserts that she translated: "Nachbarin! Euer Fläschchen!" (*Faust I*, 3834), Gretchen's request for her neighbor's smelling salts, as "Ma voisine, une goutte" (conversation with Fr. Förster, March 1828). Rather, what escapes the translators' grip are the subtleties of metric jests that underscore the ironies of boutades and situations. What Valéry is prone to mistake for Goethe's "pseudo-depths" more often than not results from the pompous or awkward tone struck by the translator, who frequently flattens out subtle paradoxes into puzzling "contradictions." When compared to the German text, they generally turn out to mark Goethe's refusal to reduce the irony of complex and ir-

resolvable problems to the platitudes of simplistic and arbitrary solutions. Goethe's shrewd irony, so close to
Valéry's wit, has a way of concealing ambiguities in re-
buses and tongue-in-cheek rhythms, which only seem to
contradict the text, while they actually serve to enhance
its semantic duplicity.

The waltz time of Faust's and Helena's love duet in
Act III is an example of rhythmic irony—a point well
made by Bahr (*op.cit.*, 161). The frivolous three-quarter-
time discreetly mocks the operatic pathos and irreality of
this scene. They are immanent, too, in Helena's equivocal
warning about her own phantom existence: "Ich fühle
mich so fern und doch so nah," etc. (*Faust II*, 9411; ["I
feel so far away and yet so near"]). This line in waltz time
provides a chiastic echo to an earlier verse in *Faust I*.
There it is pronounced by Faust who is fated to "see
Helena in every woman" (*Faust I*, 2603 f.)—as Mephisto
puts it so aptly, thanks to the brew the good Doctor had
imbibed in the Witches' Kitchen. Lusting for his Nordic
Helena of the day, Faust is misguided by his passion to
commit the blasphemy of envying the Eucharist for
touching Margarete's lips:

> *Faust*: Ich bin ihr nah, und wär ich noch so fern,
>   Ich kann sie nie vergessen, nie verlieren;
>   Ja, ich beneide schon den Leib des Herrn,
>   Wenn ihre Lippen ihn indes berühren.
>   (*Faust I*, 3332 ff.)

> (*Faust*: I am still near her and, though far removed,
>   Her image must be always in my head;
>   I already envy the body of the Lord
>   When her lips rest on the holy bread.
>   (MacNeice, p. 107)

Foreshadowing Faust's behavior in the Helena act, these lines are a prime example for Goethe's secretive irony, his manner of "hineingeheimnissen"[34]—a method of concealing "caveats" and clues in rhetorical devices and in meters that are shared by parallel passages with a common theme, no matter how far apart they may occur in the text. Both caveat and clues are doubly coded here, in the form and the substance of these parallel passages, hidden as they are (1) in the rhetorical device of chiasmus, and (2) in the rhythmical ironies of iambic feet that dance in three-quarter time:

> *F.*: Ich bin ihr (Gretchen) *nah*, und wär ich noch so *fern*
>   (*Faust I*, 3332)
> *Helena*: Ich fühle mich so *fern* und doch so *nah*
>   (*Faust II*, 9411)

This chiasmus in waltz time spans 6080 lines and the chasm of three millennia that separate the still half-medieval Renaissance milieu of the German petite-bourgeoise Margarete from the Hellenic grandeur of Helena, the tragic queen of Sparta, captured after the fall of Troy, and facing an uncertain future at the hands of her cuckolded husband. She is now deceiving Menelaos again, by delusively begetting with Faust the ephemeral Euphorion-Byron, whose era is evoked rebus-like with his tragic death at Missolunghi, and by way of the Romantic waltz beat of his "parents" love duet. These events take place in a phantasmagoria where, once again, Faust is fated to confuse his ideal fantasy world with a reality that does not exist outside his poeticizing imagination.

Both this vast chiasmus, and the three-quarter-time

---

[34] Cf. Goethe's conversation with J. von Pappenheim of May 4, 1828, and his letter to Zelter dated July 26, 1828.

rhythms of the two lines that constitute it, hint at diametrically opposed ways of calling in question that Romantic "moment of eternity"—the fusion of Faust with a
timeless ideal of beauty—for which we see him thirsting
throughout the play, in the vain hope of breaking down,
be it only for an instant, the temporal walls of creatureliness: In the Helena act, he will try to change time into
eternity and force eternal beauty to enter the temporal
world. He does so by copulating with Helena's shadow,
drawn by him from the Hades where archetypes dwell. In
the earlier Northern Romantic scene "Wald und Höhle"
("Forest and Cavern") his feverish imagination had filled
him with blasphemous jealousy for the mere symbol of
eternal life and love—the Eucharist touching Gretchen's
very real and temporal lips. In both instances, Faust is
guilty of a rather gross type of literalmindedness, com-
mitting a categorical mistake that—to lend a new meaning to a linguistic term—could qualify as a confusion of
the semantic "signified" (or object) with its "signifier"
(the symbol that stands for the object and is but sound
and fury: a multivalent myth).

15. Faust's Salvation Preordained by the Lord's Pride and Prejudice

We can now better appreciate the extent to which
Valéry, in his astute 1916 Cahier note on Faust, had sensed
Goethe's professional secret, and the particularities of his
secretive irony. He had intuitively grasped the fugal
structure of Faust II in particular: a chain of seemingly
independent but secretly interrelated scenes that, in their
totality, hint at Faust's vain attempts to escape his preordained fate. "Souvent toute une scène est un rébus, une
charade dont le mot se trouve au-delà de quelques autres

scènes" (Cah. VI, 319).[35] In its French ambiguity, "le mot"
may stand for the "creative Word" that causes Faust to be
so absurdly consistent in his tenaciously repeated incon-
sistencies; and "le mot" may be "le fin mot de la chose,"
providing the explanation of the mystery caused by the
"creative Word"—for a mystery it is, in the strongest
sense of this term. As both the "creative Word" and its
"explanation," "le mot" is pronounced before the very
beginning of the play's time, in the form of an adage—
both descriptive and prescriptive, which the Lord deigns
to coin in the *Prologue in Heaven*:

Der Herr: Es irrt der Mensch, solang' er strebt (317)

(*The Lord*: Man errs, as long as he strives.)

It would seem that the Lord's infinite bounty—or is it
his irony? or a combination of both?—is on a par with the
cruel laughter of the Homeric gods, for he dignifies
Faust's excesses and rationalizations of boundless appetites
with the noble litotes of "striving." The paradox of the

[35] Valéry's observation correctly evaluates Goethe's complex
technique of installing multiple and labyrinthine mirrors within
his work. In a letter regarding the Helena act, dated Sept. 27,
1827, Goethe explains his procedure to K. J. L. Iken in terms that,
once again, allude to "manifest mysteries": "Da sich manches
unserer Erfahrungen nicht rund aussprechen und direct mit-
theilen lässt, so habe ich seit langem das Mittel gewählt, durch
einander gegenübergestellte und sich gleichsam in einander ab-
spiegelnde Gebilde den geheimeren Sinn dem Aufmerkenden zu
offenbaren." ("Since many of our experiences cannot be roundly
expressed and directly communicated, for a long time now I have
chosen the means of revealing the more secret meaning to the
attentive reader, through opposite structures which, in a way, are
mirroring each other.") It is this mirror technique that Gide
applies in his own work, and that he describes as early as 1893
in the heraldic term of a construction "en abyme."

Christian "freedom of will" as a life sentence in the tread-
mill of "striving in erring" stands as a sad commentary on
the human condition. But, though it is divine by nature,
it is demonic in essence. It extends beyond Faust's temporal fate to the eternal condition of the even poorer devil,
Mephistopheles, whose semantic difficulties with Faust
always mislead him to "realistic" interpretations of his
client's idealized appetites, fantasies, and premonitions of
wish fulfillment, while all along Faust's "strivings" were
overshadowed by the potential miracle of Divine grace
that in the end almost predictably, to the accompaniment
of Angelic ruses, deprives the Devil of his prey.

So at least it would appear. But there are other dimensions to the problem. What is at work here—to use two
complementary terms borrowed from Goethe, the natural
scientist—is the ultimate *Steigerung*, the very *climax* of a
polarity whose tensions are meant to remain unresolved
until the very end of the play. It is the polarity between
Christian and pagan elements; between the absurd miracle of grace incumbent on the Lord's Elect, and, on the
other hand, the inescapable tragedy of classical fate which
entraps the hero in his own deeds. Even if they seem
righteous, noble, and good, these deeds can lead to his
destruction; and conversely, they may weigh in his favor,
though arising from errors in judgment, leading to rapine,
bloodshed, and arson. Both *fate*, in the classical sense, and
divine grace operate in an arcane area where the actions
of the individual are part of a supernatural over-all plan
that transcends human intentions and values. In these
arcana of Christian "grace" and classical "fate," the hero
is vulnerable or salvageable beyond all rational or moral
concepts of "good" and "evil." The classical hero's frailty
and proneness to "error," which in "strivings" beyond
good and evil seals his fate, his ἁμαρτία (Aristotle, *Poet.*

1453a), is foreseen but not predestined by the god who darkly speaks through the Pythia's oracle. The tragic flaw is always revealed *in the end* (when it is too late), as Man's ignorance of his past and/or his future. Both are *known* to the gods, though the gods' knowledge cannot change the hero's fate (e.g., Oedipus).

By contrast, ἁμαρτία, the hero's vain struggle to escape the entrapments of fate that the past or the future he ignores are setting for him, can be benevolently translated by Christian doctrine into redemption through the mysterious and all-powerful workings of divine grace. Faust's lapses were erased from God's slate before the beginning of time, by the Lord's resolve in the *Prologue in Heaven* to treat him as a latter-day Job. Hence, Faust's frailties, his excesses, his sins will miraculously convert into the kind of "striving" that counts toward his salvation. In the finale, the Angels who wrest Faust's soul from Mephisto's troops to carry him heavenward assure us that the strangely amoral qualities of the Doctor's "striving" do not even enter the equation. We are told that his redemption is brought about by the very fact of this lifelong striving for striving's sake. The conclusion to be drawn is that all human acts on Earth are erroneous strivings. They are trials to be undergone, no matter how ludicrous their nature, in view of an ultimate redemption that solely depends on divine grace; i.e., on the Lord's *predetermination* in saving or damning the individual soul. In this sense, Goethe's Angel can well put the stress on the existential virtues and saving grace of Faust's "striving" *per se*, regardless of its often deadly consequences for others:

Engel: Wer immer strebend sich bemüht,
   Den können wir erlösen. (Goethe's italics; *Faust II,*
   11936 f.)

(*Angels*: Him who always strives with all his heart /
We can redeem.)

Although Mephistopheles knows that he is "a part of
that force which always wills evil and always accomplishes
the good" (*Faust I*, 1335 f.), he *unwittingly* serves as the
instrument of Faust's salvation and of his own forever
unrelieved frustrations. For he does not know what the
Lord alone knows: the course of future events. On the
seesaw of mysterious powers, Mephistopheles can be re-
warded with evil, for evil is his domain. He can be robbed
of his seemingly well-deserved prize (Faust's soul) by the
omnipotent force that always wills the good, and whose
impenetrable council alone determines what, in the cosmic
plan, partakes of "good" and what of "evil."

Mephisto's battle for Faust's soul was lost before it had
even begun. It was lost in the *Prologue in Heaven*, in his
wager with the Lord, where the cards were stacked against
him in advance. But his losing battle for Faust's soul runs
parallel to Faust's losing battle for the conquest of an
unattainable ideal. It is a parody of Faust's heroic strivings
in erring; and, as it would behoove the Devil's condition,
it is pathetic rather than tragic. Faust's fate, on the other
hand, ends absurdly enough to fit the canon of Christian
martyrology. It is tragicomic rather than tragic, quixotic
rather than heroic. "Ein sehr ernst gemeinter Scherz," a
jest with a deadly serious meaning, it is almost like a
parody of the *Deus* (or *angelus*) *ex machina* interventions,
in Baroque drama, e.g., Lope de Vega's *Lo Fingido Ver-
dadero*, Calderón's *El Mágico prodigioso* and Rotrou's
Saint Genêt. The tragic hero, in the end, always accepts
his human limitations. Does Faust really do so, by ultimately confining his intentions to envisioning a feat of
engineering, feasible within the limits of the human po-

tential, but for which he again enlists Mephistopheles and his uncanny helpers? His problem is that of Goethe's *Zauberlehrling* (*The Sorcerer's Apprentice*): he cannot rid himself of the spirits he had conjured up to serve him. Only when it is too late does he realize that he cannot "remove magic from his path," in order to face Nature on purely human terms, "a Man, alone" (*Faust II*, 11404 ff.). If there be something tragic about Faust, it is his vain longing to find his way back into the human condition, to return to the *status ante quo*, to life without the Devil, without his Demon—in short, to regain his lost innocence. But in this vain longing, Faust is different only in degree from the rest of humankind.

On Faust's own terms, his absurd salvation could be seen as his true tragedy: it deprives him of the fruits of his Titanism, robbing his revolt against creatureliness of its tragic sense. Faust's beatification, his redemption through the intercession of Gretchen and the Blessed Virgin Mary, the Spectacle of "Dr. Faustus, Saint and Martyr," indeed makes a mockery of his lifelong struggle with Nature and the Supernatural. Faust's paradox resides in his gratuitous Christianity. He is Christian not by virtue of faith but by the law of inertia, by the sheer gravity of a habit contracted during his childhood. This perplexing fact seems acceptable to the Lord. It is driven home to us in the beginning of *Faust I*: a choir of Angels prevents Faust's suicide by singing the Easter message of Christ's resurrection; Faust reacts as a creature of habit, revealing at the same time the ungodly nature of his striving:

Faust: Die Botschaft hör' ich wohl, allein mir fehlt der
  Glaube;
Das Wunder ist des Glaubens liebstes Kind.
Zu jenen Sphären wag' ich nicht zu streben,

Woher die holde Nachricht tönt;
Und doch, *an diesen Klang von Jugend auf gewöhnt,*
Ruft er auch jetzt zurück mich in das Leben.
(*Faust I,* 765 ff. My italics)

(*Faust*: I hear your message, my faith it is that lags
   behind;
And miracle is the favourite child of faith.
Those spheres whence peals the gospel of forgiving,
Those are beyond what I can dare,
And yet, so used am I from childhood to this sound,
It even now summons me back to living.)
         (MacNeice, p. 31)[36]

Throughout the play, his pilgrimage can hardly be
called a search for the Divine. It is obviously not his
"Christian faith"—so far "lagging behind" in these lines,
and totally absent from his dying thoughts—which would
warrant the intervention of divine grace for his redemption. And yet, his salvation is uniquely determined by the
gratuitous arcana of sufficient grace. It is a salvation that
transcends the Biblical meaning of its purported model in
the Book of Job, and it does so by its strange vicinity to
the classical concept of ἁμαρτία. For it can be traced
back to that moment in eternity where Mephistopheles
enters his wager with the Lord. Mephisto's daring bet is
indeed an expression of ἁμαρτία in the Aristotelian sense
of the term. Ignorant of the future, Mephistopheles bets
against the Lord, who knows the future and who even

[36] MacNeice slightly betrays the text: "What I can dare" does
not capture the concept of "striving" in "wag' ich nicht zu *streben,*"
which actually hints at his "striving in erring," showing the
agnostic indifference of his aspirations. Far from seeking the
divine truth, his striving aims at anything but an understanding
of the angelic message.

darkly hints at the predestined failure of the Mephistophelian enterprise. But he does so in a language that
Mephistopheles, the rational spirit of absolute Negation,
cannot fully understand, although, ironically, as we shall
see, he is made to use it himself, on at least one occasion
in the play.

> *Der Herr*: Ein guter Mensch in seinem dunklen Drange
> Ist sich des rechten Weges wohl bewusst. (*Prolog im
> Himmel*, 328 f.)

> (*Lord*: A good Man in his obscure impulses
> Instinctively chooses the righteous path.)

The Lord's illuminist but dangerous pronouncement on
the essential righteousness of instinctive feelings vaguely
echoes the Gospel truth: "A good man out of the good
treasure of the heart bringeth forth good things" (Matt.
12:35). But it quotes only half the Gospel truth. For the
Lord's quotation is taken out of its context, which is an
invective by Jesus against the Pharisees. It continues with
an antinomy: "and an evil man out of the evil treasure,
bringeth forth evil things" (*ibid*.). The verse preceding
this one had been an even more violent apostrophe: "O
generation of vipers, how can ye, being evil, speak good
things? for out of the abundance of the heart the mouth
speaketh" (Matt. 12:34). The implication is that the
human heart (and hence, spontaneous human speech) is
corrupted by the stain of original sin.

Among the numerous literary derivatives from this
Biblical passage, there is one in particular that seems to be
the model for Faust's Romantic diatribe against Wagner's
predilection for the pedantry of formal rhetoric. It is
Erasmus, suggesting that the true believer should turn
his bosom into Christ's library ("Quin tu tuum ipsius

pectus bibliothecam facito Christi"), for: "Longe vividius penetrant in animos auditorum, quae de tuo pectore ceu viva prodeunt quam quae ex aliorum farragine sublegun- tur" (*Methodus*. cap. ii, "In Novum Testamentum Prae- fationis"; ["That which you produce as though it were flowing from your bosom, forces the hearts of your audi- ence much more vividly, (for) it is not like a rehash of the mixed leavings of other men"]):

> *Faust*: Wenn ihr's nicht fühlt, ihr werdet's nicht erjagen,
>   Wenn es nicht aus der Seele dringt
>   Und mit urkräftigem Behagen
>   Die Herzen aller Hörer zwingt.
>   Sitzt ihr nur immer! Leimt zusammen,
>   Braut ein Ragout aus andrer Schmaus,
>   Und blast die kümmerlichen Flammen
>   Aus eurem Aschenhäufchen 'raus! (*Faust I*, 534 ff.)

> (*Faust*: Unless you feel it, you cannot gallop it down,
>   Unless it thrust up from your soul
>   Forcing the hearts of all your audience
>   With a primal joy beyond control.
>   Sit there forever with scissors and paste!
>   Gather men's leavings for a rehash
>   And blow a little flicker
>   Out of your own little heap of ash!) (MacNeice,
>   pp. 24 f.)

In Luther's translation, the second half of Matt. 12:35 reads: "Wes das Herz voll ist, des geht der Mund über." It finds an ironic echo in the words of Faust whose heart— far from overflowing with the love of God—is full of his love for Helena; eager to step out of her classical domain into Faust's Renaissance ambiance, she is learning from him to speak in modern, rhyming iambic Pentameters:

Helena: So sage denn, wie sprech' ich auch so schön?
Faust: Es ist gar leicht, *es muss von Herzen gehn.*
(*Faust II*, 9377 f. My italics)

(*Helena*: Then tell me, how I learn to speak like you with art?
Faust: It is quite easy, it must come from the heart.)

But Matt. 12:34 turns into its own parody when, some 300-odd lines later, Mephistopheles speaks with the prudish voice of Christianity. Under the mask of Phorkyas, Mephistopheles, the inevitable byproduct of Christianity, represents its ugly side, the inverse of Lacedaemonian impassiveness and classical Beauty, against which he hypocritically upholds the sentimental virtues of a Romantic morality:

(*Mephistopheles-*) *Phorkyas*: Denn es muss von
    Herzen gehen,
  Was auf Herzen wirken will (*Faust II*, 9685 f.)

([*Mephistopheles-*] *Phorkyas*: For it must come from
    the heart
  If it is to affect our hearts.)

The Lord's decree on the righteousness of a good man's instinctive gropings has now undergone variations, going from Faust's passionately Erasmian defense of oratorical sincerity, over his operatic duet with Helena, to the operetta-like shallowness of Mephisto's pedantic adage. It is the ultimate irony of Mephisto's situation that he must speak as the ugly mouthpiece of Christian morality, whenever Faust, the agnostic who is Christian by mere force of habit, strays from its path to the brighter seductions of Pagan beauty. Here the Devil enters into the Lord's plan for Faust's salvation. Mephistopheles is Faust's very personal Demon. He keeps awake Faust's groping intuition,

antagonizing him by serving him, and serving him
through his antagonism. He prods and excites Faust's desires, so that he may never falter in his God-willed "erring
in striving."

> *Der Herr*: Des Menschen Tätigkeit kann allzuleicht
>   erschlaffen,
> Er liebt sich bald die unbedingte Ruh;
> Drum geb' ich gern ihm den Gesellen zu,
> Der reizt und wirkt und muss als Teufel schaffen.
>   (*Prolog im Himmel*, 340 ff.)

> (*Lord*: Man finds relaxation too attractive—
> Too fond too soon of unconditional rest;
> Which is why I am pleased to give him a companion
> Who lures and thrusts and must, as devil, be active.)
>   (MacNeice, p. 16)

What Leibnitz had called the only "compossible" world,
is despite its pre-established harmony but a finite and imperfect universe. Where perfection is wanting, desires
abound, and they are Mephisto's domain. Here Valéry
joins Goethe, for in *Lust*, Méphistophélès is allowed to
define his subtle task in these terms: "(. . .) je fais ce que
l'on veut," and "(. . .) je fais même que l'on veuille"
(P.II, 358). The Spirit of absolute Negation is that nagging
consciousness which *is* imperfection, nothingness striving
for being. As the intelligence of what is wanting, Mephistopheles performs his functions well within the orbits
of the divine order, and as a necessary part of it. *Instinct
et aiguillon*, he lures the Faustian imagination into creative dreams and apparent memories of a perfection whose
innumerable possibilities have no existence outside these
dreams.

16. *Conclusion*

In *Lust, la demoiselle de cristal*, Valéry had played comic variations on the theme of the Cartesian *cogito* and its carnal impediments. They were seen from the diabolical perspective of Bélial—as *la panse qui pense*. The two surviving fragments of Act IV suggest a tentative compromise, envisaged by Faust: mind and heart, Faust and Lust would try to consummate their union in a climate of tenderness and intellectual copulation. They would thus engender poetry in action, "moments of eternity." The leap that would bring together heart and mind could illustrate Valéry's concept of *la sensibilité de l'intellect* (Cah. XII, 68). It corresponds to the union of Goethe's Faust with Helena (*Faust II*, Act III), a "moment of eternity" as illusory and elusive as the marriage of Classicism and Romanticism that it darkly symbolizes. Faust's "moment of eternity" with Lust is expressed in the conditional tense, implying a possibility, but hardly a probable solution of the Faustian conflict. The uncomfortable *discordia concors* of mind and heart, their forced cohabitation, find Pascalian and Baudelairian echoes, faintly audible on and off stage.

The amusing characters of *Lust* can hardly be called akin to those of Marlowe, Goethe, Berlioz, and Gounod (not to mention Boito's unintentional Faust parody, the opera *Mefistofele*). There is none of the awesome fatefulness that turns the conventional Faust into a victim of his own hubris, and (by Goethean *fiat*) into the most unexpected martyr and saint that was ever saved by the gratuitous and somewhat operatic intervention of the Lord's operative grace. Unlike Goethe's hero, Valéry's Faust has left magic and humbug far behind him.

Throughout *Lust*, he masters, if not his appetites, at least the pursuits of his intellect. Simultaneously, he expands his highly fictionalized autobiography to absorb all the legends that have been spun about his feats. The predominant climate of *Lust* is one of whim and wit, together with an irrepressible gusto for punning. The only resemblance to Goethe's *Faust* occurs in Act ii, iii, where Mephistopheles offers to inscribe the disciple's copy of one of Faust's books with the Faustian motto: "Prenez garde à l'amour!"[37] Significantly, the title of this book, *Le Corps de l'esprit*, summarizes the main theme of the play, the paradox of *la panse qui pense*, which ironically seems to imply the vanity of Faust's advice. The passions have an almost predictable way of invalidating reason.

What *Lust* indisputably shares with *Faust I* is the "small world" of domesticity. The scenes are laid in Faust's study (Act i), his garden (Act ii) and his library (Act iii). The two published fragments of Act iv (*Mouvement I* and *Moment II*) could take place in either of these *décors*. The action, too, pertains to comfort, learning, and dissatisfaction with the meager rewards of comfort and learning; in short, it deals with the microcosm of middle-class aspirations—the pursuit of tenderness, a craving to satisfy cruder appetites, and the ambition to project a misleading image for posterity.

In *Lust*, Valéry conforms to some extent to the canon of the classical French stage: there is an apparent adherence to the three unities, and the actors are few in number. *Le Solitaire, ou les malédictions d'univers* escapes the rigors of classical restraints. Its nightmarish Act i and the

[37] The scene is a take-off on *Faust I*, 1868-2072, and *Faust II*, Act ii, 6685-6818: Mephisto's two impersonations of Faust vis-à-vis the student, who is first seen as a gullible freshman, then, years later, as a disenchanted and overbearing Baccalaureate.

operatic Interlude, *Les Fées*, are dreamlike to the extent of lifting the action out of time, and placing it into cardboard landscapes of fantasy lands that are consistent with the atmosphere of a "dramatic fairy play"; and *Féerie dramatique* is the generic designation given by Valéry to this second *ébauche* of a *Mon Faust* play.

It would be preposterous to compare its one act and "Interlude" with the grandiose ironies, the allegorical processions and masquerades, mythological encounters and bold feats of versification in Goethe's *Faust II*, which transports us across time and space from the German Emperor's court to the Pharsalian plains, the Palace of Menelaos in Sparta, and back into the sixteenth-century wars, to depict in the end a perplexing act of grace and Faust's miraculous ascension to heaven. All we see, in *Le Solitaire*, is a Faust at odds with a Pascalian monster who thrusts him into a precipice, and a Faust awakening in the Fays' fairy palace to an enchantment that seems to end with his doom. But, more likely, it heralds the cyclical return of sleep, dream, uncertain awakening, hesitations between passions and lucidity, and the misfortunes of the *cogito* in the intellect's heroically quixotic attempts to escape solipsism and creatureliness. For the stage of this liturgical drama, we have seen, is Faust's own brain, where the rational soul, in Act I, is overpowered by the Solitaire's bestial angelism (or angelic bestiality), and thrust upon its own resources, into the enchanted palace of its animal passions, prompted by the evocative powers of Memory and Imagination. Meanwhile Valéry's Faust never ceases to strive for ever-greater lucidity, although (like Descartes and Valéry himself), he finds it hard to distinguish between dream and reality. Like Descartes and Valéry, too, he is fascinated by the thin borderline between the states of waking and sleep, imagination and thought.

By contrast, Goethe's Faust, less observant in matters concerning consciousness and dream, is trapped into embracing every "semi-reality" ("Halbwirklichkeiten," Paralipomenon 70; Goethe V, 560) that Mephistopheles, the tempting source of his secret desires, stages for his imagination. Valéry's Faust is allowed to escape the ironic self-deceptions of his Goethean counterpart.

Whatever Valéry has assimilated from *Faust II* has already been discussed. It remains to be said that there exist minor affinities between formal aspects of *Faust II* and *Le Solitaire*, though they are rather superficial in nature. Both plays open vistas on the mysteries of the intellect that transcend the forces of Nature. Goethe ever so slightly lifts the veil of Divine ironies involving the mysteries of grace. Valéry refuses to stack the cards in favor of his own Faust, conceding no biased triumph of universal good over cosmic evil. His urbane and lucid Faust is pursued to the end by *les malédictions d'univers*, by those "universal curses" which condemn Man to live *in* a world that lives *within* him, as the creation of a mind that holds him prisoner of its passions, its sensitivity, and its intellectual constructs. He proudly consents to a *morale de la mort*, in the clear and distinct knowledge that there is no other way out of the curse of the human condition. Death is the logical end toward which all life tends, and the acceptance of death would seem the one sensible solution to the human lot of creatureliness, the only possible escape from the snares of delusions held out throughout life by the deceptive powers of Memory and Imagination. Faust's methodical doubt reduces the Solitaire's confused metaphysics to raging howls in the dark. Simultaneously, while his rational search for certainty does not interfere with his delight in savoring the Fays' rhapsodic poetry, it allows him to resist the enchanting visions their lyrical appeal is spreading out before him.

On an ever-rotating planet, where the physical determinants of "high" and "low"—and their moral equivalents "lofty" and "base"—are but verbal myths without correlatives, either in physics or in the plurality of ethical systems, the Solitaire's anguished exhortations are as meaningless to Valéry's enlightened Faust as are the Fays' worldly enchantments. It is in this sense that Valéry's modernized Faust, a physicist aware of post-Keplerian astronomy and versed in the theory of relativity, can turn a quackish recommendation by Goethe's Mephistopheles into a scientifically meaningful formula. We have seen Goethe's Devil send Faust to the Mothers, mythical weavers of life's eternally changing possibilities, there to fetch from the void of archetypal illusions the delusive images of Helena and Paris. Sending Faust into Nothingness and Oblivion, Mephistopheles, the mystagogue, orders him: "Versinke denn! ich könnt' auch sagen: steige! / 's ist einerlei . . ." (*Faust II*, 6275 f.; ["Sink into depth, then! I might as well say: ascend! / There is no difference"]). When Valéry's Faust echoes these words: "Tu n'as pas encore compris qu'il n'y a ni haut, ni bas," (P.II, 381), he leaves his Devil behind to confront forces beleaguering him from within in the form of confused school opinions and *idées reçues*. His words may sound hyperbolical, but they mark the intellectual gap between Valéry's Faust, exploring the unmapped regions of his brain, and Goethe's hero on stage, a centenarian standing on the threshold of death, whose wishful thinking cannot free him from his Demonic magic, which blocks his approach to Nature:

Faust: Könnt' ich Magie von meinem Pfad entfernen,
Die Zaubersprüche ganz und gar verlernen,
Stünd' ich, Natur, vor dir ein Mann allein,
Da wär's der Mühe wert, ein Mensch zu sein!
(*Faust II*, 11404)

(*Faust*: All magic—from my path if I could spurn it,
All incantation—once for all unlearn it,
To face you, Nature, as one man of men—
It would be worth it to be human then.)
(MacNeice, p. 281)

The three subjunctives ("Könnt'," "stünd'," "wär")
resound like a triple, pathetic, and ineffectual exorcism,
when it is too late for a switch from impetuous magic to
the patient research required for the practice of the natural
sciences. It is wishful thinking, a vain attempt to wipe
out the past when there is no time left to start out again,
for the game is played out and over. Damned by Marlowe, Berlioz, Gounod, etc., and saved by Goethe's Protestant God, the traditional figure of Dr. Faustus, magician
and irrationalist, is overcome in *Le Solitaire* by Faust the
scientist and rationalist, who scorns *auctoritas*, superstition, scholasticism, and the temptations of passions aroused
by the charms of Memory and Imagination. His "ni haut,
ni bas" points with scientific rigor to the fallacies of sense
perception and to the errors of accepted canons.[38] His
method triumphs over Mephistopheles, whose physics and

---

[38] In terms of Valéry's literary rhetoric, Faust's "ni haut, ni
bas" seems to allude to the modern mixture of style levels (*genera
dicendi*) that characterizes *Mon Faust* as much as it does Goethe's
Faust: a freedom from classical and traditional fetters, allowing,
wherever necessary, the intrusion of *genus tenue* (the probing and
didactic qualities of colloquial speech) and *genus medium* (the
polite elegance of elegy and lyric) upon the gravity of *genus
grande* (the grandiose style level of epic and tragic poetry). It is
this stylistic flexibility which allows both Goethe and Valéry to
run through a wide variety of vastly differing situations, calling
for an equally broad variety of style levels and mixtures, from
the burlesque (e.g. *Auerbachs Keller in Leipzig*, and Act III,
scene i of *Lust*) to tragic proportions (e.g. *Mitternacht* in *Faust
II*, and the finale of *Les Fées*).

metaphysics had already been shown outdated in *Lust*, phantasmagoric and removed as they are from all efforts of empirical verification.

The physical lesson in relativity is paralleled by one in relative ethics. For, morally, "ni haut, ni bas" teaches the reversibility of good and evil that Goethe's God had taught in the *Prologue in Heaven*, although in purely theological terms, by choosing Mephisto as the mysterious instrument of Faust's preordained salvation. Valéry's cold and scientific approach to the human condition enables him to reduce his theatre to the interior stage—the brain, where the emancipated intellect cuts giants down to size, to reveal them as little more than the windmills they are. Here Faust, having left behind such superstitious fantasies as his companion, Mephistopheles, meets the greater temptations of angelism (the Solitaire), from whose lofty, forbidding heights the protagonist is hurled down to the gentle but even more insidious temptations of Memory and Imagination. Resisting their sirens' appeal to the passions of the mind, the groping intellect finds the path of self-reflection and methodical doubt as both the means and the end of a lifelong progression toward always-provisional answers, with death as the sole certainty. It is an ending by far more prosaic and open to revision than the Christian apotheosis of Goethe's Faust. Yet it seems to offer a more honest solution: less ironic than Goethe's, to be sure, in many ways it is more dignified. It leaves intact the hero's refusal to be duped by forces outside his control, although it does not shield him from their dupery, nor from the solipsism of the *cogito* that threatens him from within. Nor does his caution protect him against the passions of his mind, and against the distractions with which they curse the striving intellect.

SELECTED
Bibliography

VALÉRY

1. *Editions*

Paul Valéry, *Cahiers*, 29 vols., Paris, 1957-1961.
Paul Valéry, *Oeuvres*, vols. I and II, ed. Jean Hytier, Collection de la Pléiade, Paris, 1957, 1960.

2. *Selected Criticism*

Bémol, Maurice, *Paul Valéry*, Paris, 1949.
——, "Le jeune Valéry et Goethe. Étude de genèse réciproque," *Revue de littérature comparée*, vol. 34, 1960, 5-36.
Blüher, Karl Alfred, *Strategie des Geistes. Paul Valérys Faust* [Analecta Romanica, Heft 10], 1960.
Crow, Christine M., *Paul Valéry. Consciousness and Nature*, Cambridge, 1972.
Fähnrich, Hermann, "Paul Valéry und Goethe," *Neue Folge des Jahrbuchs der Goethe-Gesellschaft*, 31. Band, Weimar, 1969, 192-212.
Freedman, Ralph, "Paul Valéry: Protean Critic," in *Modern French Criticism from Proust and Valéry to Structuralism*, ed. John K. Simon, Chicago and London (n.d.).
Gaède, E., *Nietzsche et Valéry. Essai sur la comédie de l'esprit*, Paris, 1962.
Garrigue, F., *Goethe et Valéry*, Paris, 1955.
Gide, André, *André Gide–Paul Valéry. Correspondance, 1890-1942*, Paris [1955].
Hytier, Jean, *La Poétique de Valéry*, Paris 1953.

Ince, W. N., *The Poetic Theory of Paul Valéry. Inspiration and Technique*, Leicester, 1961.

Lawler, J. R., *Form and Meaning in Paul Valéry's "Le Cimetière Marin,"* Melbourne, 1954.

———, *Lecture de Valéry. Une étude de "Charmes,"* Paris, 1963.

———, "The Serpent, the Tree, and the Crystal," *L'Esprit Créateur*, IV, 1964; 34-40.

———, *The Language of French Symbolism*, Princeton, 1969.

Lettres á Quelques-Uns, 1889-1943, Paris, 1952.

Lorenz, Erika, "Der Name *Lust* in Paul Valérys erstem Faustfragment," *Romanistisches Jahrbuch* XXII, 1971; 178-190.

Maurer, Karl, *Interpretationen zur späteren Lyrik Paul Valérys*, Munich, 1954.

Maurer, K. W., "Goethe et Valéry," *Universitas* (Manitoba), IX, 1967.

Noulet-Carner, Emilie, ed., *Entretiens sur Paul Valéry*, Décades du Centre Culturel International de Cérisy-la-Salle, nouvelle série 7, Paris, 1968.

Pire, F., *La tentation du sensible chez Paul Valéry*, Bruxelles, 1964.

Raymond, Marcel, *Paul Valéry et la tentation de l'esprit*, Neuchâtel, 1946.

Richthofen, Erich von, *Commentaire sur "Mon Faust" de Paul Valéry*, Paris, 1961.

Robinson, Judith, "Valéry's *Mon Faust* as an 'Unfinished' Play," *Australian Journal of French Studies*, VI, 1969; 421-439.

Scarfe, F., *The Art of Paul Valéry. A study in Dramatic Monologue* [Glasgow University Publications XCVII], London, 1954.

Wais, Kurt, "Goethe und Valérys 'Faust,'" in *Mélanges de litterature comparée et de philologie offerts à Mieczyslaw Brahmer*, Warsaw (n.d.), 555-579.

Walzer, P.-O., *La Poésie de Valéry*, Genève, 1953.

GOETHE

1. *Editions*

Gedenkausgabe der Werke, Briefe und Gespräche, herausgegeben von Ernst Beutler, Zürich, 2nd edition, 1962; 26 volumes.

Goethes Werke. Vollständige Ausgabe letzter Hand, Stuttgart und Tübingen, 1827 ff.; 56 volumes.

Goethes Faust. Der Tragödie erster und zweiter Teil. Urfaust, kommentiert von Erich Trunz, Hamburg, 1963.

MacNeice, Louis, translator, *Goethe's Faust, Parts I and II*, an abridged version, translated by Louis MacNeice, New York, 1960.

Eckermann, Johann Peter, *Gespräche mit Goethe*, Leipzig (n.d.), 3 volumes.

2. *Selected Criticism*

Bahr, Ehrhard, *Die Ironie im Spätwerk Goethes . . . diese sehr ernsten Scherze . . .* , Berlin, 1971.

Diener, Gottfried, *Fausts Weg zu Helena. Urphänomen und Archetypus*, Stuttgart, 1961.

Emrich, Wilhelm, *Die Symbolik des Faust II*, Berlin, 1943.

Friedländer, Paul, *Rhythmen und Landschaften im zweiten Teil des Faust*, Weimar, 1953.

Kommerell, Max, "Faust zweiter Teil. Zum Verständnis der Form," in *Geist und Buchstabe der Dichtung*, Frankfurt a. M., (n.d.).

Meijer, Herman, *Diese sehr ernsten Scherze. Eine Studie zu Faust II*, Heidelberg, 1970.

Mommsen, Katharina, *Natur- und Fabelreich in Faust II*, Berlin, 1968.

Staiger, Emil, "Faust's Heilschlaf," *Hamburger Akademische Rundschau* 2, 1947-1948; 251-257.

DESCARTES

1. *Editions*

Oeuvres de Descartes, publiées par Charles Adam et Paul Tannery, Paris, 1897 ff.

Oeuvres Philosophiques de Descartes, Textes établis, présentés et annotés par Ferdinand Alquié, Paris, 1963 ff.

2. *Selected Criticism*

Baillet, *La Vie de Monsieur Descartes*, Paris, 1691.

Gilson, Etienne, *Discours de la Méthode*, Texte et commentaire, Paris, 1962.

PASCAL

Pascal, Blaise, *Pensées et Opuscules*, publiés avec une introduction, des notices, des notes par Léon Brunschvicg, Paris (n.d.).

Index

PRINCETON ESSAYS IN LITERATURE

ADVISORY COMMITTEE: Joseph Bauke, Robert Fagles,
Claudio Guillén, Robert Maguire

Library of Congress Cataloging in Publication Data

Weinberg, Kurt.
The figure of Faust in Valéry and Goethe.

(Princeton essays in literature)
Bibliography: p.
Includes index.
1. Valéry, Paul, 1871-1945.   Mon Faust.   2.   Goethe,
Johann Wolfgang von, 1749-1832.   I.   Title.
PQ2643.A26M5138   842'.9'12   75-30211
ISBN 0-691-06304-4